Flabas

0   1   2   3   4   5 Km

Bois
d'Haumont

Haumont

Bois des Caures

Bois de
la Wavrille

Bois
d'Herbebois

JUMELLES
D'ORNES

Beaumont

CÔTE
344

Bois
des
Fosses

Ornes

W
O
E
V
R
E

Louvemont

CÔTE DU
POIVRE

Bois
de la
Vauche

Bezonvaux

HAUDROMONT

cherauville

Bois
Chaufour

Village

Douaumont
Fort

Bois
d'Hardaumont

Ravin de la Dame
ou de la Mort

Tranchée des
Baïonnettes

Bois de la
Caillette

Village

Bras

Ossuaire

Ravin du Bazil

Étang

Vaux
Fort

Village

CÔTE DE FROIDETERRE

Ouv. de Thiaumont

Bois de
Vaux-Chap.

Bois
Fumin

arny

Ouv. de
Froideterre

Fleury

Damloup

Chapelle Ste Fine

Bois de
la Laufée

Ch.de fer
v. Etain

Fort de Souville

Tunnel

Fort
Tavannes

Eix

Village
Belleville

Fort

Fort St Michel

Fort
Moulainville

V E R D U N

Village

Faubg Pavé

adelle

Ch. de fer
vers St Mihiel

La Meuse

Fort de Belrupt

P. Simonet

VERDUN

BY GEORGES BLOND

VERDUN

GEORGES BLOND

Translated by Frances Frenaye

THE MACMILLAN COMPANY

New York

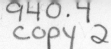

CONTENTS

1

"DRY YOUR TEARS, LOUISE"

―――――――――――――

AT THE BEGINNING of the second week of February 1916, everything in the north and east of France was damp and cold. So too were life and death and the narrow terrain between. The army train was rolling at twenty-five miles an hour through the icy night. Pale rays of moonlight were visible, at intervals, amid the falling snow.

The train was very long, made up of both passenger and freight cars. These last were packed with soldiers, except for a few at the rear, which served as kitchens and for the transportation of horses. The engine was anything but powerful, for all available rolling stock had been called into use, and on the slightest grade the train's speed slackened. At such times there was a sound of singing of melancholy, nostalgic songs, alien to the French countryside. The people of the invaded regions, close as they were to the German border, were not yet used to these songs, or to the poignant band music of the Sunday parades in the village squares, with its stifled bugles, shrill fifes, and muted drums.

And yet the German soldiers aboard the train, men of General von Zwehl's Seventh Reserve Corps, did not seem to be particularly homesick. The fact that they belonged to a Reserve Corps did not mean that their duties were performed behind the front line. There were very few raw recruits among them. Almost all of them were hardened soldiers, with a professional lingo and manner of their own.

In the passenger cars, which carried commissioned and noncommissioned officers, gas jets were burning. Airplanes might easily have spotted the caterpillar-like motion of the train, but in February 1916, few airplanes flew by night. In the freight cars, in defiance of orders, the soldiers had set up lanterns on the straw in order to play cards. Winter nights are long in the northeast of France, and the temperature was too low to favor sleep. Some of the soldiers' knapsacks were stuffed with comforts they had picked up during their furlough; but they could not eat the whole night through, or play cards either. So it was that they began to sing:

> "Dry your tears, Louise,
> Wipe your eyes;
> In spite of what they say,
> A soldier never dies. . . ."

Or else, because someone had jokingly said, "I tell you, boys, we're going to Strassburg," they broke into *Du wunderschöne Stadt* or any one of a dozen other popular airs.

Someone occasionally peered through a crack in the side of the car and tried to make out the features of the landscape. Wooded hills and valleys and fields . . . "Is that a French tree or a German tree?" The landscape was very much the same, the same clods broken by the plow, the same foliage, the same cows and chickens, the same dog barking in the farmyard at night. So what did it all add up to? The songs had a way of dying on the lips of the singers.

And yet the beginning of the war had been marked by a genuine feeling of exhilaration. Marching soldiers and trains leaving for the front had been bombarded by bouquets of flowers. In the schools entire classes had signed up as volunteers, while the teachers, weeping with joy, had scrawled on the blackboards the slogan *Nach Paris!* and the idolized veterans of the War of 1870 had harangued them:

"Groups of sharpshooters advance on the double. Officers

lead the way, sword in hand. At the right are the scouts, and at the left the company commanders, the buglers at their side. At definite intervals the bugles ring out: *Ta-ra-ta-ra, ta-ra-ta-ra . . . "*

Many soldiers of the Seventh Reserve Corps knew this bugle call, for it had not changed; it was still as staccato, by virtue of sheer repetition, as ever. Incredible that once upon a time it should have been the signal for a charge. Only yesterday, yet so many things had changed it was an eternity away. The war had emptied a large number of words of their meaning; it had turned them inside out, like gloves tossed away on muddy ground. Dust and mud, these were the epitome of war. What words were left were stark and crude, inventively realistic; the others were devaluated and meaningless.

The little freight cars carrying the soldiers of the Seventh Reserve Corps were rolling at twenty-five miles an hour through the icy night, and dozens of other trains were rolling that same night, and had on the night before, and would be rolling in the nights to come from almost every point of the compass, from Germany and the invaded regions. Theoretically each train was moving toward a destination of its own, quite independently of the others, but their glimmering caterpillars made up a network of lines, all converging upon a single invisible point.

Sometimes the trains came to a stop in a station. They stopped at Sedan, Neufchâteau, Bastogne, Arlon, Luxembourg, Longwy, Thionville, Briey, Conflans, Chambley, and Thiaucourt. The men nearest the doors leaped to the platform, looking for a drinking fountain, a canteen, a latrine, anything that might furnish an excuse to stretch their legs and ask questions, although their sergeants warned them not to go too far because the train would leave soon. Officers made hasty purchases of cigars and then returned to their seats. The canteens were taken by storm. When several trains arrived almost simultaneously at the same station, the men shouted to one another, their warm breath forming a mist in the cold air; even the officers leaned out of their windows to exchange greetings. The sergeants continued to call the men back, but the train showed no sign of moving. Yardmen and dispatchers walked across the tracks, swinging lanterns and making no more than monosyllabic replies to the soldiers' joking questions. Their faces were drawn and sullen, and they had every reason to be tired. Since the beginning of January, sleepless nights had been the rule, and they lived in a state of constant disquiet and irritation.

Orders had dropped on them like bombs, as the German railway system, the most elaborate in the world, gradually built itself up into an almost perfect organization. The frontline zone was divided into so many sectors, each with a forward station that had behind it a feeder and behind that a marshaling yard; the rolling stock was divided among the yards and kept in balance by a system of intricate communications. Now the system worked as smoothly as a well-oiled machine, ingeniously geared to the necessities of war. Everything was accounted for, including air-raid alarms and even front-line battles. The stationmasters had prepared instructions for any of half-a-dozen eventualities; upon receipt of a single code-word telegram they knew exactly what had to be done. The system was as efficient as that of the General Staff; perhaps, to tell the truth, even more so.

Just now the orders seemed to verge upon madness. Some eighty battalions were to be poured into a zone only about eight miles square, and with them their arms and supplies and medical equipment. There were trains loaded with barbed wire, stakes, boards, sandbags, cement and gravel, enough material to build a city. There were carloads of rails and ties, for the laying of hundreds of miles of narrow-gauge tracks. Guards, squatting on piles of shovels and buckets, watched over great areas of this assembled material, their faces unbelieving. What was to be built so close to the front? The Tower of Babel?

The protests and objections of the railway officials had been brushed aside. Orders had come from the very top level, from Olympian heights where even a corps commander would have trembled to enter. And so they had had to take apart and destroy with their own hands the apparatus which they had so painstakingly put together, in order to make way for hundreds of trains pouring in from the east, southeast, northeast, and from the combat regions of the north, through which men and equipment were being transferred, even from as far as Russia. The heavy guns that had pounded Liège, Namur, Maubeuge, Antwerp, and Novo-Georgiyevsk, Kovno, and Grodno jostled one another along the rails leading to this narrow zone of the Western Front that was their new destination, and the trains that had carried them were shuttled back immediately to the marshaling yards to be reloaded. The operation was working well, and the railwaymen should have been pleased and proud; but they were reeling with fatigue, and none of them had really recovered from the shock of the initial disturbing orders.

The trains with the soldiers finally pulled slowly out of the stations, the stragglers running down the platforms and even leaping from tie to tie until they caught onto the last car and their comrades hoisted them aboard. At intervals during the night they were sidetracked, in order to let the guns go through. As often as not an artillery train was drawn by two engines, whose smokestacks shed a train of sparks and a red glow around them. On each gun carriage a canvas-covered cannon raised its mouth toward the sky, like a sorrowful animal, a continuing procession imploring forgiveness for the future carnage. Only when the gun carriages had passed and were succeeded by cars carrying horses did the sidetracked soldiers recover their speech and call out a greeting to these creatures of flesh and blood, more akin to their own humanity. The horses' ears were visible between the slats; at the sound of human voices they raised their heads and opened their mouths, their white teeth gleaming through the dark.

The destination of all these convoys was an official secret. According to regulations only the officer in charge of the train knew it. At the beginning the secret was kept intact, but with time the noncoms and even the common soldiers began to guess at the existence of the lodestar to which everything was attracted. By now every car rang with the sound of a French name, a name that had never before been pronounced below the highest level, so that it was set apart and enveloped in a majestic and terrible shadow: Verdun, or *Verdoon,* as the Germans pronounced it; the name seemed to explode out of the most innocent sentences.

Geographically, the region of Verdun has nothing re-markable about it. "A landscape almost totally devoid of charm," was the way Baedeker described it. A region studded with small villages, unpretentious fields and wooded hills, traversed in every direction by ravines. In 1916, even before the great battle, the sparsely leafed woods were narrow and stunted. One ravine, deeper than the others, crossed the area from southeast to northeast. This was the winding valley of the river Meuse, with meadows, farms, gardens, roads, and church spires on either side.

For over two months the officers of the French Operations Bureau had watched the front line in this region with special care. The German trenches ran uphill from Consenvoye, on the Meuse, to a point opposite the forest of Beaumont, down-hill to the forest of Caures, then up to another high point— the one farthest east—near Azannes. After that, the German line entered an area of low-lying fields, sluggish streams, and dense woods. It ran as far as Étain, before turning south and crossing the valley of the Woëvre as far as the heights of Combres, where it met the hills of Lorraine. We need remember only that this irregular line formed a semicircle with a radius of about eight miles and that at its center was the lodestar whose pull was now felt as far away as the center of Germany. Here it was that hundreds of trains were converging.

"A good thing," some of the soldiers were saying. "Let's attack for a change. Anything to get moving."

"Moving straight into hell!" said others. "Are you in such a hurry to die?"

New recruits were not the only ones who longed for action. Among the troops there were veterans who had been half dead with thirst and fatigue in the retreat from the Marne, up to their ankles in mud along the Yser, nearly drowned at Ypres, and then ordered to repel the French offensives of Champagne and Artois. Nothing in the world was more loathsome to them than the trenches, with their dank chill and filth and rats, the sickly-sweet smell of dead bodies, the foul stench of excrement, and the fear that descended upon them at the words, "The enemy is coming!" when they were already almost at the end of their physical resources. A clean-cut attack, with all the chips down, was infinitely better. As they moved out of northern France, they shouted from the train:

"Goodbye, rattrap, pigsty!"

Verdun? A place as good as any other. Apparently the General Staff was playing for all or nothing.

"A hundred hours of softening up by the artillery, fellows!"

No one knew whether this phrase, which had reached the ears of even the humblest wagon driver, had originated with a boastful artilleryman, a staff orderly, or some propaganda outfit. False or not, it was reassuring, and so was the sequel:

"After that, the infantry can advance with their guns slung from their shoulder straps."

In the lamplight skeptics laughed such slogans down.

"You young idiots must want to die! What about the Verdun sector?"

Some of these skeptics had taken part in the capture of the spur of Éparges, eight miles south of Verdun, in September 1914, and between the following February and April had held it, in a sea of mud, against perhaps fifteen French attacks, interspersed by counterattacks of their own. They had seen whole platoons shot up into the air by mines charged with twenty or thirty tons of explosives laid as deep as a hundred and fifty feet below the ground. They had fought with rifles, hand grenades, bayonets and knives on the slopes of yawning holes, strewn with corpses, while from behind the lines, on either side, the artillery aimed at the billowing smoke and slaughtered the survivors.

Other skeptics had conquered, lost, and reconquered half-a-dozen times with rifles, grenades, and machine guns, the heights of Vauquois, twelve miles west of Verdun. They had stumbled into gaping holes and trenches, first French and then German, lined and sometimes filled to overflowing with dead bodies in various stages of putrefaction, bodies that in themselves formed a hill on top of the hill and became a bone of contention between the two mingled groups of those who were about to die and thus add their own bodies to the sinister pile. The General Staffs called it "Combat for an observation post" or "A local action undertaken to boost morale."

Men who had lived through such things might have been expected to prefer anything to the slaughter involved in this type of war of "position" or "attrition." The Verdun sector seemed to have a curse upon it. But their feelings were divided. "Anything rather than this hell," they said to themselves, "but there might be a hell even hotter." In their way they were prophetic.

At General Headquarters the Intelligence officers spoke of Verdun in strictly technical terms:

"A mainstay of the French front, in an extraordinarily favorable position. The forts of Bois Bourrus and Marre dominate the left bank of the river valley; to the northeast, Belleville, Saint-Michel, Souville, Tavannes, and Moulainville protect the hills of Lorraine, half a dozen other forts shield the southeast and south, while the powerful twin bastions of Vaux and Douaumont jut out to cover the hills to the north. Among these forts there is an aggregation of concrete shelters and secondary supports and a network of trenches. All the ravines are blocked, and there seems to be no possibility of a flank attack."

The regimental officers—majors, captains, lieutenants—in the troop trains had heard fewer rumors than the soldiers, but they had a clearer idea of what lay ahead. Most of them felt that the dark lodestar which had drawn men out of the heart of Germany and even from the Russian front was going to turn into a furnace. Verdun had been the great block to the 1914 invasion, untouched and untouchable even when the German troops had nearly reached Paris, and ever since, on a semicircle stretching northward and eastward, it had held them at bay, like a crouching dog, by its growl alone. An attack on the strongest point of the enemy line must have some strategical reason. Every officer, even the most closemouthed, foresaw a colossal bloodletting.

Among officers and soldiers alike a counter-rumor spread for a few days. There was no question of attacking Verdun. The sector was being reinforced for fear of a French attack; the troop movements were purely defensive. But this comparatively reassuring idea quickly lost ground. The closer the troops came to their goal, the greater was their anxiety.

The Seventh Reserve Corps, commanded by General von Zwehl, ended its journey at Longuyon on February 9th. Snow was still falling, blown by the wind, and equestrian statues, draped in white, stood sentinel around the station square.

"Hussars!" the soldiers exclaimed. "What the devil are you doing here?"

One of the statues shook the snow off his cloak.

"Traffic police," he replied. "You'll soon see what that means."

The town was crowded with soldiers, but the snow muffled their footsteps, and in spite of their heavy boots they moved as silently as ghosts. The new arrivals were quartered in the southern section, which had not been as much damaged as the rest of the town. But the requisitioned houses were full, and there was hardly any place for billets except in the cellars, where at least the temperature was higher than aboveground. Field kitchens made the rounds, and the soldiers who had money bought extra food out of their own pockets. The officers were divided among the dining rooms of three hotels, where orderlies put bouquets of snowdrops on the tables, and sullen-faced girls carried the trays. Rumor had it that part of the population had recently been evacuated.

All day long, troops, guns, trucks and wagons passed through the town from north to south on Route Nationale 18. Toward evening the soldiers who were out looking for a supplement to their rations—and for girls not too shy to speak to them—found themselves near a sort of covered market, where a sentry was mounting guard.

"What's in there?" they asked him.

"Stores."

"Stores of what?"

"I have orders to keep my trap shut."

But under pressure he admitted that the stores were munitions.

"Shells and cartridges. The place is emptied and filled up again three times a day. There was never anything like it."

The optimistic counter-rumor—of defense against a French attack—was exploded. Some of the soldiers, passing from one extreme to the other, began to expect a night march, but they were simply ordered back to their quarters. After dark, Route Nationale 18 became a thundering torrent of men and matériel. The horse-drawn artillery wagons made as much noise as the heavy trucks with their hard rubber tires.

Around two o'clock in the morning, unable to sleep, most of the soldiers got up and stood in the doorways, aroused by what sounded like the roar of a railway locomotive on the street. The sight that met their eyes was even more surprising. Two monstrous machines, spitting sparks, emitting steam, and piercing the snow with enormous spotlights for eyes, were rumbling by. They were steam-driven trucks, hauling guns, 420's, so huge that the houses were dwarfed beside them and so heavy that it seemed the pavement might crumble. At the edge of the town this monstrous convoy uprooted a tree.

That night, and on the nights that followed, similar convoys could have been seen rolling through Montmédy, Bazeilles, Audun, Spincourt, Piennes, Nantillois, Vilosnes, Romagne, Muzerey, Baroncourt, Chambley, Conflans, and other towns behind the German front. Here, before reaching the front-line railway terminus, the infantry got off the trains and continued on foot. Men have legs with which to walk, unlike shells and sacks of potatoes, and there were barely enough railroad trucks to carry this valuable matériel all the way.

After twenty-four hours of rest, the soldiers began their march to the front, as far as they could to the beat of their regimental drums. The soldiers sang, the officers rode up and down the line on horseback, quite as they had done in earlier wars. The captains kept careful watch over their companies. Any soldier who, because of weariness or carelessness, unhooked the collar of his tunic was punished by being made to carry the rifle of the man behind him as well as his own.

New conditions had made for a certain softening of field regulations, but officers still inflicted on their men a rigorous discipline. Manifestations of passion, and hence of potential disorder, are always erupting in the German soul, and an unhooked collar might have marked the beginning of a catastrophe. Of course, the rules were relaxed during actual combat, but up to the very end of the war the German infantryman was better disciplined than the French poilu. This does not necessarily mean that the German officers were inhuman. The accusation of brutality, of men kicked and whipped into a charge, is a piece of wartime propaganda. Every army has its share of sadists. In 1916 the most brutally treated common soldier was probably the Russian.

In some of the villages through which the troops passed, there were still civilians—women, children, old men, boys and girls. The women, in their dark peasant dresses, were seldom beautiful, and yet their presence to many of the soldiers was disturbing, so near to the empire of death. The civilians were hostile in some cases, indifferent in others; no general rule determined their attitude. As for the German soldiers, they did not, for the most part, hate the French, and they could understand why the French did not love them. "We're trespassers, after all, and war is no joke."

War was present to the German infantry not only in the form of demolished houses and in their own foreign uniforms but also in the more obtrusive shape of their artillery. At Romagne thirty 210's and two batteries of 420's were installed only a hundred yards beyond the last house in the village. Covered with canvas and camouflage, they were the core of a compact military concentration, to which they had been carried over a specially constructed narrow-gauge rail line.

Beyond this formidable concentration the infantry marched along a road with woods on either side. Here too, heavy guns—210's, 150's, and 105's—were lurking. The woods of Tilly, Clairs Chênes, Le Penard, Foameix, and Baty were all artillery assembly points. In the woods of Tilly alone were more than a hundred artillery pieces and their caissons, brought all the way from Metz. To the infantry such a sight was both frightening and reassuring. At every halt they listened for artillery fire. On February 8th the French had bombarded Saint-Maurice, but since then there had been silence, except for the occasional boom of a heavy German gun.

"Testing the range," the old soldiers said. "Whatever's brewing is well under way."

There were other groups of buildings along the road, not half-destroyed French villages but brand-new German creations, which explained the huge amount of construction material that had been moved up to the front. Hastily thrown-up wooden barracks were raised above the swamps like prehistoric lake villages, linked by hard roads or narrow-gauge rails to more solid ground. Certain large units, like that at Fontaines-Saint-Clair, housed five thousand men and three thousand horses. The Douâ River had been funneled off to feed a reservoir on top of a hill, and drinking water was piped down to the military settlement. The officers led their men to the barracks, numbered and spotlessly clean, from which the former tenants had only just moved on.

"There's a canteen," they told them, "and you can send letters home."

This last sentence had something ominous about it. A little earlier, at the end of January, troops had stayed for several days at a time in camps of this kind, but now the transition period was shorter. Sometimes the new arrivals had time to exchange news with the regiments moving out.

"Three army corps are going into line."

"With three million shells to get them going."

"February 13th, at eleven o'clock in the morning."

This was the last contact among the regiments that had gathered from north and south and east, from the heart of Germany and the conquered outposts in France. From this point on, there were no more drums, no more songs. The men carried pup tents on their shoulders, two allotments of fresh rations and two of hard rations in their knapsacks; 150 cartridges, two or three hand grenades, empty sandbags, a bucket and a gas mask on their belts. The sappers were equipped with wire cutters, dynamite, and flamethrowers.

The officers guided the heads of the columns by intermittent beams from their flashlights. When their boots sank into the mud, with a curious sucking sound, the men swore beneath their breath. All of them realized they were reaching the combat zone. The guns were silent. The whole sector seemed dead.

The field kitchens halted, under orders to protect themselves by camouflage. The marching columns proceeded more slowly, often led by a guide. These guides seemed to spring up out of the ground, with flashlights in their hands. How long had they been waiting in the darkness? They murmured a few words to the officer in command, and then made their way to the head of the column.

"No talking!" said the officer. "Let them by."

The men were quite sure that they had reached their journey's end when they saw the figures of their comrades ahead of them grow smaller. The road sloping so abruptly down obviously led to a trench or a shelter. But the German soldiers arriving at the trenches of the Verdun sector in 1916 found a surprise awaiting them.

The word "trench," so generically employed in relation to the First World War, designated various kinds of excavations, from the trench proper, over six feet deep, with vertical walls and sometimes a grating at the bottom or a roof which classified it as a "shelter," to the barely indented furrow. There was wide variation among the shelters as well. Some of them were underground passageways, others mere dugouts or shellholes, which afforded an illusory protection. The *Stollen* which the German High Command had prepared for the offensive of Verdun were underground bar-racks, fifteen, thirty, and even forty-five feet deep, perfectly safe from bombardment. They were to serve as the quarters of the first-line reserves, who were to be called up to attack as the occasion demanded. Steps led up to the departure and communication trenches.

The *Stollen* in the woods of Consenvoye, less than twelve hundred yards from the French trenches, had a capacity of twelve hundred men. Earth is a good conductor of sound, and the French listening posts in the wood of Caures had heard the German excavations at Consenvoye. The inter-rogation of prisoners had revealed the presence of other similar installations nearby. French Intelligence officers at the General Headquarters of Chantilly had studied the various reports and sent a summary of them to the Bureau of Operations. The conclusion reached by the Bureau of Operations was this: "The *Stollen* had been dug for purely defensive purposes."

The German occupants had no such misconception. Any lingering doubts were dispelled by the expression on the faces of their captains when they called the companies to-gether and read them the following message:

> *"After a long period of stubborn defense, His Majesty our Emperor and King, calls us to the attack. Let us all fortify ourselves with the knowledge that the Fatherland expects great things of us. We must show our foes that the iron will to victory is still alive in the hearts of Germany's sons and that the German army, when it advances, beats down all resistance. In the firm confidence that all ranks will give of their best, I order you to advance. God be with us!"*

This message was read during the night of February 11 and 12, 1916.

2

A CATASTROPHIC
TERRAIN

---

*Just behind the French lines on the Western Front
there are objectives which the French command must defend to the last man. If it so defends them the French army
will be exhausted by its bloody losses in the inevitable combat, regardless of whether or not we win the objectives immediately. If, on the other hand, it lets them go, the
damage to French morale will be enormous.*

This statement of von Falkenhayn, the German Chief of
Staff, in *The German General Staff and Its Decisions, 1914–
1916,* is cloudily and clumsily phrased. But another German,
Werner Beumelburg, put it more bluntly:

*We must apply a suction pump to the body of France,
and gradually but steadily drain the strength from its half-
open veins.*

In short, a bloodletting. I can almost hear von Falkenhayn
enlarging upon this theme:

"It wasn't my idea. As a professional soldier I couldn't
have been so stupid. I knew that a war of attrition is double-
edged, that it bleeds both sides alike. My idea was to make a
breakthrough and follow it up. If you don't believe me, read
Liddell Hart, a first-rate strategist, even if he is an Englishman. He has shown that my idea of progressively exhausting
France was elaborated only after the defeat of my offensive
at Verdun and that all the time I really wanted to strike a
blow and win a decisive victory. You must remember that,

even then, time was working against us. Behind the lines, milk, butter, and meat were lacking; workers were on strike and women were demonstrating in front of the shops. Time always seems to work against German generals. But any army leader worthy of the name could not fail to hope for a break- through. Trench warfare is the complete negation of mili- tary science."

"Thank you for your confession, General. But why didn't you write the truth? Why did you let it appear that you favored a gradual bloodletting?"

"Because I was concerned with the verdict of history. As soon as we generals, to whatever country we belong, put pen to paper we are obsessed by the urge of self-justification. We apply our ingenuity to fitting the final results to our inten- tions."

I apologize for putting words in the mouth of a ghost, but here we have, in a nutshell, the origin of the battle. The ghost is so anxious to tell the truth (and so constrained, also, because, in the place where he is, truth may bring either punishment or reward, but it is the only coinage), that I am tempted to ask him a few more questions. My method is not really so artificial, because von Falkenhayn has answered most of them in his memoirs, and besides, his answers are military axioms.

"General, what makes you say that trench warfare is the negation of military science?"

"The art of war is movement. Half a hundred historians have explained why the Great War—that's what we called it —turned out to be static."

"Not all our readers are informed on this subject. Can you explain it further?"

"Yes, and quite briefly. There was a moment in history when the defensive power of firearms was greater than the offensive one, and that's when the trouble began. The war got off to a good-enough start, from a professional point of view. We knocked the French around at Charleroi, and they had to retreat to the Marne. After the Battle of the Marne we fell back upon a line of trenches prepared by our reserves. Then the French discovered the idea I have exposed above. It was as simple as this: Three men and a machine gun can stop a battalion of heroes. So they too dug trenches. Two great armies sat staring each other in the face. The front became a wall."

"And you wanted to break through it, did you?"

"So did Joffre, in Champagne, in Argonne, and (after Verdun) on the Somme."

"You massed enormous quantities of men and matériel. Why didn't you break through?"

"That's obvious: tanks hadn't been invented and armies weren't motorized. The infantry advanced on foot, just as in the time of Napoleon and Julius Caesar. The general whose line was broken knew that the enemy couldn't advance more than fifteen miles a day, granting that it met no resistance. Actually, the advance was even slower, because artillery and supplies had to be moved up as well. The defenders had time to bring up their reserves and dig more trenches. 'Consolidating,' the tacticians called it. This ugly word became so fashionable that it was still used in your communiqués of 1940 and in ours from the Russian front in 1942 and after. It had become quite meaningless, but a General Staff never throws an old word away."

"Let's get back to Verdun. Why did you decide to break through at what you knew to be such a strong point of the French front?"

"There were psychological considerations. Among us Germans the name of Verdun had even more prestige attached to it than in France. It was there, over a thousand years ago, that the German emperor whom you have annexed to your history under the name of Charlemagne chose the two-headed eagle as symbol of his power. We had conquered

Verdun, after a hard battle, in 1792 and again in 1870. Even an ordinary private soldier was aware of this historical aura. I thought that the conquest of Verdun would give a tremendous boost to our morale. And from a tactical point of view my choice is quite defensible. Have you looked at a map of the front as it was at that time?"

"Yes, I see the great fortress at the center of a semicircle."

"That meant that a great body of artillery could strike converging blows. The numerous small woods allowed for the effective concealment of the guns and for the protection of the troops from observation, and a network of rails was available for bringing the men and matériel together. On the French side, communications were poor; of the two regular railway lines, one we had already cut off and the other was within range of our guns. There remained only one narrow-gauge line and a single road. It was this particular advantage that caused me to make up my mind. I saw the impressive mass of Verdun connected to the rest of France by a slender umbilical cord, and I said to myself, 'Our best bet is there!' "

*　　*　　*

At the beginning of February 1916, the city of Verdun, formerly of twenty thousand, now of five or six thousand inhabitants, seemed from an altitude of three hundred feet to be intact. At its site several branches of the Meuse, flowing among sharply outlined hills, came together. On the heights of the left bank stood the cathedral of Notre-Dame, beside it the imposing Bishop's Palace, and a little farther on something that looked like a stone star, half buried in the ground, the citadel built by Vauban.

Even when we come down from our bird's-eye view, there are no visible wounds. Indeed, the city had barely been scratched. The two worst bombardments, resulting in the fall of some fifty shells from 380's, had caused a few deaths and injuries, but not enough damage to leave any perceptible scars. Let us look at the streets. A certain number of houses had closed shutters, but the sidewalks were as animated as those of any town behind the lines. There was only one difference: most of the strollers were in uniform. A few cars were passing by—with engines and chassis high above the ground, and spindly tires—how times have changed! More interesting are the men, women, and children, our parents and grandparents, perhaps our infant selves. How remote they too seem to us today! For one thing they seem small, making us aware of the general increase in human height over the last fifty years. And how somberly they were clad! The faded sky-blue of the soldiers' uniforms stood out among the dark colors of civilian clothes. From behind, no woman seemed less than fifty years old, because of the austerity of her dress. Hair was pinned up in sober knots, and a scarf covered every head. The lack of rouge and lipstick did not account for the pallor of the women's complexions. The children too, clumsily bundled up in thick hooded coats over their school smocks, were pasty-faced. Could it be that these people did not have enough to eat?

On the walls were posters put up by the Subprefect's Relief Committee, and where there is Relief there are empty stomachs. And yet all over the city foodstuffs were on display, as if everyone were buying or selling them. Tins of ham and sardines were piled up in a music-shop window; barrels of wine lined the entrance hall of an empty hotel; oranges and cheese were on sale at the entrance to a moving-picture theater; and wild rabbits hung in front of a café. Passing soldiers stopped to look and sometimes to purchase, but the civilians, for the most part, passed indifferently by. The general atmosphere was somewhat uncanny.

Until the middle of 1915, Verdun was an exceptionally lively and agreeable place. There was an unusual number of soldiers, but business flourished, as it had in Savannah at the beginning of the Civil War. But all wars last too long, and with the first evacuation of the civilian population the city began to decline. The civilians were transferred to Normandy and Brittany, but also, for some inexplicable reason, to the north, where they soon found themselves in invaded land.

"Deported to Germany," that was what people murmured about them. And the enemy bombardments, the first of which took place on June 4, 1915, did not make for good cheer. "Within range of the enemy's heavy artillery . . ." This phrase was obviously depressing. Many people had gone away of their own will; the others remained simply because they had no place to go. Money, jobs, and consumer goods were all scarce.

Who bought the foodstuffs of which we have spoken? Of course, there was not so much as it might have seemed from the display. There were soldier buyers, as we have seen, because some soldiers are richer than others, a fact which historians seldom take into account and to which we shall return later. As for the rest—just look at this woman passerby, in a fur-trimmed coat and hat and high-heeled shoes, with an almost insolent prosperity. There is a word, born of the First World War, which has lost its sting: *profiteer.* I can remember how scornfully the poor used to pronounce it.

But let us forget this woman and continue our survey; let us look from close by at the citadel which was the heart of the city. Different types of soldiers are to be met on the way. Oldish men, wearing caps and gray moustaches, obviously territorials or members of the Quartermaster Corps. At the foot of the citadel's wall a company has come to a halt and broken up into small clusters. Verdun was a replacement center, and soldiers often stopped there for a few hours or a day before moving toward or away from the trenches. These soldiers were not dirty or tired enough to be coming back from the front; they must have moved up from the rear.

Let us examine them from head to foot. Not merely because only two out of three, at the most, would ever return, but also for documentary purposes. What Frenchman under fifty years of age really remembers the getup of the infantrymen of 1916, the poilu of Verdun? Our story will soon come to a point where the action is so rapid and confusing that there will be no time to notice the protagonists' appearance. Let us scrutinize it while we have time.

The poilu wore a helmet of the "Adrian" type, which took the place of the *képi,* or peaked cap, in the second year of the war, when it became evident how many wounds were inflicted upon the head. The helmet weighed a little over a pound, and *L'Illustration* described it as "elegant," adding, however:

> *Let strict traditionalists be reassured. The* képi *remains the official headgear of both the Infantry and the Light Cavalry. The helmet is intended strictly for combat and the trenches, and as soon as a soldier comes back from the front he will put the* képi *back on his head at an individual and jaunty angle.*

Such was the heroic tone of the press of the time.

Now let us look at the face. In the drawings, lithographs, and water colors of artists like Georges Scott, which were meant to give civilians a not completely unrealistic and vaguely comforting picture of the war, we can see a gradual change in the French infantryman's expression. 1914: a resolute eye, gazing at the spire of a church in far-away Alsace, a moustache and sometimes a short beard; 1915: a fiercer and less dreamy look in the eye, a pipe between the lips, a moustache and beard that can only be described as luxuriant; 1916: more moustache and less beard, the look of a hardened veteran, able to stand up to anything the Boche may try to put over. The change is true to life. The moustache is the denominator common to all stages. For various reasons these soldiers appeared older than those who are of the same age today.

Certainly their uniform had nothing youthful about it.

No longer did an exaggeratedly long coat come down over a pair of red trousers. The sky-blue model was shortened early in the war, but we should find it still too long, as well as heavy and badly cut. The infantryman was strapped into a combat pack called the *barda,* a sort of harness made up of a cartridge belt and a pair of leather straps crossed over the shoulders, to which were attached a canteen, a pouch, a bayonet, a gas mask, and a knapsack. In military jargon the knapsack was often called "Azor" (Fido) because once upon a time it had been made of dogskin. The *barda* was jokingly referred to as a "bazaar" or, more often, a "bordello."

The boots, "clodhoppers," had nothing very special about them. Over these were worn the cloth puttees, an amazing relic of the time of the Franks or the Merovingians. *"Puttees outlined the muscles of the calf of the leg and accentuated the swing of its stride."* The rifle was a Lebel. Let us refer again to a newspaper description of two articles that I forgot to mention in connection with the harness:

> *On the chest, under the pouch, was a Browning-type revolver, and hanging from the belt a startlingly long knife in a sheath. All the* Kultur *of 1916 had brought us back to the* miséricorde *of the sixteenth century.*

This modern version of the knife used to put an enemy mercifully to death was used for "mopping up" a captured enemy trench, which was the function of the grenadiers. Here is a description of this function from an Infantry manual:

> *The grenadier's task is to clean out, first with hand grenades and then with a knife, the dugouts from which lurking enemy soldiers may attack our advancing men from the rear. Sometimes they take refuge as far as thirty feet belowground. Real courage is required to go down into these dangerous holes, where well-armed and combative enemies may be in hiding.*

And yet the soldiers we see walking up and down at the foot of the wall of the citadel have nothing very savage about them. Their faces are for the most part benign. Apart from combat the average infantryman was a good fellow.

* * *

Citadel: "a fortress that commands a city"; *fortress:* "a fortified place, capable of sheltering a large force." Sébastian Le Prestre de Vauban, the greatest soldier of his time, had studded the north and east of France with powerful fortresses. Let us penetrate the stronghold of Verdun. The first impression is favorable. Before us there opens a broad gallery, wider than a subway tunnel, with side galleries running out of it at right angles. The glow of a multitude of electric-light bulbs shines on the slightly pink stone walls. Underfoot there is fine sand. The heating is unequal; in some places the air is warm, in others cold and damp. The atmosphere is very much alive. Some of the galleries are dormitories, where soldiers can stretch out on their cots, write letters, or put their equipment in order.

But here is something less rosy: two galleries are packed with civilians, men, women, and children, with mattresses, bundles of household effects, and cooking utensils. These are refugees from nearby villages, waiting to be sent on their way to some other destination. Why had they been evacuated? What was there to fear? Did someone have an idea that the German *Stollen* were not for purely defensive purposes?

In any event, no *Stollen* could match the spaciousness and comfort of the citadel of Verdun. We have seen from the air its passive protection, the thickness of the star-shaped stone structure built by Vauban. What about the active protection, in other words, the number of guns, available for its defense? The answer is: There were none. During the second half of 1915 the collective brain of the General Staff had given birth to a new idea, one quite logical and indeed very advanced for the times.

"Stationary fortifications are outdated. A heavy artillery bombardment destroys or cripples them. Their large consumption of ammunition necessitates supply routes which are wide open to bombardment. A besieged fortress, deprived of ammunition, is bound to fall into enemy hands. Look at the fortresses of Liège, Namur, Antwerp, and Maubeuge, not to mention an equal number of examples in Russia."

If the General Staff had been endowed with clairvoyance, it might have added, "Look at the Maginot Line and the Atlantic Wall." But the idea, even as it was conceived in 1915, was premature. The strategists did not clearly see that in their Great War, based on "position," on trenches that were no more than ratholes, the slightest elevation, the least fragment of wall, the shallowest shellhole with a few yards of barbed wire in front of it, was defensible.

On August 5, 1915, the governor of the fortress of Verdun was placed under the orders of the commander-in-chief; on August 9th the fortress ceased to be an administrative unit and was reclassified as "the fortified region of Verdun," an area including fifty miles of front lines, under the orders of General Herr, who was subordinate in his turn to General Dubail, commander of the Eastern Armies Group. At the same time General Dubail was informed of the General Staff's intentions: "(1) The safety of the country is entirely dependent upon the armies in the field. The troops hitherto assigned to fortresses would be better employed in building up the front-line defenses. (2) The heavy artillery, of which there is so great a need, can best be obtained by dismantlement of the fortified places." At once General Dubail sent word to General Herr to the effect that he should proceed at once to remove the artillery pieces, ammunition, and personnel of the fortified region under his command. The "fortified region" did not consist of the citadel alone; it included the "belt of surrounding forts" of whose strength the Germans spoke respectfully. But the General Staff thought that these forts, too, no longer served any purpose, that they were relics of the past, which could be stripped down to their framework. By October 15, 1915, forty-three heavy batteries had already been removed from the fortified region of Verdun. The Germans, of course, had taken heavy artillery away from the fortress of Metz. But Metz was not in the combat zone.

The French General Staff persisted in its resolution. The auxiliary 75's were removed and the garrison troops reduced in number or done away with altogether. Marshal Pétain has written, in his characteristic, poetically melancholy vein, of the results of this operation:

> *Above the heights of La Chaume, Saint-Michel, Souville, and Belrupt, which surround the frequently flooded fields of the Meuse Valley basin, the forts of Marre and Vacherauville, on the left bank, and of Douaumont, Vaux, and Tavannes on the right, stood in silent abandonment. The massive Douaumont dominated them all, but it seemed as if nothing had been done to ensure its protection.*

This last phrase is a typical military euphemism, but a little farther on, Pétain speaks more clearly:

> *If we had trusted, from the beginning, the ingenuity of our engineers, the battle for Verdun would have developed quite differently. Had the fort of Douaumont been regularly defended it would never have fallen into enemy hands. With its overhanging position, its tested shelters, its armored observation posts, and with covering troops capable of carrying out a flanking action, it would have discouraged the enemy from the start.*

The passage is flawless in style, but the conditional tense of the verbs deprives it of any historical interest. There are too many "ifs." These quotations reveal to us the inner weakness of the fortified region the Germans imagined as so hard a nut to crack.

* * *

We must speak now of the citadel's outlying defenses: of the trenches, tunnels, shelters, mounds, sandbags, and entanglements that immobilized the two greatest armies of all times and the greatest firing power ever assembled. If we are to understand the terrain of the Battle of Verdun, we must have recourse to other documents of the time. Readers who are impatient of these details can go on to the next chapter, to the beginning of the battle itself. But in my opinion this collection of facts and textual quotations has a certain tragic grandeur; it is a fitting prelude to the slaughter that lies ahead.

On December 16, 1915, General Gallieni, who had been Minister of War since October, wrote to General Joffre:

Reports from various sources concerning the organization of the front call attention to certain weaknesses in our defense system. In the Meurthe, Toul, and Verdun sectors the network of trenches is not as complete as in other places. This situation may well turn to our disadvantage.

On December 18th Joffre replied with a threat of resignation, adding:

I can assure the government that the two main defensive positions present obstacles sufficient to ensure their protection. The attached maps of defenses show that in the sectors to which you refer in your communication of December 16 three or four adjacent positions are completed or on the point of completion.

During the same week General Herr (the future scapegoat, who only a short time later, at Chantilly, was to be threatened with execution) wrote to General de Serrigny, Pétain's second, the commander of the 33rd Army Corps:

Every day I am fearful. If I were to be attacked I could not possibly hold out. I have reported as much to Headquarters, but no one pays any attention.

Not only did he receive no attention, but every time he asked for extra artillery, more batteries were taken away.

"You won't be attacked," Headquarters told him. "Verdun is not an enemy target."

In January 1916, General Herr managed to get an envoy

from General Headquarters, General de Castelnau, Chief of
Staff of the armies in the field, to come and inspect his sector.
On the spot Castelnau made an official statement: "The
organization of the forward position on the right bank of
the Meuse responds completely to the directives from Headquarters." Obviously Castelnau did not wish to dishearten
the troops or to sow panic among the civilian population. In
his statement there was also—let us face the facts rather than
burn incense before even the most time-honored figures—
an element of the diplomacy and solidarity that high-ranking
officers practice toward one another. Castelnau was not blind,
and he ordered, "as a safety measure," the construction of
fortified underground shelters (at last an equivalent of the
Stollen!) and reinforcement of the flanks of the second line.
The report he made to Joffre upon his return to Headquarters was a cry of alarm. The third-line positions, which Joffre had termed "completed or on the point of completion,"
existed—splendid in their blueprints—only on paper. The
second-line trenches were abandoned and falling to pieces;
those of the first line were shallow and in some places discon-
nected.

January 21st. General Chrétien, recently appointed 30th
Corps commander, came, in his turn, to inspect, and found,
to his dismay, that barbed-wire was lacking, that the battle-
ments did not afford a sufficient firing range, and that the
shelters were barely able to stand up against shelling. Another and more alarming detail: the communication
trenches were too few, and often no deeper than furrows, so
that reinforcements could not be moved into the front lines
unless the enemy benevolently ordered his artillery to let
them pass. "A catastrophic terrain," he concluded. Let us add
another quotation from Pétain, in the usual poetically melancholy vein:

> *Between the forts and beyond, everything was in a state*
> *of dilapidation. Trenches had collapsed, the network of*

barbed-wire covering the ragged woodlands of the banks of the Meuse and the muddy plains of the Woëvre was in pieces, roads had turned into swamps, and matériel lay scattered about, with the wood rotting and the metal collecting rust under the rain. The battle languished; there were only rare explosions of shells, bombs and grenades, which did not awaken the invisible troops from their slumber.

"We will not believe in an attack," replied most of the officers of the Bureau of Operations at Chantilly, "until aerial photographs show us parallel approach trenches 150 yards from our lines."

Approach trenches were usually dug at the very last moment, and in a very advanced position, so that the attacking troops should have the least possible exposure at the time of their attack. The Germans had built no such approaches before Verdun. Their deep, comfortable first-line trenches were from three hundred to eight hundred yards or more from those of the French. Because no attack had ever been launched from such a distance, it was presumed that none would be.

Ever since the beginning of January, German deserters had crossed the lines. Among them were conscripts, who had no taste for the coming battle, and Alsatians who felt no loyalty to the German flag. The deserters told of the enormous building program behind the German lines, of the thousands of tons of cement poured by French and Russian prisoners to make heavy-artillery platforms, of the digging and equipment of the *Stollen,* of the convergence of troop trains just behind the front. Some of them brought a word-for-word account of the Crown Prince's order of attack for the night of February 11th and 12th, explaining that the attack had been delayed because of bad weather which prevented the sighting of the heavy guns; others described the assault companies suffering from the low temperature, the indigestible cold rations, and the tension of expectation and postponement. It was natural enough that the deserters' stories should be imprecise and contradictory. A simple soldier does not see the overall picture, and may misinterpret what he knows. The contradictions made Headquarters mistrustful. Deserters may, of course, plant false information. As Pétain has put it:

> *Between February 18 and 21 reports were so inconsistent that the High Command wondered if the German attack might not be made on the Eastern rather than the Western Front.*

On February 17th the Verdun region was swept by heavy winds and gusts of snow. February 18th was cold and foggy, but during the night there was rain. The French soldiers welcomed this letup as affording a chance for reinforcements to arrive before it was too late. The ordinary soldiers and noncommissioned officers had no doubts at all about whether the German attack was to be made on the Eastern or the Western Front. They did not belong to the small, privileged group whose function it was to take a broad view, to think along general lines, and come to a decision uninfluenced by petty details. All they knew was what their eyes and ears told them. They had witnessed the erection of the German observation post at Romagne, a miniature Eiffel Tower, and every night for weeks they had heard clanging iron and rumbling wheels just behind the German front lines. For their own part they were taking advantage of every hour of darkness, no matter how bad the weather, in the second line and even the first, to lay barbed wire and deepen the trenches.

February 19th. In spite of the rain there was cannon fire on both sides. General Joffre came to Verdun and "congratulated General Herr on his preparations."

February 20th. General Herr, encouraged by Joffre's favorable opinion, requested and received more supplies. Headquarters had begun to think that something might be going to happen.

*   *   *

February 20th: 6:00 P.M. In the dusk three German soldiers belonging to the 143rd Infantry Regiment, Fifteenth Army Corps, commanded by General Deimling, emerged, one after the other, out of a shelter trench in the German lines near Étain. Their rifles were swung from their shoulder straps; their tabs were rolled back, and they carried cooking utensils in their hands. As they proceeded toward no-man's-land they were stopped by one of their own patrols.

"Where are you going?"

One of the soldiers explained that he and his comrades had been sent out to distribute rations and had lost their way. He spoke correctly but with a visible effort.

"What's the matter with you, anyhow?" asked the patrol sergeant. "Have you been drinking?"

"Oh, no, nothing like that!"

"Well, get along with you, then! You want to stick to the right-hand side of the road."

The front was silent; the only sound was the characteristic sloshing of the soldiers' boots in the mud. Each one of them could also hear his own heart pounding. Soon there was the sound of heavy breathing as well, for they were walking as fast as they could. At their left was a pale white ribbon of road.

"We'll be crossing over soon," said the soldier who had answered the sergeant. "That's where we'll have to put on speed."

This time he did not speak in correct although halting German, but in Alsatian dialect. Suddenly the man beside him stopped in his tracks.

"Count me out," he said. "It's too risky. I want to go back."

Before he had finished, two rifles were poked into his chest. His heart beat even more wildly than before, and he nodded his head.

"All right. I'll go along."

It is incredible how clearly a road can stand out in the darkness. Here and there German lookouts, crouching behind their machine guns or with their rifles braced against their shoulders, peered into the night. Finally Private Emile Didier of the 143rd Infantry, Fifteenth Army Corps, the leader of the little expedition, whispered:

"Let's go!"

A second later the road was behind them.

"Throw down your guns! Flat on your bellies!"

Soldiers of the First World War were quite used to crawling through the mud. It was slow going, hard on the elbows and hips and heart. The three soldiers stopped at every shellhole just long enough to catch their breath or until a sudden noise, perhaps that made by one of the many rats, caused them to move on. The minutes and hours dragged by. The shellholes were invariably filled with water, and the men were soon soaked to the skin, although a coating of mud gave them some protection. Luckily they did not run into much barbed wire; we have seen how inadequately Verdun was defended. Eight times, however, they had to take out their clippers, cut the strands, and then worm their way through. Their hearts pounded now, not so much from fright as from sheer fatigue.

Emile Didier, who was crawling ahead of the others, stopped and waved his arm. About thirty yards ahead were the outlines of half-destroyed houses. Didier's calculations had turned out to be correct: these were the ruins of Mongerville. Among the crumbling walls, on the irregular surfaces that had once been streets, in formerly fenced gardens ghostlike forms moved to and fro. The only sound was the clink of the metal objects they were transporting. Two men were leading—of all things—a donkey, with a roll of barbed wire strapped on its back. Someone must have taught the donkey not to bray. It was ten o'clock, four hours after the three

Germans had left their own lines. Emile Didier raised his chest out of the mud and shouted in his best French:

"Don't shoot! We're Alsatian deserters!"

His outcry caused the French soldiers to freeze in their places. Then there was the click of a cartridge slipping into a rifle breach.

"Don't shoot!" Didier repeated. He scrambled to his feet and ran toward the houses, his hands held over his head and his comrades behind him.

"Your guns! What did you do with your guns? How many of you are there? Where are the others?"

A quarter of an hour later, a French colonel, sitting on a chair in his shelter, stared at the three motionless, mud-caked figures before him and made notes of what one of them had to say. Finally he lifted his pencil.

"Have you had anything to eat?"

"Yes, sir. But we'd like most of all to be taken away. If they were to catch us . . ."

"Very well. I'll have you taken to Verdun. You say it's for five o'clock in the morning, do you?"

"Yes, sir, five o'clock. That's when things will start to move."

3

THE OUTBREAK

February 21, 1916. The earth turned with absolute regularity on its axis. On the coral sands of Pacific atolls natives roasted fish over wood fires; drunks fell to the floor in the waterside taverns of Brooklyn; camel caravans wound their way through the deserts of Asia and Africa; hundreds of millions of men were barely aware of the fact that Western Europe was the seat of a so-called Great War. The site of the carnage was no more than a scratch on the surface of the globe; to many people, even in France, war was only a word.

In Paris, 125 miles from the front, life went on much as usual, except for the shortage of coal and the lack of men, of whom so many had been called up by the Armed Forces. On their way to work Parisians eyed with curiosity and surreptitious amusement the women ticket-takers on the buses and subways. For the first time women were working, not only in shops and factories but also in the public service. Women of all classes of society wore forage caps, the more fashionable among them rigged out with veils and tassels, as tokens of their eternal remembrance of their dear ones at the front. Actresses and theatergoers, at seven o'clock in the morning, were still asleep. The theaters had reopened on December 12th, when Marthe Chenal, enveloped in a French flag, sang "The Marseillaise" at the Opéra-Comique. For a short time thereafter only classical pieces were given,

but soon this Spartan rule was relaxed; after all, soldiers
on leave needed lighter things to distract them. And so, at
seven o'clock in the morning of February 21st, many women
were still asleep, waiting for their maids to bring them a
cup of creamy hot chocolate. Alone or in company, regretting
their loneliness or enjoying it—such sensations were un-
changed, except for the obvious fact that men were increasingly scarce and that this scarcity lent added interest and
savor to casual affairs of the heart.

Paris woke up by degrees, from the working-class section
in the eastern part of the city to the fashionable one in the
west, in accordance with the revolution of the globe. People read in the papers the items concerning General Kuro-
patkin's assignment to the command of the Russian armies
of the North and the enthusiasm caused by the British
"Military Service Act" of January 27th, calling up all single
men between eighteen and forty-one years of age. Then there
was, of course, the latest official communiqué:

> In Flanders the enemy made a vain attempt to cross the
> Yser Canal near Boesinghe. Russian front: hard-fought
> battles and Russian gains on the Dneister, at Bukovin.

"Vain attempt" and "Russian gains" were both reassuring.
Of course, the war was in the back of everyone's mind, and
many people had already suffered privations or were in
mourning. No one was to blame if airplanes and zeppelins
failed to bomb the city every day and it was not within range
of the German guns. The fact was that Paris belonged to
the world of the "rear," a protected world as different from
the "front" as day from night, where life went on in normal
fashion and indeed had to go on for the very sake of the
war effort. The stabilization of the front had created this
cleavage, which lent the Great War, "the war to end war,"
a character all its own.

In Paris and all the other great cities of France the clocks stood at seven. Their hands moved as regularly as the earth, and soon they would stand at a quarter-past seven and then at half-past seven; the day would progress like any other day, and life would go on almost as it did in time of peace, in spite of shortages and absences and the black symbols of mourning.

*   *   *

A high-wheeled, horse-drawn wagon, carrying a big barrel of water, was moving slowly along the country road that led through the forest of Caures. The driver, with his legs hanging down over the front of the wagon, looked almost as bulky as the barrel itself, and from a distance their two bulks seemed to merge into one. He was muffled in a coat whose color—or lack of color—would have defied a painter's palette, and had a blanket wrapped around his legs, a sheep-skin thrown across his shoulders, a scarf crossed over his chest and another tied around his head, revealing no more than a pair of bright eyes and bushy eyebrows. Only an army helmet revealed the fact that he was a French soldier. Charity begins at home, but he had extended his efforts to keep warm to his horse, which was covered with a patchwork quilt of burlap sacks, sewn irregularly together. The animal was a yellowish-gray draft horse with a heavy mane and evidence of being well fed, no longer young but still spirited enough to whinny at the sight of an artillery mare. Every now and then the man in his wagon stopped at a group of soldiers to ration out his water in their pannikins.

The forest of Caures, covering a hill in front of the German-occupied village of Ville-Devant-Chaumont, was a strip of woodland a mile and a half long and half a mile wide, running from southwest to northeast, like a weapon aimed in the enemy's direction. A weapon indeed, since it was held by the 56th and 59th Light Infantry battalions, three hundred reservists, none of them very young and most of them in civilian life miners, farmers, and factory workers from around Saint-Quentin and the region of the Orne and the Meuse—in other words, stout, stolid fellows, hardheaded, careful of their lives, but courageous.

Nevertheless, from time to time one of these stolid men swore under his breath, tore up the newspaper he was reading, and threw the pieces onto the ground. The soldiers who came from the invaded regions had every reason to be downhearted, since the fate of their families was a matter of concern. The slanted news, the tendentious commentaries, and even the pure fabrications, which have always been the pap handed out by propaganda bureaus, had filled them with apprehension of German atrocities. Letters and food parcels from benevolent Red Cross ladies did nothing to relieve their anxiety.

These soldiers were under the command of Colonel Driant, Parliamentary Deputy for Nancy. On August 22, 1915, Driant had told Paul Deschanel, the presiding officer of the Senate, that within the next six months the Germans would "unleash a massive attack on the Nancy-Verdun line" and that all efforts should be made to fortify the terrain. Since then he had several times repeated his prophecy and asked for more men and matériel. His soldiers were unaware of these things, but they knew that their colonel was always ready to listen to their troubles, and never turned them away with mere words for an answer. Those who survived the Battle of Verdun are unanimous in their expressions of regard. The commander of the 56th Battalion was a Major Renouard, previously assigned to General Headquarters. Parliament had decided that all Staff officers should see service at the front, and Renouard was one of the few who did so wholeheartedly. Following the example of Driant, he had won the loyalty of all those who were under his command.

On February 20th the storm had abated. During the night the clay in the earth and its covering of snow froze over. The water carrier drove his wagon the whole length of the forest of Caures, distributing water to the soldiers who, under Driant's orders, were working to strengthen the defenses. In the frigid early-morning air they looked like peacetime woodcutters or foresters or intrepid winter campers. Only among themselves could there be any understanding of the continuing tension they felt at the closeness of the enemy.

It was nearly a quarter-past seven, and in the forest the almost horizontal rays of the rising sun shed a rosy glow over the snow-covered branches. Even the smallest twig had its coating of snow. Then something happened. Before even the slightest noise, before the whole northeast horizon began to crackle, the soldiers saw the snow on the branches quiver and fall. Before it had time to reach the ground, a stifling sensation shot through their breasts. A few minutes later General Passaga hastily scribbled in his diary:

> *Through the earthen floor of my shelter I can detect an incessant rumble of drums, punctuated by the pounding of big basses.*

General Passaga's shelter was near the Lac Noir in the Vosges Mountains, a hundred miles from Verdun.

*   *   *

Nothing existed but a roaring, thundering monster that lashed and ripped the earth, tossing huge chunks of it up into the cloud of smoke, dust, and debris which had replaced the breathable air. A rain of branches, stones, fragments of metal, cloth, and human bodies fell uninterruptedly from the yellowish sky. No other movement was possible; the human presence was reduced to flattened terror. In every man not yet smashed to bits the violence of the shock produced a constriction of the blood vessels that wiped out every feeling but sheer animal fear and the desire to hide underground the palpitation that still persisted in the center of his body, just above the diaphragm. Men's eyes were not closed but wide open, their pupils dilated; they did not blink when, a few yards away or even within reach, the bodies of their fellows were transformed into a flat spot beside them or torn to pieces or erased from their sight. Unable to move, the soldiers stared at the rain pouring around them. They were not divided into the living and the dead; there were also wounded men, whose shrieks and groans had even less chance of being heard than the crackling of an uprooted tree.

The water carrier had instinctively reined in his horse when he heard the thunder on the horizon. But within a split second the barrel had burst open and the wagon had turned over, with one shaft sticking up in the air. The horse's intestines formed a smoking gray mass on the ground, rapidly disintegrating under the falling debris. The bony structure of his head, neck, and ribs was laid bare under the torn flesh, and the quaking ground shook what was left of his body in the tangle of harness. As for the driver, he existed only in the form of a few shreds of skin stuck to the nearby trees until they too were shaken to the ground where everything found its eventual resting-place.

The cannons—77's, 88's, 105's, 130's, 150's, and 201's—were raking the first, second, and third French lines. The front lines were also assailed by the whistling projectiles of mortars (the German equivalent of the French *crapouillots*) nested in the German trenches. A few batteries were sending tear bombs into the ravine between the Hautmont woods and Vacherauville. Six *Drachen* (observation blimps), with planes hovering protectively above them, were directing the barrage.

The cannonade had opened along a six-mile curve between the Meuse and the village of Ornes; two hours later it extended from Avocourt on the left bank of the Meuse to Paroches on the right. At the same time it increased in depth, as 280's, 305's, 380's, and 405's came into play, to strike crossroads, forts, and villages behind the lines, the railway tracks at Sainte-Menehould, and the bridges between Troyon and Verdun.

Under normal circumstances both French and German soldiers were quick to detect by ear the caliber of the projectiles falling nearby or even over their heads. The roar of the big shells aimed at the rear, the whir made by 75's, 77's, and 105's have been described by countless veterans of the Great War. But on the morning of February 21, 1916, the breadth and intensity of the bombardment did not allow any such distinction. The fiery deluge swept with equal violence over the positions in the forest of Caures, at Ville, Herbebois, Haumont, Cap d'Espérance and, farther to the rear, over the woods of La Wavrille, Les Fosses, Louvemont, over the heights of Hardaumont and several villages close by. Equally frightening was the sight of ruined field positions and that of shattered human bodies and trees. Trenches of normal depth in the course of a few minutes were opened up as if by a giant hand, and turned into deep pits lined with corpses and fragments of corpses.

These human remains did not always lie on clean or at least decent ground. It was characteristic of the Great War that bombardments did not fall upon a terrain disputed by two moving armies but on one where for months men had been dragging out a miserable, almost subhuman existence and where corpses had been barely covered with earth or even left to rot on the surface. In many places pounded by the attack of February 21, 1916, wounded and dead men and survivors were commingled into one mass of tin cans, split helmets, slats of wood and metal that had made up the support or furnishings of their wretched trenches, and dead soldiers' boots and bones and the contents of cesspools the bombardment had uncovered.

Textbooks on war repeat over and over again that any bombardment is less destructive than it seems to those who are involved in it. This is to a large extent true. Even a hardened soldier cannot objectively sum up the extent of the damage around him. The murderousness of this particular attack may be judged by the fact that in the trenches of Herbebois one man per company was killed every five minutes. This figure may seem small when we think of Hiroshima, but the Verdun attack lasted not for just a second but for nine hours in succession. At the rate at which the slaughter was progressing, there would have been no one left alive after sixteen hours.

The examination of written accounts, together with the testimony that I have gathered from a few survivors, proves that the great majority of men submitted to this hail of fire had few and fragmentary thoughts: *I'm still alive. I'm going to die. I'm in pain. I'm going to choke. God forgive and protect me!* (There were more acts of contrition than one might expect.) Survivors have told me that after the first hour they realized that they were exhausting themselves by the emission of a continuous plaintive sound. Very few lost control of their bladders or bowels. Anxiety and apprehension cause these organs to relax, but the fear of immediate death has the effect of contracting them.

After a certain length of time a few soldiers managed to think in less elementary terms, or rather they found themselves voicing a protest aroused by awareness of their situation: "Where is the God-damned artillery?" The French artillery, of course.

*   *   *

We have no heavy artillery. No heavy artillery. Unfortunately we have no heavy artillery. The Germans have heavy artillery.

A child's memory is a perfect tape recorder, and I can still hear even the tone of voice in which adult voices spoke these words during the first years of the Great War. They served as an explanation or an excuse on every occasion that the French Army was defeated.

Along the six-mile central segment of the German semi-circle alone, a thousand pieces of artillery were assembled, including 540 heavy cannon and 152 mortars. The opposing French artillery numbered 270 pieces in all. The 140 French heavy cannon were either of the Rimailho type, which had a ridiculously short range, or else old Banges which had been taken from dismantled forts. Everyone has heard of the famous 75, hailed at the outset of the war as the weapon that would ensure victory. It was pictured on postcards; miniature replicas were sold as trinkets or charms; and there was even a celebration of one or more 75 Days. The 75 was a cannon with a low trajectory, unsuited to the hilly Verdun region, and no match for the short-range but heavier German 150's and 210's. The French had a reserve of 15,000 shells, for all their guns; the Germans had allotted 3,000 shells to every battery.

But the lack of guns and ammunition was not responsible for the inadequate French reply to the German cannonade. The fact was that no battery commander received orders to open fire. All telephonic connection with the rear was cut, and the signal flashes could not be seen through the cloud of dust raised by the bombardment. Undirected, random firing through this cloud would have been a completely wasted effort. Moreover, the battery commanders and their gun crews were in no condition to wonder whether or not they should fire, because of the hail of shells around them. In many artillery positions the chances of survival were as slim as in the front-line trenches. All but one of the men of a battery of 240's in the Haudromont ravine were wiped out by a single salvo. The lone survivor somehow managed to hitch the undamaged guns to a linker and convey them to safety. A battery of 75's suffered the death or disablement of twenty out of its twenty-four men in the space of only two hours. Horses, blinded by tear gas or wounded, threw themselves against trees or into ravines, and the explosion of ammunition wagons added to the general turmoil.

"The instinct of self-preservation is always the same," writes Ernst Jünger. "It is a mistake to believe that soldiers toughen and become more brave in the course of a war. What they gain in technique, in knowing how to deal with the enemy, they lose in nervous exhaustion. There is only one support, and that is a sense of honor which it is given to few men to possess." Quite so. At the beginning of an attack, the hardened veterans are just as shaken as the new-comers; experience enables them to mask their emotion, but only in a few cases completely to master it. The bombardment of February 21, 1916, had been going on for some time before the "few" to whom Ernst Jünger refers were able to collect their wits and think clearly. They were, for the most part, line officers, who had learned on the spot the special technique of trench warfare.

Their train of thought was not very startling; it was, in fact, elementary, but it was a distinct achievement to progress from the phrase "Where is the God-damned artillery?" to "We must get guns to fire back." There was no hope that the French artillery could silence the German, but at least it could hold it in check. The infantry officers were thinking: At any minute the Boches may move to the attack. If we don't bombard their front line, they'll come at us in full force and wipe us out with hand grenades.

Even if the French guns were to cause little actual destruction, they would raise the defenders' morale. Even civilians know that the sensation of being a helpless target can become psychologically unbearable. Already some French soldiers had gone mad.

The lines were cut; any field telephone still to be found in an intact shelter was a mere curiosity. The only way to communicate with a command post was to send a runner.

The front-line soldier of today has no difficulty in getting in touch with his command, with faraway tank or artillery units, or even with planes and helicopters in the air above him. "Walkie-talkies," radio transmitters and receivers, all of which have become more and more compact and efficient, have brought about the disappearance of the soldier or non-commissioned officer who used to carry messages from one place to another. During the war of 1914 this man, when he was a private soldier, was called a runner.

The runner's task was particularly dangerous, and yet I have never read or heard that there were any shirkers. It accorded with the French soldier's high degree of individuality, his desire to be singled out for his intelligence, to function outside the limits of everyday discipline, and in some way to share the secrets of his superiors. In return he was ready to use his wits and to outdo himself in daring.

Now the officers who had realized the necessity of re-establishing communication asked for runners. Where the regular runners had been wounded or killed, there was no lack of volunteers. When the runners started out, the officers who were sending them, and many of the soldiers as well, raised themselves from the bottom of the shellhole or trench against which they had flattened themselves for protection to speed them on their way. And in spite of the instinct of self-preservation that nailed even the most hard-bitten among them to the ground, the runners got up on their hands and knees, and then began to run. Of course, they did not run as if they were in a cross-country race or the Olympic games. Bent over half double they advanced for a few yards, fell flat on their bellies, and then got up to run on. The soldiers left behind grimaced in agony when geysers of smoke and mud rose up out of the ground around them. Some had not gone very far before they fell never to rise again. In the trench more volunteers offered to take their places, but their officers held them back, thinking that one attempt was sufficient. Those who survived continued to advance sporadically until they disappeared in a curtain of smoke lighted by the flash of exploding shells.

*   *   *

An incessant rumble of drums, punctuated by the pounding of big basses . . . Such is the vivid description of General Passaga. How very different from the drums that, in the old days, had led the infantry to the attack! To the German High Command the artillery in this battle was to be queen. The big guns were to clear the terrain, and the infantry was simply to occupy it. This classic doctrine had up to now been theoretical, a dream of the staffs. In practice, both sides expected the infantry to fight and conquer, after an artillery preparation. Now the Germans seemed to be following the book.

The hundreds of thousands of German shells were not being fired at random. Fieldpieces and medium guns were battering the near areas, while the heavy guns reached out beyond them. Within this pattern there were variations; in military terms: *Hammering over a broad area, with concentration on picked objectives.* Among these objectives were villages like Haumont and Beaumont, evacuated by the civilian population, which housed nests of machine guns and hence served as points of defense. The soldiers who occupied their cellars could distinguish, in the hail of projectiles, the occasional big shells that razed entire buildings in the vicinity to the ground.

Farther to the rear the bombardment fell on Bezonvaux and Vaux, where men, women, and children took to whatever shelter was closest at hand. Shells ripped through rooms where the beds were still warm, where the kitchen stove was still burning. Out onto the street tumbled bureau drawers filled with underwear or linen, crockery, broken glasses, corsets, women's hats, flowerboxes, mantelpiece decorations, photograph albums, and other intimate treasures.

Still farther behind the lines, in villages like Thierville, the shells fell less frequently. Some of the inhabitants hid in the cellars, but others packed their few belongings and ventured out, clinging to the walls, hoping to work their way out. In Verdun itself the civil population took refuge in the citadel and in underground shelters. Beginning at 8:50 A.M., shells from medium to heavy began to fall. But, perhaps because of the large number of troops in the city, the people of Verdun were not really downhearted. Many of them thought that the result of the battle would be that the enemy would be driven farther back from the city. Life would then return to something like normal.

* * *

The runners who reached their destinations had the aspect of ghosts. Even those who were not wounded bore marks of the dust and heat through which they had come. They had crossed one, two, and three miles of uneven ground, studded with shellholes of all sizes, and crumbling trenches, which offered them precarious protection as they crouched among dead and dying men, skeleton-like woods littered with the trunks of fallen trees, ravines polluted by tear gas, and bombed villages, where temptation whispered in their ear: "You'll never make it! Creep into a cellar and wait until this hellish storm blows over."

The panting runners, their dirty faces channeled by sweat, unclenched their fists and held out a scrap of paper with a scribbled message which they knew by heart not only because this was the rule but also because it was quite impossible for them to have forgotten it.

Counterbattery fire was easy enough to ask for. The artillery colonel or lieutenant colonel, responsible for his own small sector, whom the runner eyed as a possible deliverer, suddenly felt the whole weight of the world upon his shoulders. "Where is our own lousy artillery?" Here it was again: the eternal reproach from the front lines. He sent the runner off for food and rest, and telephoned to brigade headquarters.

"I'll fire two 155's more or less into the air. At least they'll know we're here."

Such firing, except for moral support, was sheer waste.

Through the murk of the bombardment the German lines were completely invisible. The 75's, if they had not been smashed or had not lost their crews by the time the German guns lengthened their range in order to permit the assault troops to advance out of their trenches, might have served some purpose, if they still had ammunition. But before this they were completely useless. The heavier guns, with no target, had no function whatever. There were planes whose job it was to direct the artillery's aim, but for the moment the Germans had complete mastery of the air. Their squadrons of ten pursuit planes each gave ample cover to the observation balloons and held the French planes at bay. The isolated French flyers who managed to fly over the battlefield on the morning of February 21st found the landscape below them almost unrecognizable. Over the hills bordering the Meuse and the valley of the Woëvre the smoke was as dense as that of a factory region. The German lines were a roaring furnace of flames, and the forest of Spincourt was "a mass of fireworks."

* * *

Five miles back, at Dugny, Staff Headquarters for the fortified region of Verdun, the bombardment was almost as audible as at the front. From the heights above the Meuse there came an uninterrupted rumble. And yet, two hours after the action had begun, all that was officially known was that shells from 380's were falling on the city. The area of the bombardment was undefined, and so were the number of casualties and the extent of the destruction. No one knew whether or not the German infantry had begun their attack, and there was even doubt as to whether an infantry attack was part of the German plan. Some officers held that the rumble was unusually loud, while others swore that there was nothing "out of the ordinary" about it.

At eleven o'clock there was still the same lack of awareness. The only possible excuse lay in the fact that there were no telephone communications. Actually, all army headquarters are singularly uninformed. Whenever something starts to happen, there is a period of confusion during which nothing is known. The staff officers pace up and down the halls of a requisitioned manor house or chateau, smoking cigarettes and pausing from time to time to ask the telephone operators, with a studiedly nonchalant air, "The line's still dead, of course, isn't it?" The collective personality of any headquarters (as I know from direct experience) is fussy and suspicious. Only the most precise information, that which fits in with preconcieved standards and an established frame of reference, is accepted as true; all the rest is dismissed as negligible. The fussiness and suspicion have some reason for their existence; without them, Headquarters would be overrun by unconfirmed bits and pieces of news and even by stupid rumors. The drawback is that some time must elapse before the true picture of a sudden event can be known.

At Dugny, even after the receipt, examination, and checking of the runners' messages, relayed by the artillery command posts, the picture was that no counteraction was possible. What could be the target? Who was to aim the guns? What reinforcements were necessary? Yes, the bombardment *was* out of the ordinary, but exactly how was it to be described? Heavy, powerful, very powerful, massive, continuous —which adjective or adjectives were appropriate? (*"Easy there. If nothing comes of it, then we'll look silly. Doesn't it sound a little less loud already?"*) In short, after the usual period of hesitation and inaction Headquarters at Dugny decided, not without some apprehension (*"They want to hear something definite; that's what's awkward about it!"*), to send on, in very nearly their original form, the scraps of information it had collected, to the next echelon, that is, to Headquarters of the Central Armies at Avize.

Such a simple retransmission was totally inadequate. The

picture of an event cannot be sent higher up without inter-
pretation, without being placed in its general context, freed
of everything contingent and superfluous. As it travels it
must lose its original dimensions and reach the higher spheres
in an outline as clear as a Chinese drawing.

Avize Headquarters, for its part, had nothing with which
to collate the picture sent by Dugny except some vague reports from aerial observers, which spoke of *"a forest of flames
. . . a mass of fireworks . . . German batteries almost wheel to
wheel."* And so the report forwarded from Avize was simply a
recast version of the patchwork of feverish messages that had
arrived from Dugny.

The next echelon was the holy of holies, G.H.Q. (Grand
Quartier Général) at Chantilly. The final messenger was a
certain Major Thouzelier, known as "Toutou," who knocked
on a door, a paper in his hand, then opened the door and
closed it behind him. An interminable time elapsed. The
lapse was always interminable. The officers of the Operation
Bureau still paced up and down, smoking cigarettes and
pausing to ask the telephone operators, "The line's still
dead, of course, isn't it?" The news of an "out-of-the-ordinary" bombardment (this unsatisfactory adjective-phrase had
somehow survived) had reached its final goal. Now it was a
question of waiting until the door reopened. But the door
remained closed. To the stout man sitting at his Louis XVI
desk, behind the closed door, time was of no importance. Or
rather, he had come to the point where he thought of himself as the incarnation of time, impervious to any human
attempt at regulation.

"For two years," wrote Jean de Pierrefeu, "the whole
world had venerated the victor of the Battle of the Marne
as if he were a god." Every day, from every quarter of the
globe, he received gifts of chocolates, wine, champagne,
game, flowers, fruit, objects of art, clothes, cigars, pipes, inkwells, paperweights. His head was reproduced, like that of

Napoleon, on pipes, inkwells, paperweights, and glass bottles. Every day he received letters from schoolchildren (some of whom addressed him as "Our Father"), from old people who wanted to make him their heir, from women who wanted to don soldiers' uniforms and go to the front, to serve as nurses or in any other capacity, from madmen who begged him, as the Savior of their Country, to exorcise the evil spirits that tormented them or the children and relatives who subjected them to persecution.

I have neither seen these gifts nor read these letters. (Joffre used to shut himself up to examine them and sign his letters of thanks.) But the image of "Papa Joffre" is clear in my memory. In our school notebooks he was very close to God. No one told us that on Good Friday of 1915, when fish was served him, he pounded the table with his fist and said: "Bring me some meat! I'm a republican general!" If we had been told we shouldn't have believed it; and besides, this episode has nothing to do with the conduct of military operations. The most important thing, in relation to this most unscientifically waged war, was his incredible self-confidence. (In 1914, when Colonel Penelon submitted to him the design of a new helmet, he answered: "My friend, there's no time to produce it. I'll have wiped up the Boches in the next two months.") Self-confidence and perseverance. But let us not be too harsh. When a man carries so great a weight of responsibility, we have no right to pass summary judgment upon him.

Still the door did not open. Joffre must have resented the intrusion. Not that he was sleeping (he did not habitually fall asleep at his desk, as his detractors insinuated), but because he was probably absorbed in the elaboration of his master plan for a French offensive on the Somme, scheduled to take place in July. Not just another attack, but one that was to be irresistible, based on a formidable concentration of troups and an artillery barrage such as had never been seen before. Artillery would be queen of the battle, and the infantry would have only to march in. The preparation of this final blow required the strength of a Titan and the wile of a Machiavelli, for it involved parliamentary as well as military strategy. "Joffre was a born politician," says André Tardieu, "a lobbyist of the first order."

Amid such preoccupations the passive defense of Verdun was a detail that he had, quite naturally, left to his subordinates. Now there was a bombardment, described as "out-of-the-ordinary." This presented a dilemma: "Either I move up reinforcements or I wait to see what happens next. If I send more men into the cul-de-sac of Verdun and it turns out that the bombardment is only a feint to cover up an attack in another sector, then I'll be in trouble. On the other hand, if Verdun turns out to be the real thing, it means serious trouble." Lucky Napoleon, who marched into Italy with an army of forty thousand men! Joffre had millions to think about, and to maneuver them meant straining an almost unbearably cumbersome machinery: troop trains and trucks, guns and munitions, and, behind them, quartermaster and medical units.

No wonder the door did not open. Joffre was taking his time and thinking it over. Events usually move more slowly than we imagine, and although the postponement of a decision may cause one chance to be lost, there is always another to be seized later on. The officers of Joffre's staff found fault with his somewhat affectedly blunt speech, his southern accent, and his crude manners (when the Duke of Connaught was his guest at Chantilly he summoned him to the table with a "Sit where you please, Your Highness"), but they did not object to his deliberation. It was of a piece with his self-control and coolheadedness, his refusal to be stampeded into a decision. In the collective personality of General Headquarters, these are qualities without price. Joffre's phlegm was a French-peasant variation of the Englishman's attitude of "wait and see."

By now some of the staff officers were looking at their

watches. Although it is true that almost everything can be postponed, there was one point that required immediate attention, and that was fifteen hours (then called 3:00 P.M.), the hour of the daily communiqué. In printing plants all over France the managing editors of the evening newspapers were looking at the rectangular space in the middle of the front-page form, into which every day the official war bulletin was inserted. The text they received from Chantilly, at an hour when, only 150 miles away, the air was still filled with smoke and debris and the ground littered with the wounded and dying, ran as follows: *Artillery on both sides mildly active all along the front, except north of Verdun, where there was more pronounced activity.* Evidently Joffre was still thinking it over.

* * *

In a deep German trench, with six inches of mud at the bottom, men quivered, and plugged their ears with icy fingers. Even the mud quivered, moved by the deep shaking of the ground below. The men's nerves were no less tense because the shaking was caused by their own guns; such a storm cannot be unleashed with impunity. At times the passage of the great mass of a 420 shell over their heads threw them against the wall of the trench, and they heard a rumble like that of a hundred subway trains under their feet.

Three o'clock in the afternoon. The men's heads were feverish and hot, but they were shivering with cold; the snow had begun to fall. On the French side the snow was barely noticeable; it melted in the fiery air before reaching the ground, but here it fell in great flakes, climaxing the fall of rain that had gone before. For nine days the assault troops had occupied the front-line trenches. Several times the corps commanders had petitioned for their relief, only to be told, "No, the attack will probably take place tomorrow morning." And so, from one morning to the next, the period of anxious expectation dragged on. Discomforts multiplied from day to day: wet feet, stomachs upset by cold field rations. . . . "Over the top with shit in your pants!" This was one of the favorite jokes of the *Stosstruppen.*

But no one really felt like joking. The men had spent their last pfennigs at the canteen, before reaching the front. What can a dead man do with money? Not that they really thought they were going to die. Underneath the contracted skin and muscles and digestive organs there was still the murmur of the life force: "Somehow you'll get through." But the images and voices that passed through their throbbing brains were all overshadowed by the age-old figure of the front-line soldier's last sweetheart, Death. There was the image of the church at Merles, transformed into a field hospital, with mattresses lined up in the nave and surgical instruments lying on the altar. The voice of a hurrying, preoccupied doctor: "They'll have to go by train, because an ambulance rolling over these bumpy roads would kill them." The face of the Crown Prince as he addressed the front-line troops, in a heartening tone, to be sure; but all the while the observation blimps floated overhead, nodding in the wind, like great heads that answered: "No, no, no . . ." The Crown Prince didn't get around to all the troops; some of them saw only the track left by his tires in front of a hotel. "He was here a moment ago, but he's gone." At Romagne a soldier who was slightly the worse for drink (having spent his last pfennigs at the canteen) bent down and touched the tracks with his hand. "All honor to you Kronprinz!" he muttered, half respectfully, half joking. A sergeant slapped his wrist, and he fell flat on the ground, as if Death had already struck him. Closer still the image of the captain, standing up in the trench and calmly asking the lieutenants, "Did you remember to name your substitutes?" Then the voice of the corporal jocularly announcing, "Here are the bonbons," as he distributed the grenades, the last handout before the attack. The conglomeration of beer and sausages gulped down at the canteen: perhaps that was the reason for the bellyache.

Now there was this earth-shaking thunder, which inflamed the brain and contracted every muscle of the body, inflamed and contracted them more violently than ever when the fatal words came down the line: "Five minutes more!" Atrocious words, even more inhuman than the next and last which were to follow: "Platoon, forward!" beyond which nothing was imaginable. The forts of Verdun loomed up like monsters, spitting death from their maws. The thunder of the German guns that seemed to sweep everything in its path was not completely reassuring to these men, not even to the most hardbitten veterans—to them, perhaps, least of all. In Champagne, during February of the year before, the German artillery had seemed to flatten everything in its path, and yet when the soldiers leaped out of the trenches to "occupy the terrain," dozens of them staggered and fell in the first twenty yards. The terrain was occupied, of course, but by dead bodies; that was the catch in the story.

The French guns were firing—feebly, to be sure. (Incredibly enough, the first haphazard French salvos, intended to comfort the prostrate defenders, were better heard by the Germans, who anxiously counted every shot.) The French shots were desultory, quite ineffective in comparison with those of the Germans. But the men waiting in the German trenches knew what this meant. The French were not so crazy as to waste their ammunition at this stage of the game. Just as in Champagne, at the moment when the Germans lengthened their range and the first assault troops leaped out of the trenches, the French 75's would come into play. The weight of the soldiers' helmets was almost more than they could bear. The lieutenant was holding up his left wrist, his eyes glued to his watch. Only one more minute to go.

4

THE PARAPETS OF CORPSES

THE READER should take advantage of the lapse of time and the perspective it affords to raise himself for a few minutes above the murk and mud and look from a bird's-eye, strategical point of view at the snowy landscape around Verdun. The coming struggle must not present itself to him in a state of confusion. The numerical strength and the unit designations of these masses of men about to come to grips, the names of the places where they clashed are part of history. If two veterans of Verdun start talking, they seem to express themselves in a code language of numbers. "The 351st, the 59th Light Infantry, the 1st Battalion of the 324th, the 2nd Sharpshooters, the 2nd Zouaves, the 61st R.A.C." If Germans are included in the conversation there is still the same almost secret code: the 24th Brandenburgers, the Twentieth Army Corps . . . We cannot mention every number without falling into the very confusion we are trying to avoid, and so we shall limit ourselves to the larger formations. They are not an abstraction: they exist not only on paper but as parts of the landscape before us.

Three German Army Corps—the Seventh Reserve Corps, under General von Zwehl; the Eighteenth Corps, under General von Schwenk; the Third Corps, under General von Lochow—occupied the right bank of the Meuse from west to east, from Consenvoye to the vicinity of Ornes, and were slated to strike the main blow. The Fifth Reserve Corps, which had held this ground until the arrival of the assault troops, had retired, for purposes of regrouping, to the rear and did not go into action until February 24th. In the Woëvre region, from Ornes to Éparges, two divisions of the Fifteenth Corps and the 5th Landwehr division were ready to advance as soon as the French front gave way. The disposition of the German troops, with their supporting artillery and complex supply organization, had been planned down to the last detail. At the moment when the first-line section leaders were looking at their wristwatches and preparing to give the signal for attack, the German masses, from front to rear, were practically intact. Few and far between were the shellholes made by the French artillery on the German terrain.

We have already seen that, on the French side, General Herr with his headquarters at Dugny was in command of the fortified region of Verdun, and subordinate, in his turn, to General de Langle de Cary, commander of the Central Armies Group with his headquarters at Avize. On the right side of the Meuse, from the riverbank all the way back to Ornes, facing the first three Germans Corps mentioned above, was the Thirtieth Corps, under General Chrétien with his headquarters at Souville. The Thirtieth Corps included the 51st and 72nd Infantry divisions, under General Bapst and General Boulangé respectively. The 14th Infantry Division, also a part of the Thirtieth Corps, was held in reserve east and south of Ornes. The left bank of the Meuse, as far as Avocourt, was held by the Seventh Corps (29th and 67th Infantry Divisions), under General Bazelaire. Farther south, in the Woëvre Valley, was the Second Corps (3rd, 4th, and 132nd Infantry divisions), under General Duchêne. General Herr's reserves, the 37th and 48th Infantry divisions, were stationed eight and sixteen miles south of Verdun, toward Souilly and Chaumont-sur-Aire. General Balfourier's almost legendary Twentieth Corps, famous for its striking power, was on the way from Charmes to Bar-le-Duc.

Let us remember, in relation to what follows, that the two railway lines that normally connected Verdun to the heart of France were both cut. The one running up from the south, by way of Commercy, had been cut in 1914 by the German salient at Saint-Mihiel; the other, from the west, by way of Sainte-Menehould, had been severed at seven-fifteen on the morning of February 21st. Bar-le-Duc was now the only railway center for the passage of reinforcements and supplies. But the railway was a winding narrow-gauge line, in a state of disrepair, known as the "Meusien," supplemented by an unpaved secondary road. These formed the ridiculously inadequate "umbilical cord," which von Falkenhayn had asserted could so easily be blocked off or broken.

At four o'clock in the afternoon, the range of the German big guns lengthened. As if moved by a single hand holding a watering hose, the hail of fire ceased to rake the French front lines and started to spray the rear. The intermediary space was like the calcified surface of the moon or some other dead planet, with smoke hanging overhead. The desolate ground was covered with long necklaces, whose beads were bomb craters, outlining the former French trenches. Where there had been woods, all the branches had been lopped off, leaving an assembly of charred, bare trunks, a sort of tree cemetery, blanketed in snow. This was the terrain over which the German assault troops were now to advance.

*   *   *

In a dark moving-picture theater the screen images of an attack never fail to thrill the audience. Soldiers leap in waves out of the trenches with fixed bayonets, while geysers of smoke raised by enemy shells spurt up from the ground around them. Single figures disappear in the smoke, but others go on. The enemy machine guns go into action; the attacking line grows thin; soldiers stumble, gasp, drop their guns, and fall on their faces; but another wave takes their place and pushes ahead, heedless of losses. The men of the second wave finally jump, holding their bayonets in front of them, into the trenches on the enemy side.

I saw all this, just lately, at a revival of *All Quiet on the Western Front,* and the pictures were so realistic that I fancied myself an actual participator. Such infantry charges undoubtedly took place during the First World War. But if we wish to picture the German assault of February 21, 1916, we must imagine something entirely different.

The heavy guns still boomed in a funereal tempo. Their heavy helmets making them look like beetles, the German soldiers came out of the trenches. But they did not leap or run or advance in waves. They proceeded at a slow walk, each line led by a corporal or sergeant; and some of the officers did not even hold their revolvers in their hands. This was no dream of the General Staff. Infantrymen actually wore their guns swinging from their shoulders; grenadiers did not take the grenades out of their belts. They walked with lowered eyes, watching out for unexploded shells, across the three hundred to fifteen hundred yards of aptly named no-man's-land. Let us look, in our turn, at the crater-studded ground. What is this charred fragment of a beam? Is it a remnant of trenchwork or just a piece of wood that has been rotting for months in the mud?

At certain points the Germans crossed the French front lines without even knowing it, without seeing the least sign of trenches, dugouts, sandbags, wooden crates, or human beings. The defenders had been pulverized, almost like the inhabitants of Hiroshima, their bodies mingled so closely with the earth that flesh and earth were one. This was a feature of the early stages of the Battle of Verdun, this total annihilation of the front-line positions.

Let us follow the advance. This small-scale countryside is rolling rather than flat. We go up and down, over hillocks and along narrow ravines. The stripped trees are uncannily still amid the gusts of snow.

Not quite everything has disappeared. Our watchful eye distinguishes the necklaces of shell craters outlining the former French trenches. Every now and then we hear a plaintive cry. War stories often expatiate upon the moans and groans of wounded soldiers. Here they are drowned out by the roar of the artillery; only an occasional shriek from his immediate vicinity reaches the advancing German infantryman's ear. This is the time to unstrap his rifle or hold a grenade in his hand, for often the first complaint of the wounded precedes the defenders' machine-gun fire. In any case we must pass the wounded by. Later on, stretcher-bearers will pick them up, without regard to nationality, but only after the advancing infantry have left them behind. In his passage a German may finish off a wounded enemy in case he props himself up on his elbow to throw a treacherous or (from the opposite point of view) heroic hand grenade. Few wounded men, however, retain sufficient presence of mind to make any such gesture.

On and on. The officers do not look steadily ahead of them; according to instructions, they turn their heads from side to side, with a birdlike motion, in order to maintain contact with the other lines and to make sure that their own men are following them. This tiresomely slow advance seems ten times slower to those who are actually making it. Each man has a vivid memory of other occasions when the monotony was broken by the crackle of machine-gun fire and the sight of comrades falling around him.

The right wing of the Third Corps and the left wing of the Eighteenth are converging on the northenmost edge of the forest of Caures, a ridge which forms a salient facing toward the German lines. "Torn to ribbons" is the only phrase with which to describe the forest. Even the bare trunks of the trees are slashed from top to bottom, but at least their black, ghostlike forms do not cry out in pain.

Ra-ta-ta-ta. Ra-ta-ta-ta-ta. Flashes of light and the crackle of machine guns. Men swear or shout as they fall; men drop in silence like sacks of potatoes. The defense of Verdun has begun.

* * *

Jacques Péricard tells us that the German grenadiers armed with flamethrowers and wire cutters who penetrated the woods of Haumont, northwest of the forest of Caures, found French infantrymen asleep. Two battalions had practically melted away in the course of the ten hours since the beginning of the offensive. The survivors were so nervously exhausted that as soon as the range of the German guns lengthened and the shells began to fall beyond their position, they fell into a deep sleep, and the Germans discovered them, sleeping amid the dead bodies of their comrades, while shells still whistled through the air.

It is even more amazing that, not only in the forest of Caures but in the woods of Haumont and Ville and to the east, and at Herbebois as well, men who had survived the cannonade, when they saw the Germans advancing, were able to set up their machine guns or shoulder their rifles and open fire.

During the Second World War, on Pacific atolls which had been flattened out by American ships and airplanes, Japanese soldiers came out of their shelters and threw hand grenades in the very second before they themselves were finished off by flamethrowers, while others threw themselves like living explosives under the advancing tanks. At Stalingrad, Russians and Germans gave equally astounding examples of fighting to the end with destruction all around them. There are relatively few examples in history of such determination, and some are more psychologically explicable than others. The Japanese, of course, were motivated by racial and religious fanaticism. But the defenders of Verdun had no great hate for the *Boches*. Indeed, some of them had probably taken part in the truces that at intervals were tacitly declared between the opposing lines. The trenches were for such a long time so close together that French and German soldiers came to know each other's voices and coughs, the sounds and even the smells of daily life, more closely than if they had been living on the same floor of an apartment house. Under such conditions it was inevitable that there should be moments of spontaneous relaxation, which allowed for the exchange of cigarettes and newspapers and for expeditions to bring in the wounded of both sides. Officers on the spot tolerated this state of affairs, but the High Command stigmatized it as "fraternization."

Because there were, in the First World War, neither racial nor ideological differences, the front-line survivors at Verdun knew that they could, without fear of torture or mistreatment, give themselves up to the advancing enemy. Thus, some of them were taken prisoners, either from nervous exhaustion or the lack of weapons and ammunition, or because their position was surrounded and they saw helmeted Germans with flamethrowers and machine guns all around them and heard the German guns pounding their second lines to cut off any prospect of escape. In their physical and psychological position we must honestly admit that we might have done the same thing. It is all the more surprising that other survivors should have pulled themselves out from under a comrade's corpse or even shoved this same corpse in front of them to serve as a parapet, wiping the blood and brains off their hands and placing their machine gun or rifle in position. Yet such French soldiers were not exceptions to the rule. In relation to the total number of front-line survivors, those who pulled themselves together and fired their weapons were actually a majority.

*   *   *

Detailed accounts have come down to us, including one of the attack on the forest of Caures, with large-scale maps showing the trenches, shelters, communication trenches, outposts, first-aid stations, tool-storage boxes, and even the pigeon houses belonging to the unusually well-planned defensive organization of the chasseurs of Colonel Driant. On the maps we see the name and position of every noncommissioned officer at the moment of the attack; and the accompanying account minutely describes the circumstances and successive phases of the battle:

> *A battalion takes position S.8 from the rear. . . . Between S.7 and S.8 the Germans have installed a machine gun and a quick-firing gun. . . . Sergeant Legrand who, along with six men, occupies Trench 16 . . .*

An extraordinary reconstruction, a sort of historical cross-word puzzle, but one that we have no time to follow in the midst of so grimly realistic a situation.

The first factual element in the picture of the forest of Caures is this: out of Driant's original 1,300 chasseurs only 350 were still alive, and they were in a state of complete bewilderment. We can see from the combatants' stories that the willpower of certain officers, both commissioned and non-commissioned, was what held things together. Men who at first refused to react ("They hesitate and mumble something about pulling back; they are brave but quite naturally want to go on living. . . .") did not dare disobey orders, even from a simple sergeant: "Nothing doing, we're to stick it out here," and, cursing him roundly they fumbled for their cartridges. Others decided of their own accord to stay and fight, and among these emerged a small number of genuine heroes.

In one part of the forest of Caures, where there had been sporadic machine-gun fire, the Germans advanced in single file through a communication trench until they came to a bend where a lone Frenchman felled them, one by one, with hand grenades. The dead bodies blocked the Germans' way

and served the Frenchman as a rampart, but finally one man
had the sense to crawl out of the trench, make a wide semicircle, and hit the Frenchman over the head with his rifle butt,
from the rear. German riflemen, flamethrowers, sappers, and
grenadiers were closing in from three sides on the outpost at
the northwest corner of the forest, held by Lieutenant Robin
and his 9th Company, now reduced to the size of a platoon.
During an occasional lull in the bombardment Robin's men
could hear the hoarse voices of the German wire cuttters,
answering their impatient officers as they crawled, among
the trees, across the ground. Though they were advancing
with difficulty, they did advance, and hundreds of their comrades followed behind them. The so-called attack on the
forest of Caures was in reality a slow infiltration. "Good
God, here are some more of them! Now they're coming from
this side!" And all of a sudden German figures loomed up
only a few yards away.

Though there was nothing remotely resembling a charge,
there was bayonet fighting. Men held their guns at arm's
length, poking among corpses and rubble; they crept from
one vantage-point to another and flattened themselves
against trees like so many red Indians, while bullets whistled
like a magnified hum of bees, punctuated by the coffee-
grinder sound of the machine guns. The French defenders
first heard their enemies' breath and then felt it on their
faces as they engaged in hand-to-hand struggle. Soon they
were drawing trench knives and ripping each other's bellies.
On both sides men wrote home, "I'll never forget the expression on his face!"

Half or even a quarter of a mile from this melee, disarmed French prisoners were marching quietly toward the
German lines. For the German advance consisted of infiltration on one side and a flank movement on the other.
While Robin withdrew the survivors of his company to another small outpost, fifty yards behind, where they held out

for two more hours, two German assault battalions were edging their way toward the south end of the forest. In the woods of Haumont and Ville and at Herbebois, men singly or in tiny groups held on to barely perceptible rises and indentations of the ground. Twelve inches are no distance at all, but a twelve-inch rise is sufficient to protect a prone human body. At Herbebois a few such men, under the command of a sergeant-major not only survived but caused a German section to beat a retreat.

* * *

The Germans had a definite numerical majority. On the morning of February 21st there were seventy-three battalions on the German side and thirty-six on the French. But, although estimates have been made, there is no absolute certainty as to how many men the German command sent into the infantry attack that followed the bombardment. Certain positions, like the village of Haumont, were dealt with by the artillery alone. The battle had just begun, and the German command intended to conduct it methodically. The softened-up area was to be occupied at the least possible cost, and the next day the big guns would once more go into action. Artillery, rather than infantry, was to be queen of the battle.

There was still snow in the air when night came; but, later on, stars were visible through rifts in the clouds, and moonbeams fell upon the stripped trees. The German attackers and an ever-dwindling number of French defenders carried on their ghostly combat. The Germans had orders to lie low for the night in the conquered French positions, but when the Frenchmen resisted or even counterattacked this was out of the question. Besides, among the assailants, there was a spirit of excitement and aggression. Close-quarter combat adds primitive violence to the instinct of self-preservation.

The German guns were still booming. A few French guns

had begun to reply, but their aim was bad, and the shells fell, not on the German lines, but on the combat zone. Runners were still carrying their messages. Making their way through the darkened countryside, they conveyed word of the condition of the defenders of the forest of Caures and the Woods of Ville and Herbebois (no word came from the woods of Haumont, which had fallen into enemy hands). The return messages which went out from General Chrétien's headquarters at Souville were extremely simple; they simply said: Stay where you are. Hold on. In the case of the forward positions, this order was easy to obey; most of their occupants could not move because they were dead.

Meanwhile Headquarters was working on plans for a counterattack, to be carried out by the survivors. Some eight miles behind the lines reinforcements were beginning to move. They were heading for the secondary defense lines, which had not yet been attacked by the German infantry but were being softened up by the big guns. Snow was still falling. In shellholes and crumbled trenches along the way, wounded men cried out for water or a pistol shot in the head, calling their mothers and wives by name. But the enemy shells made it impossible to go to their rescue, and for the most part they were not even heard through the snow. The first night was drawing to a close. The gunfire did not let up; indeed, toward morning it grew more intense. This was the beginning of the second day.

*   *   *

The village was slowly sinking into the ground. At seven-thirty in the morning German assault troops captured the southern end of the woods of Brabant. From the woods of Haumont their officers stared down through their field glasses at the village of the same name. They focused upon it about every ten minutes, and after every such interval the village seemed to have sunk, like a floundering ship, deeper into the ground. It was a village of no particular charm, probably not even very clean, no different, certainly, from many others of its kind, except that it seemed to have been singled out for concentrated destruction.

There was something reminiscent of the Napoleonic era in this procedure of looking down on a battle as if from a box at the theater. The German officers paced up and down the snow-covered ground, exchanging impressions between one cigarette and another. The noncommissioned officers stood at a discreet distance, and beyond them were certain well-disciplined enlisted men. There had been occasions, since the beginning of the war, when discipline had gone by the board, but now in the excitement of battle it seemed to have stiffened. The officers were mindful of the fact that other units, belonging to the Third and Eighteenth Army corps and the Seventh Reserve Corps, would go into action at noon.

Lines of French prisoners were winding their way up the heights above Brabant and the woodland paths of Haumont. The stunned expression on their faces reflected the violence of the bombardment, and some of them, suffering from minor wounds, were helped along by their comrades. The German officers spoke to them quite without malice, joking about the changing fortunes of war and occasionally offering them cigarettes. At the beginning of their captivity French prisoners were always surprised to find out how many German officers knew their language.

Now the officers turned back to their field glasses. Through them, at moments, they saw flights of birds passing across their fields of vision. Migrating birds had long since flown south in order to escape from the winter weather, and these late-starters were the sparrows that usually hibernated in bushes, caves, and holes in the ground. Sometimes a faint ray of winter sun caused them to chirp, and many a German soldier let his thoughts wander toward his distant home.

But something was sure to happen to remind him that

this was war. The conquered terrain looked perfectly empty, an area of chaos increasingly draped in snow. Only field glasses revealed groups of heavy-helmeted German machine gunners in the former French positions. Occupation of the conquered terrain had been methodically planned to synchronize with the lengthened range of the bombardment.

In the onlookers' sight Haumont was still changing. It looked more flattened out than before, but there were still bits of wall standing. It takes time to raze a village to the ground. One stone seems to have a way of staying on top of another. And what of the inhabitants? Some of them must have been caught in the debris and have cried out, until, under a load of rubble, they were buried alive. Perish the thought! No officer can function if he gives way to pity. The French were not particularly tenderhearted, either. From this divided and contentious people there had risen up an army as tough as if it were made of professionals. France is a paradoxical nation, one that the Germans were perhaps fated never to understand.

At about half-past eight the bombardment of Haumont was suspended, and an infantry reconnaissance force appeared on the scene. Through the field glasses it was easy to see two long lines of men, with their rifles hanging from their shoulders. Toward the front of the lines the platoon leaders were insisting that they hold their guns in their right hands, a precaution which seemed quite ridiculous in view of the deathlike immobility of Haumont, with wisps of smoke floating above it. And yet, through their field glasses, the officers saw the men of the advancing reconnaissance groups throw themselves to the ground. The observation post was too far away to allow them to hear the spitting guns, but it was clear that some ambushed French soldiers had opened fire from the ruins.

The two reconnaissance groups beat a prudent retreat, without losing a single man. This maneuver paid credit to the tactical ability of their leaders, but they were none the less disappointed. A precisely timed and successful attack on an objective of this kind might have won them the Iron Cross. As it was, the German artillery started pounding Haumont again, less violently than during the preceding hour, but with patient determination.

Toward half-past eleven messengers brought word that the French defenders of the Ville woods were falling back. This was good news. Everything would have been under control, if only the men could have had some hot food. The field kitchens had arrived late or failed to arrive at all. On the way they had had to give precedence to marching troops and truckloads of ammunition. Like Moloch, the front devoured thousands of cases of shells, cartridges, and hand grenades. The maintenance of an even flow of supplies had been carefully planned and was now being carried out successfully. The only flaw was the delay of the field kitchens.

At noon the German gunfire slackened, and the battalions at the edge of the woods of Haumont and Brabant received orders to advance. Objective: the village of Beaumont. The officers put away their field glasses and took up their posts at the head of their men.

* * *

Since dawn the French soldiers in the forest of Caures had been pounded not only by distant gunfire but also by the mortars and howitzers the Germans had installed in the conquered front lines. From the sound of these projectiles it was clear that the forest was hemmed in on three sides and that the only possible escape route was in the direction of the woods of Fays and the village of Beaumont. There was no sign of an infantry attack, but, with danger sharpening their senses, the defenders could feel that the Germans were infiltrating not only the edges of the woods but also their interior.

At noon, when the bombardment diminished in intensity,

they received orders to come out of their shelters. Colonel Driant stood outside his command post, a rifle in his hand. At 12:10 the German attack actually came. Of course, it was not an old-fashioned charge. Helmeted figures moved across the snow; there was an exchange of shots and occasional machine-gun fire, with mortars in the background. By degrees the German figures became more numerous, while each of the Frenchmen discovered that there were fewer of his comrades beside him. This gradual increase of the one side and decrease of the other had something unreal and intolerable about it.

Overhead, a few shells, apparently coming from the French lines, to the southeast, exploded. The soldiers cursed their artillery, but four machine gunners came to tell Driant that these shells were from a German 77 that had just been set up on the road to Ville.

Orders to the forward positions were still just as simple as before: to hold on at all costs. Driant was temperamentally averse to calling a retreat, and in any case, to withdraw under the fire of a 77, added to that of the German infantry, would not have been a safe solution. He was itching to get at the gun, a bulky yet vulnerable foe, and said to his machine gunners in fatherly fashion:

"Boys, it's quite easy. Set up your gun facing the road, and that'll be the end of the 77."

Witnesses say that the gunners hesitated, but a lieutenant induced them to go ahead. Soon afterward the French infantrymen heard the machine gun's characteristic rattle. The gunners fired for several seconds at the gun, just long enough for the Germans to train it directly on them. A moment later they had all gone up in the air. Not long after this, a wounded soldier arrived at Driant's command post with the message: "Sir, Lieutenant Robin's 9th Company has been wiped out." Reports were becoming as laconic as orders.

One after the other the French positions in the forest of

Caures were surrounded. Lieutenant Robin had carried his regimental papers to his last command post. When he saw the Germans advancing from every side, he burned them, then picked up a rifle. A few minutes later, the Germans had taken him prisoner.

Little by little the Germans occupied all the French emplacements. In what was left of the trenches French soldiers who were out of ammunition fought with gun butts, picks, and shovels. Within the forest, during the day, there were many small but furious combats, which in spite of their restricted scope deserve the name of counterattacks. Short lengths of trench were recaptured and held for several hours. But it was impossible to stand up against the organized drive of the German assault troops.

Four o'clock. The situation was increasingly critical. After conferring with Major Renouard and Captain Vincent, Driant decided to withdraw his men, "in order to continue resistance more effectively from the rear." The withdrawal was effected in good order, with one company serving as cover for the rest. Because Driant had reluctantly issued the command to retreat he himself lingered near the fighting, at a first-aid post. Here he saw the rearguard of the covering company annihilated. A soldier was hit beside him, and with a bandage from his own first-aid kit Driant tied up the wound. Then he moved on, taking shelter momentarily along the way in a bomb crater. As he came out of it he staggered, threw out his arms, made a half-turn, and fell to the ground, dead.

A hundred yards away Major Renouard fell, in his turn, with a bullet in his forehead. Throwing their last hand grenades behind them, the soldiers continued to retreat. The Crown Prince writes in his book, *My War Experiences:*

> *The Eighteenth Army Corps had orders to take the forest of Caures, at any price, before the day was over. By afternoon it had effected a deep penetration of the forest*

at the level of the road between Ville and Vacherauville, with two other corps carrying out a flanking action to support it.

Out of Driant's 1,300 men, only 110 survivors reached Vacherauville.

When Colonel Driant fell, the German bombardment of the village of Haumont came to an end. Of the eight companies of the 362nd Infantry, which had been holding the area, there were some 300 men still alive. The German flamethrowers assigned to mopping up the cellars were amazed by the dust-covered, deafened, and stunned individuals, blinking like owls, who emerged into the light of the winter afternoon. Nevertheless some fifty men in this condition, pursued by machine-gun fire, managed to escape, among them Lieutenant Colonel Bonviolle and five other officers. When Bonviolle reached Samogneux, a mile and a half away, he wrote a report which ended: *Our orders were to hold on to the end. These orders have been obeyed.*

"To the end of what?" we may well ask, when we consider that this part of the front had been pounded for thirty-three hours. And yet at some points small groups of survivors fought so hard that the Germans mistook them for newly arrived reinforcements. Actually, the plan of a counterattack for the purpose of "regaining lost ground," elaborated at General Chrétien's Souville headquarters the night before, for execution in the morning, was never carried out. The counterattack battalions were still moving slowly up from the rear, under artillery fire which the Germans hoped would destroy them before they reached even the second lines.

The communication trench leading to Haumont, which the 324th Infantry was attempting to follow, was at certain spots literally filled with corpses. The men of the 208th, on their way to relieve the 327th at Beaumont (bombarded but not yet attacked), wept with pain as they tore their icy fingers on the barbed wire. One of the many shells that landed upon them left fifteen dead and ten wounded. Tree trunks and human limbs went up into the air and fell back down together. On the left bank of the Meuse the French artillery was answering the Germans with increasing vigor, but on the right bank there was a confused situation. The artillerymen attached to the field batteries, functioning under almost impossible conditions, were torn between the desire to support their exposed and martyred infantry comrades and their fear of hitting them. Those who had been cut off by the bombardment from their sources of fresh ammunition suddenly saw German soldiers rising up before and even behind them, and had to surrender their guns without firing a shot.

Guns were what the French army particularly lacked. This is not the place to ask why the Ministry of War, to which the government had, since the beginning of hostilities, voted unlimited credits, countenanced this state of inferiority. On July 11, 1915, Premier Viviani had asked the Minister of Supplies, Albert Thomas, "Are we manufacturing more than the necessary number of 75's?" To which Thomas answered, "Alas, we are not!" Pétain has termed the superiority of the German artillery seven months later, at the start of the Battle of Verdun, "overwhelming." No one was more aware of this state of things than General Chrétien, whom several historians have described as "a born winner." He it was who sent the order to all the infantry positions within reach to "hold on." But at the same time he realized that there was no purpose to throwing away the inadequate French artillery power, and during the evening of February 22nd he ordered the "most exposed" batteries to withdraw.

Infantry troops were, on the contrary, abundant. Although at the beginning of the battle they found themselves outnumbered by as much as four to one, this was because of the great concentration of the German forces in the weeks immediately preceding. Such an advantage could not be expected to endure. Even if (on this point French and German historians do not agree) the Germans enjoyed numerical superiority on the front as a whole, they could not have hoped to maintain it in such high proportion at Verdun without stripping other sectors. If the battle continued, it was reasonable to suppose that sufficient French reserves could be brought into action to halt the German thrust.

"If you want your men to fight to the death, then lead them," General Patton told his officers during the Second World War. "Troops are like spaghetti; you can't push them around, you have to pull them." And he put his principle into action by visiting the front lines and marching at the head of his men. Such a practice was frequent both before and during the war of 1914–1918. But at Verdun, where the spaghetti was stretched out along an extended front, it was obviously impossible. The French infantry, composed of about 1,200,000 men, was divided into army groups, armies, army corps, and so on; but actually they formed an unwieldy, sprawling mass, whose movement from one point of the front to another was beset with difficulties. In 1916, a general was called upon to possess the qualities of a stationmaster. And while the mass was being shunted from one supporting position to another, the front line had to stand its ground. This was why General Chrétien had issued the order to hold on, whatever the price. This was why, knowing that a leader has to ask for more then he actually hopes to obtain, he proceeded, on the morning of February 23rd, to call for a counterattack.

That morning, in the forest of Caures, the woods of Ville and Herbebois, and indeed wherever combat was in progress, an order to counterattack was only a scrap of paper. The front-line officer to whom it was addressed had barely time to read it. Even the generals of the two divisions involved, at their forward command posts, said to themselves that if their troops could temporarily contain the attack and then retreat in good order it would be a positive miracle. During the night between February 22nd and 23rd General Bapst had seen the garrison of Brabant—what was left of a battalion of the 351st Infantry—about to be surrounded. Because Bapst happened to be the sort of general that thinks last-ditch resistance should allow for some freedom of movement and that withdrawal is preferable to annihilation, he signed an order, at 12:45 A.M., to the effect that the battalion should move back and reinforce the garrison of Samogneux, a mile and a half to the rear. This disengagement was carried out, with intelligence and precision, between 3:00 and 6:00 A.M., in fog and a blinding snowstorm. At once Bapst informed his superiors of what he had done. From the Central Armies' Group Headquarters (General de Langle de Cary) came, later in the morning, this reply:

> *Every defense point must be held, even when overrun or surrounded. Such resistance, no matter how hopeless or futile it may seem, may have incalculable consequences, serving to slow up the enemy advance or to facilitate our counterattack.*

And, as a corollary:

> *Hold on, at any price, waiting for the counterattack, whether it can reach you or not.*

General Chrétien gave his version of this reply in an order transmitted to Bapst: *"Counterattack. Recapture Brabant."*

At this very moment the men of the 351st Infantry, who had fallen back from Brabant to Samogneux, were wondering how many quarters of an hour they could survive amid the flaming ruins. The only intact shelters were those dug, like mine galleries, sixty feet below ground, in the side of a hill. Here crouched the men who were supposed to recapture Brabant. The command post of the lieutenant colonel in charge of the battalion was completely isolated, without a telephone or bicycle or horse; all the runners he had sent to the rear had been killed, half his officers were dead, and the violence of the bombardment made it impossible to move. What did the lieutenant colonel and the men around him do? They held on. When a major and two soldiers on a dangerous reconnaissance mission dropped in on him, he sent them back with the penciled message: "The 351st is tired, but it is holding."

The orders to hold at any price caused much less of a protest among the soldiers than one might believe. The only thing that really irritated them during this phase of the war was the local offensive, what was known at headquarters as the "nibbling" operation. Experience had taught them that such an action served no purpose, even if it resulted in the temporary conquest of a piece of ground. The gain of a few hundred or a few dozen yards did not justify the loss of thousands of human lives. Fortunately, no one soldier knew the total of the losses incurred in such operations during the year 1915. But almost everyone suspected that two-thirds of these local offensives were launched by generals anxious to get the name of their sector in the news.

On the other hand, most of the soldiers were ready to obey their orders even under the atrocities of this bombardment. We have quoted Ernst Jünger on the sense of honor, which was given to a few of them. But the soldiers who stuck it out against hopeless odds were not just the few. They were motivated by a far more primitive, almost animal, feeling: they were defending their own soil. They were holding their ground in obedience not so much to their officers as to an obscure law of nature. Every one of them felt that he was defending a line beyond which were his wife and children (in animal terms, his mate and his offspring). This war, stupid as it was from the point of view of military science, nevertheless on occasion drew upon certain deep-seated biological resources.

Certainly if the order to hold on at any price, so tactically debatable, had met with protest, the French would never have put up such amazing resistance during the first days of the Battle of Verdun. There is a definite sameness in the accounts of the defenders of Herbebois, Beaumont, and the southwest section of the forest of Caures. Everywhere the German artillery was massacring men who were yielding ground foot by foot, sheltering themselves behind the last vestiges of every defensive position, the smallest fold in the ground; if need be, as many witnesses tell us, behind a parapet of corpses. All the accounts end somewhat as follows: "The enemy has filtered into the area between Herbebois and the forest of Caures and surrounded our position. . . . We are under fire from both left and right, and have no alternative other than withdrawal. . . . There are 20 men left out of our original 160 . . . 10 of them are going to make a break for it through the machine-gun fire. . . ." Few witnesses can bear to mention the plight of the wounded, too numerous so far to receive any attention.

West of Herbebois, on the heights of La Wavrille, the Germans broke through the first line and captured an entire regiment. Three other battalions escaped capture only by falling back on the run in the direction of the woods of Fosses. All over the map German reserves seemed to be pouring in; at Fays a regiment in spic-and-span uniforms moved to the attack *singing*. At four o'clock General Boulangé of the 72nd Division took it upon himself, without contradiction, to order a withdrawal of the survivors of Herbebois. At the end of the day the two divisional commanders, Boulangé and Bapst, realized that the continuous bombardment, the lack of sleep, and the threatening shortage of food and water made it imperative that their troops be relieved. But their messages to General Chrétien received only the reply: *Counterattack. Recapture La Wavrille.*

* * *

At nine o'clock in the morning of February 24th a rumor went the rounds among the German infantry occupying

Haumont that the attack would be resumed before noon. They were to move out of one set of ruins into another. The guns had rumbled all night long, and toward morning it seemed as if the bombardment were as violent as on the first day.

"One more push," said the officers, "and we'll be relieved. None too soon, either."

Prisoners taken that very morning had revealed the fact that Samogneux, one of the new localities subjected to the concentrated fire of the German artillery, had also been pounded by the 155's of a French fort on the left bank of the Meuse. For the Germans such a sign of disorganization argued well.

The officers knew that the new attack would be launched not only from Haumont but also from La Wavrille, Herbebois, the forest of Caures, Brabant, and all the other razed villages and stripped woods occupied by the French the day before. In the woods around Haumont reinforcements were assembled, regiments from the Fifth Reserve Corps, which had held the front-line trenches before the battle and then enjoyed a short respite at the rear. The others were those that had been involved in the push since the beginning. They were tired and dissatisfied with their field rations, but the scent of victory was in their nostrils. Even the most reluctant among them, the veterans disgusted by the slaughter at Les Éparges and other death traps, the raw recruits who had trembled as they waited for the order to go "over the top," were now caught up in the rhythm of the big guns. With this devastating firepower at their shoulders, they had a feeling of invincibility, even when they saw their comrades fall at their side.

Toward eleven o'clock, when the bombardment of Samogneux was lifted, four battalions emerged from the ruins of Haumont, with flamethrowers carried by the first line. No defenders of Samogneux were visible. On the slopes covered with hardened mud and snow there were only dead men, dead horses, and smashed guns. To the men with the flame-throwers, proceeding in good order, their officers in the lead, their noncommissioned officers bringing up the rear, this terrain littered with corpses spoke eloquently of a French defeat. As the flames licked the ground a few survivors came out, like rats, from their hillside shelters, throwing down their rifles and raising their hands in surrender. One group was said to be resisting furiously at the north end of the village, but was already surrounded. One battalion was left to mop it up, while the rest continued to advance, following in the wake of the destruction wrought with such precise timing by the artillery behind them.

Observation balloons and planes moved freely over the French positions, guiding the artillery fire. At two o'clock in the afternoon the French were still fighting stoutly at the north end of Samogneux, but the main body of the Germans had thrust on to their next objective, "Hill 344." Officers who acted as guides, when they stopped to look at their maps, were hard put to it to fit the printed page to the deceptively level, snow-covered landscape before them. Fortunately, the ruins of villages and the trunks of trees stuck out above the snow, and crippled guns and caissons dotted the fields, just as in old battle paintings. The tide of the German advance was slow-moving but irresistible. From the woods of La Wavrille, conquered the day before, a ribbon of gray uniforms unrolled in the direction of Beaumont; from Herbebois the movement was in the direction of the woods of Le Chaume, Les Caurières, and Les Fosses, and the villages of Chambrettes and Louvemont. The general advance was sporadic but continuous. From the low-flying planes one wave of soldiers could be seen fanning out toward the woods and villages where French machine guns were still waiting.

The German soldiers advancing on Hill 344 cursed as they

stumbled over remnants of barbed wire. The hill was a white sea, in which the bombardment threw up dark geysers of earth. Then the artillery fire, as carefully regulated as usual, was suspended. Suddenly the attackers became aware that French machine guns were still there. French survivors raised themselves on their elbows and fired across the intervening whiteness.

From their headquarters Generals von Zwehl, von Schenck and von Lochow, and the divisional generals under their command, followed the harmonious progress of the advance. The bombardment was still raking a wide area, from the west bank of the Meuse to a point fairly far east in the region of the Woëvre. But the infantry attack, in terms of both time and space, was assuming the form of a funnel. Since the first day the front had been gradually narrowed, in order to obtain, as in a steampipe, a greater power of compression and propulsion. At the center of the funnel's still wide-open mouth lay an objective which the soldiers had not yet heard of but which occupied a prominent place on the map and an obsessive one in the minds of the German generals— Douaumont.

The soldiers whose fingers were congealed on their rifle butts or scorched on machine guns, the grenadiers who marched and threw their grenades like robots, the men wielding flamethrowers, with smoke in their eyes, were all of them unconsciously advancing toward this same objective. But no single one of them felt the advance to be as continuous as it seemed to the strategists in the rear. First there was a forward push under the French machine-gun fire, then a halt while another group pushed ahead in its turn.

In the villages there was time to rummage in bombed-out bureau drawers, to pick up bits of civilians' belongings. There was no real looting; powerful as this instinct may have been, the battle was too close to allow any time for its satisfaction. In such a short time, what could be taken away?

The refugees had not left any small objects of value behind them. The soldiers were moved rather by simple curiosity, by the desire to escape for a moment from the inhuman violence of war and find some trace of everyday life. While half a platoon was routing a sniper out of a church tower, the other half was standing around a fire, passing a photograph album from one hand to another. Such bizarre scenes were common on both sides. In a cellar in one village, bombed to bits and littered with corpses, ten French soldiers sat drinking, smoking, and playing cards by the light of three candles. When the Germans burst in, the Frenchmen rose to their feet and surrendered without saying a word, while huge rats that were sharing their refuge ran off in every direction.

"One more push," the officers had said. From the soldiers who were storming Hill 344 the push required a superhuman effort. Wave after wave went up its bare side, only to be mowed down, as if by a scythe, by the French machine guns. At four o'clock in the afternoon the grim harvest was still in progress, when beyond the machine gunners propped up on their elbows in the snow, beyond the riflemen behind parapets of corpses, the attackers noticed the presence of new arrivals who behaved not like hard-pressed defenders but like conquerors. In the melee that ensued the most unbelievable things took place. Officers with drawn swords led their men in a bayonet charge on the machine gunners; a colonel with a swagger stick in his hand went into battle thirty feet ahead of his men. These anachronistic scenes took place so rapidly that the survivors wondered if they had not seen them in a dream. On this day anything was possible. Some wounded Bavarians were laid out in a barn where a few forgotten lambs were bleating with thirst. The least seriously wounded among them, who a few minutes before had been concentrating their attention on killing their fellowmen, dragged themselves out to get the lambs some water.

As night fell, French and German soldiers alike curled up

on the ground, often so exhausted that they did not concern
themselves with looking for even the most primitive shelter.
Snow was still falling.

*   *   *

The first reinforcements traveled in trucks as far as Verdun, under the falling snow. Traveling in the opposite
direction came the refugees. They trudged beside long
wagons with slat sides and canvas covers, vehicles that seemed
to have been built centuries ago in the East, filled to overflowing with mattresses and bundles of linen, beside dust
carts and even baby carriages, whose rubber soon gave way.
Where the road was narrow, this pitiful column was squeezed
close to the ditch to let the army trucks roll by. The soldiers,
bumping on their wooden seats, could see through an opening in the back of the canvas cover a row of umbrellas, and
under them tear-stained or strangely indifferent faces. On
the wagons women were nursing their babies; their hands
reddened by the cold held their milky-white breasts. This
sight was not one that inspired the soldiers to their usual
lewd jokes. They cursed beneath their breath and spat between their feet on the floor.

From time to time little donkeys, loaded with sandbags
and boxes that might have contained anything, including
munitions, were led by heavily bearded soldiers through the
space left between the line of steaming trucks on one side
and the refugee wagons on the other. The soldiers shot them
a friendly glance, as if they were comrades moving into the
same danger. Yes, the donkeys' bones might be mingled on
the battlefield with those of the men who were watching
them go by. But the soldiers had no such morbid clairvoyance; they were concerned, rather, with the holes in the
narrow road and the two rivers of traffic, each of which had
left overturned vehicles in the ditches on either side. Straining their eyes to see the endless ribbon of mud ahead, they
spat, and mumbled: "Getting off to a good start! . . . Who
knows what kind of mess there is farther on?"

Since the early morning of February 21st heavy shells had fallen incessantly upon Verdun. For the first two days the civilians, installed in well-equipped cellars and shelters, were not too badly off. Family groups shared their supplies, and in the underground parts of the citadel, where several hundred refugees were quartered, children played hide-and-seek. Everywhere people were saying, "The Germans will be driven back, and then we can return to normal."

But by February 23rd the lack of oxygen and light had begun to make themselves felt. The children were cranky, and the women were looking fearfully at the doors. Word went round that the Germans were coming, that the Germans were there. At six o'clock in the evening an almost prostrated elderly captain told the refugees in the citadel that within three hours they were to be evacuated. "Where you're to go? Wherever you can." At ten o'clock the little convoy set out in the darkness. The next day the evacuation order was extended to the entire civilian population, which was largely composed of women, children, and old people. The soldiers arriving in trucks from the rear ran right into the start of this exodus. "Keep going!" they were told. There was no time to hold the bundle of a woman with four children clinging to her skirts, to reassure a little girl frightened by a fire, to lend a hand to one of the old men, painfully walking, with the aid of a cane, toward the outskirts. The bombardment was scheduled to increase, progressively, in intensity. None of the new arrivals could guess that if he came back from the front this mutilated and burned-out city would seem like heaven.

*   *   *

Every defense point must be held, even when overrun or surrounded. . . . There can be only one order: to hold on at any price, with an eye to the counterattack, whether it ever actually arrives or not.

How long a time had gone by since General de Langle de Cary, commander of the Central Armies Group, had signed

this order? Less than twenty-four hours. Now, on the evening of February 24th, at his Avize headquarters, he was
poring over a map with his Operations officers, working out
an order to evacuate the whole Woëvre Valley. This meant
the surrender without resistance of an area twice as large as
that which had been fought over inch by inch since the first
attack, at the cost of 60 percent of the troops in the forward
positions.

It is one thing to send orders to the front line, and another
to make an important strategical decision—that is, if the
painful movements of a hunted beast can be dignified with
the name of strategy. Even a corporal, looking at the general's
map, would have seen that the protuberance formed by the
French front north of Verdun had dangerously narrowed,
with a salient to the east that might easily be cut off by a
flank attack. The defense of Verdun would be even more
difficult if the troops and artillery in the Woëvre Valley were
to fall into enemy hands. Therefore the decision of General
de Langle de Cary was that of "a withdrawal to the heights
of the Meuse." He telephoned to Joffre for approval, which
had been given, and then signed detailed orders to the local
commanders.

For the sake of its psychological interest, let us pause
briefly over the "storm of protest on the part of the generals
of the Verdun region," of which many military historians
have spoken. The staff officers at the headquarters at Souville
(Chrétien, Thirty-third Corps) and Dugny (Herr, in charge
of the fortified region) knew perfectly well how badly things
were going, and had indeed spent a good part of the day
drawing up orders for the destruction of the bridges over the
Meuse and other key points. Now they sat back in their offices, without any risk of ultimate responsibility, and decided
what they would have done. (There was no reason for them
to worry, since they did not have the power to implement
their brilliant alternative solutions.) In any case reality had
passed them by. The convoy of troops and guns moving up

from Souilly to Verdun found the narrow road crowded with pitiful sights. Beside the overloaded wagons an interminable line of women, children, and old people staggered under heavy burdens across yawning holes in the pavement and along the edge of crumbling embankments. Among the refugees was the Bishop of Verdun, pushing a baby carriage before him. And all this time the German artillery roared overhead.

Once the reinforcements had passed through the flaming ruins of Verdun and crossed the Meuse, they found themselves in an area of complete chaos. German shells were falling out of the darkened sky on convoys of wounded making their way to the rear, on trucks carrying supplies to units that no longer existed, on retreating artillery batteries, and on other relief troops who were unable to find the officers supposed to direct them to their positions. The German guns were their only guides, and these filled the entire northern horizon with their noise. Colonels were obliged to ask private soldiers driving trucks for the latest news.

"News? The Germans have broken through our front lines. We're fighting in open country."

And from his ammunition wagon an artilleryman called down:

"Our guns? Don't worry! The Germans are looking after them."

On his face there was a look of ironical despair. The pace at which the reinforcements were moving through the icy night was exasperatingly slow. Over and over again they were brought to a complete halt by the stream of refugees, to find themselves the targets of the bombardment. Not all of them traveled in trucks. The men of the 95th Infantry, for instance, had covered twenty-five miles on foot. Every time there was a halt they dropped to the ground, as if they were already dead. When their colonel sent a runner to brigade headquarters asking for a period of rest, the answer was, "Get your troops into battle as soon as possible, and to the last man!" Where the battle was to be engaged the brigadier did not know, having received four contradictory orders from divisional headquarters within the last few hours. Colonels, majors, captains, and even lieutenants had to search, not for their assigned positions but for any location that they thought could be held, that could be shaped into something like a front. But they too were swamped by reality. The situation was definitely out of hand. Too many men without orders, commanders, or ammunition were surrounded, captured, or wiped out before they had a chance to fight. At the edge of the woods of Haudromont, just north of Douaumont, on an abandoned artillery emplacement, a battalion of the 95th made a parapet of empty ammunition boxes. But the ground was too frozen for them to dig a trench, even with pickaxes, behind it.

In the low-lying Woëvre Valley men were chilled to the bone. In their disorderly retreat they had abandoned many intact batteries. Together, those who were obeying the withdrawal order and those who were involuntarily retreating noticed with anxiety the slackening of the German bombardment during the night. Every soldier knew the reason. The big guns were being moved farther south; the next day the cannonade would be more terrible than ever.

On the morning of February 25th, in answer to a call from Joffre, General Pétain, commander of the Second French Army, came to Chantilly. Since the evening before, he had known that he was to be assigned to the command of the sector of Verdun.

By now the situation at Verdun was so acute that it was understood even at General Headquarters. The shadow of disaster was visible on the faces of the officers with whom Pétain exchanged a few words before entering the holy of holies. Many of these officers had spent a sleepless night;

some of them were calling not only for General Herr's recall but also for his execution.

Finally an aide-de-camp opened the door. Joffre looked as if he had slept well, having, as usual, gone to bed very early. General de Castelnau, Major General of the Armies, had rashly violated instructions and disturbed him in the middle of the night with the latest news of Verdun. But Joffre had quickly returned to sleep. Now, at a quarter-past eight in the morning, he was rested and in good humor. When Pétain entered his office, Joffre got up and moved somewhat clumsily around his desk. With a kindly smile on his face he clasped his visitor's hand.

"Well, Pétain," he said, "things are not going so badly."

5

"DOUAUMONT IST GEFANGEN!"

T HE P R O C E S S repeated itself with almost monstrous precision. The range of the German artillery lengthened, leaving a pulverized village behind it, and the beetle-headed,
gray-uniformed soldiers began to advance. When the men
with flamethrowers were a few hundred feet from the ruins,
the French machine guns crackled, casting tiny sparks into the
mass of dust and smoke around them. "Platoon, flat on the
ground! . . . Platoon, about-face; fall back!" To a drill-
master's eye, the movement was executed to perfection. Then
the artillery hammered again at the target. The operation
was repeated as many times as necessary. On this morning of
February 25th the target was Louvemont.

Louvemont, a little over a thousand feet above sea level,
in peacetime is a village of little consequence. The main objective, of course, was Verdun. But directly in front of Verdun there stood a more impressive elevation, the fort of
Douaumont, east of and overhanging Vaux, with a ravine
between them. Louvemont was nowhere near; it was north of
Douaumont. But even a Bavarian corporal could have seen
that Douaumont could not be attacked from one side alone.
In order to move infantry up to the fort through the ravine,
it was necessary to capture the hill known as the Côte du
Poivre, to the northwest. And the key to the Côte du Poivre
was Louvemont.

Louvemont had been under fire since the day before, February 24th. Already it was a cross between a graveyard and a heap of débris. The defenders who brought their machine guns into play every time the German range was lengthened were the survivors of other bombardments, men who had fought their way out of encirclement with bayonets and hand grenades. These men who had somehow survived without surrender, without giving in to the temptation to run away, were superhuman, in some way hardened to the nightmarish conditions under which they existed.

On the morning of February 25th German flamethrowers had theoretically mopped up the ruins of Louvemont, and yet at half-past twelve the second battalion of the 85th Infantry was still holding out. At one o'clock, when Colonel Theuriet said to his men, "We're going to counterattack with bayonets," not a single one of them retorted, "The colonel is crazy!" On the contrary, they attacked, Colonel Theuriet himself at their head, a cigar between his lips and a swagger stick in his hand. No man can advance very fast with a lighted cigar in his mouth, and the colonel's nonchalance did not make for his men's safety. Nevertheless they followed blindly after him. The sight was so extraordinary that the German officers imagined that the French were coming forward to surrender. As soon as the German machine gunners saw the gleam of bayonets they opened fire. A minute later all the French officers were dead except for one second lieutenant, who gave the order to withdraw. The withdrawal resolved itself into an attempt to clamber over heaps of dead bodies without becoming one of them.

One of the most frequent phrases in reports of the First World War is "held in reserve." While the second battalion of the 85th Infantry was being annihilated at Louvemont, the first battalion was "held in reserve" in the ravine of Bras, a mile and a half to the south. Here is what was meant. . . .

The downpour of heavy shells was almost as terrible in the ravine of Bras as at Louvemont, and there was no shelter from them. The men were waiting for orders which, in view of the continuing deterioration in the French situation, had little chance of reaching them. There were no communications, and all the runners were lost or dead. Their disappearance did not really matter except to their families, because the orders they were carrying came from their superiors who had not the slightest idea of what was going on. Even those who were in the midst of it could know nothing outside a radius of a very few yards. Here, then, were the soldiers of the first battalion of the 85th Infantry, together with some remnants of the 273rd and the 310th, all of them "held in reserve" in the ravine of Bras, where there was no shelter from the shells of the 210's falling upon them. For those to whom the number 210 has no definite meaning, let it be said that a shell of this caliber that exploded against a tree in the ravine of Bras that afternoon caused death or wounds to sixty-seven men.

After the fall of Louvemont (at three in the afternoon), things began to move fast. Below Louvemont was the Côte du Poivre, from which parallel ravines led toward the village of Douaumont and its fortress, five hundred yards to the right. The German infantry occupied the ridge of the Côte du Poivre, swarmed over the summit, and then moved down toward their objective.

*   *   *

The 95th Infantry, defending the village of Douaumont, was the regiment we saw slogging it out for twenty-five miles toward the front, which had met ambulances, baby carriages, weary and ironical artillerymen and even deserters along the way, and which had arrived, utterly exhausted, in an area of chaos, whose colonel had received the order, "Get your troops into battle as soon as possible, and to the last man!" Into what battle and where? Perhaps the corpses piled up on the ground could give an answer; there was certainly no other source of information.

They reached a gutted village, one of many like it, until voices called out, "It's Douaumont!" The colonel had a clear idea of the local topography and knew exactly where the village was in relation to the fort. At once he set up his command post and immediately began to organize his defense: one battalion within the confines of the village, another in front of it. The east side was protected by the fort. "There are Zouaves," some villagers kept repeating, but no one seemed to know where they were or how many of them there were. The fort was what mattered; it was like a powerful right hand. To the west, in other words on his left flank, the colonel placed his third battalion, and soon afterward some messengers came to tell him that there were other troops just beyond them, some of the 85th, who were to fight at Louvemont the next day.

The bombardment was still going on, but in a desultory fashion, because the German artillery was moving up. For a few hours there was some chance of survival. So it was that, in the midst of the darkness and confusion, the colonel was able to plan his defense. He and his fellow officers, each in his own small sector, were trying to join together the shattered fragments of the front. They were not making their moves according to a master strategical plan, but simply patching things up on a local level.

The colonel of the 95th Regiment was not responsible for what was going on beyond the fort. He had no way of knowing that there, during the night between February 24th and 25th, the front would be broken. What elements went to make up this front no one could say. "A few thinly stretched battalions, forming an anything but solid line." Most of these men had hardly had a chance to compare notes and make themselves known before the German flamethrowers loomed up before them, raking the ground, and by the light of the flames they could distinguish the silhouettes of the grenade throwers. Three German divisions had been thrown into the attack, but the defenders never had time to count them. Two hours later their bodies were as cold as the frozen ground.

The bombardment resumed its intensity on the morning of February 25th, at about the hour when Pétain walked into Joffre's office at Chantilly. Louvemont, as we have seen, fell at three o'clock in the afternoon, and soon afterward the Germans made their way down the slopes of the Côte du Poivre in the direction of Douaumont and its fortress, five hundred yards east of the village proper.

The 95th Infantry was still holding, although no longer the regiment it had been. The battalion to the west no longer existed, and whether or not the one to the north was still there no one could tell. A cloud of smoke, shot through with flashes of fire, overhung Douaumont. Trees were torn up and smashed; rocks and dirt geysered into the air; the low-flying shells exploded almost without interruption. Deafened by the noise the defenders exclaimed, "When will the stinkers attack?" They clung to what cover they could find; knowing that the artillery range would be lengthened at the moment of the infantry assault. Nothing could be worse than the shelling, because if it lasted long enough none of them would survive.

The men of this last battalion could see to their right the massive, crouching outline of the fort, invulnerable, it seemed, to any explosion. The surrounding noise and smoke prevented them from noticing a strange phenomenon. Not a single shell, not a bullet had been fired by the fort's defenders.

Everywhere else on the battlefield the least remnants of trench or fortified position, a hillock, a mound, a dead body provided a place from which to shoot or to throw a grenade. Yet the German heavy shells fell without apparently causing so much as a scratch on the fort sunk halfway into the ground. But the fort itself seemed like a huge elephant, dead on its feet or paralyzed by some strange disease.

* * *

To the soldiers of the 24th Brandenburg Regiment the silent immobility of the fort had something uncanny and nerve-racking about it. This regiment was part of the three divisions that formed the left wing of the assault, and during the night and at dawn pulverized the thin French brigade to the east of the fort. Under cover of their artillery the Germans had advanced without difficulty, taking a considerable number of prisoners on the way. Only when they were close to the dry fortress moat itself their troubles began. In the smoke, their artillery had lost sight of the rockets signaling to lengthen the range, and the artillery continued to make the fort its target.

"We're going to take it by storm," a company commander cried, and the sappers had already begun to cut the barbed wire. But the idea of leaping down into the twenty-four-foot-deep dry moat was most unattractive to the 24th Brandenburg, especially since their own artillery was dropping shells into it. Moreover, it seemed impossible that from the ramparts of the fort the French machine gunners, who must be lurking there, would not open a murderous fire. The fort's heavy guns did not have to be called into play to repel an attack, when the machine gunners could so easily take care of it.

An iron grille over six feet high surrounded the entire fortress moat, but the Germans had found a breach, and beyond it, a section of the counterscarp in disrepair. Now that the barbed wire had been cut, the way into the moat was easy. But German shells were still falling on the fort itself, dangerously close. The company commander scrambled down, with some of his men following, others lingering behind. Turning, the captain called back: "Men, you won't let me do it alone, will you?" At once they joined their

comrades, although once down in the moat they moved
cautiously. The idea of being killed by one of their own
shells was demoralizing. Still there was no fire from the
ramparts. With loudly beating hearts the attackers began
to climb on all fours up the slope of the parapet.

The captain ordered one of his men to wave a signal flag
from the roof of the fort to the guns. But apparently the flag
was not seen, for the 210's kept falling. Suddenly machine-
gun bullets began to pelt the cement; the firing came from
the village, where the remaining defenders had spied the
German uniforms on the ramparts.

The men of the 24th Brandenburg were now running
freely all around the fort. Half a minute later they had made
their way, at several different points, into the interior. In a
corridor lighted only by kerosene lamps hanging from the
walls, they met an old territorial with a flashlight in his
hand, whistling to himself. Suddenly he halted, and his
mouth fell open.

"The Boches!" he exclaimed, as if he had never heard of
the Battle of Verdun, or indeed of the war.

"You're a prisoner," said the captain, adding, to his men,
"Take him to the command post."

The sappers cut all the electric wiring so that the fort
could not be blown up. First French voices, then German
were heard. Another company of the 24th Infantry, the 8th,
under Lieutenant Brandis, had penetrated the fort from
another side at the same time, and had already lined up
some of the defenders in the courtyard. They consisted of
fifty-seven elderly territorials and one old artilleryman.
There was not a single officer among them. Leaderless and
without orders they had remained to be captured, completely passive. At the moment when both German companies had scaled the walls of the moat, the main entrance
to the fort (but this they could not know), was open and
the drawbridge down.

During the evening German artillerists brought ammunition for the 155 and the two 75's in the turrets. From the morning of February 26th these were to be used against the French troops fighting in the open fields around the fort.

* * *

Many of the stories concerning the capture of Douaumont are long and complicated. The simple error that causes a disaster seems to call for some detailed explanation. The brief story above is based on facts as they are known to us, and the process leading up to the disaster can be told no less directly.

Douaumont was the most important single unit in the fortress of Verdun. Its concrete walls, four to eight feet thick, were ample protection for five hundred men with supplies and ammunition.

In the second chapter of this book the reader will remember the order of August 5, 1915, regarding the dismantlement of the forts. For various reasons, the quick collapse of the fortresses of Liège, Namur, Antwerp, and Maubeuge, and of their equivalents in Russia, had caused the military hierarchy to lose faith in their usefulness.

After February 11, 1916, when the German intention of attacking Verdun had become overwhelmingly evident, the High Command finally decided to put the "exterior defenses" of Verdun in order. We have seen how General de Castelnau arrived to examine the front-line installations, how General Chrétien insisted that the trenches be deepened and the barbed wire repaired, and how, under rain and snow and cover of darkness, the French soldiers worked to effect these improvements until the moment of the first German bombardment. So urgent was the need for this work that it was done, not by engineers, although a regiment of engineers had been assigned, but by the very troops who had to withstand the assault a day or two later.

But nothing was done to prepare the defenses of the forts; for them there was no modification of the order of

August 5, 1915. In all the documents or reports relating to
Verdun, we find no officer rising up at a staff meeting to
protest and say: "After all, the fort of Douaumont may be a
good deal more useful than a trench. Why don't we rearm
it?" By some chance the three artillery pieces—the 155 and
the two 75's—had not been removed. In the face of an
enemy attack it would have been only logical to man these
guns. But, as we have seen, there was only one artilleryman
among the small group to whom the German attack came as
such a complete surprise.

Let us be exact. On the morning of February 25th there
were other troops in the fort besides the fifty-seven territorials captured by the Germans. There were some "reserve
units" of a territorial regiment which had been stationed in
the Woëvre Valley, in the direction of Étain. If we choose
to penetrate the circumlocutions of official military style, we
shall see that the fort was used as a sort of barracks. The
reserve units were later referred to as a "garrison," but they
were in fact nothing of the sort, being quite unschooled in
the technique of the fort's defense, and in any case there
being no ammunition for the guns.

Still, they might have done something to defend it. The
fact is that when the two companies of the 24th Brandenburg Infantry arrived upon the scene they had already left
the fort. We know that, the evening before, General de
Langle de Cary had ordered a withdrawal from the valley
of the Woëvre to the left bank of the Meuse. Doubtless he
did not have in mind the tiny "reserve units" at Douaumont,
and he was quite justified in leaving such a detail to his subordinates. But the reserve units themselves felt quite sure
that they were included in the general order, and they were
all too happy to obey it. How many they were and under
exactly what circumstances they cleared out is not clear. We
may surmise, however, that at some points of the Verdun
front the fighting spirit was lower than at others.

Even after reserve units had gone the fort could still have

been defended. The Germans who leaped down into the ditch had every reason to fear a murderous machine-gun fire, and the fifty-seven members of the garrison were quite numerous enough to provide it. If they did nothing it was because there was no officer to tell them what to do.

Various military historians have sought to parcel out the blame for this state of affairs, but there is little satisfaction to be obtained from their pages. The disaster seems to go back to the dismantlement order of August 5, 1915, and there is no valid explanation of the fact that, even after the beginning of the German offensive, the fort should have remained unmanned and asleep.

One of General Chrétien's staff officers has, in apology, quoted his chief as stating that on the evening of February 24th he had drawn up an order "instructing the divisional generals to install and maintain garrisons in the forts of their sectors." Unhappily, as the general himself has to admit, this order was still, "by mistake," on his desk on the morning of February 25th, when General Balfourier, the Twentieth Corps commander, arrived to replace him. Still more unhappily, there is no evidence that the order ever reached those for whom it was intended.

Another one of Chrétien's officers has sought to cast the blame on somebody else. "It is incomprehensible and inexcusable," he writes, "that the commander who had the powerful fort of Douaumont under his jurisdiction should not have taken it upon himself to occupy it, especially in view of his valiant defense of the village of the same name." The "commander" to whom he refers is Colonel de Belenet of the 95th Infantry. We know enough about the circumstances under which this regiment arrived at the front and the conditions it found when it got there to understand how impossible it would have been for Colonel de Belenet to "take it upon himself" to occupy the fort. What is incomprehensible is the writer's lack of contact with reality.

Even if the colonel had had time to think of the fort, he

could not have imagined that he was responsible for it. His direct superior, General de Reibell, commander of the 31st Brigade, relates quite clearly that General Chrétien told him twice—during the morning and evening of February 24th —and in the presence of two witnesses, that he need take no thought for the fort of Douaumont, which had a garrison of its own. It was during this same evening (which was indeed the very last moment) that Chrétien drew up the order to the effect that the territorial reserves (euphemistically called the garrison) should hold the fort. He had every reason to believe that one of his staff officers would see to it that such an important order did not sit all night long on his desk and then disappear into thin air.

*   *   *

Let us not hesitate to use the hackneyed expression "powder train" to describe the effect produced upon the German troops by the news of the capture of Douaumont. *"Douaumont ist gefangen!"* These three words ran like wild-fire along the front lines and back to the rear, provoking a series of explosions of joy that went far to counterbalance the pressure and anxiety of the days that had gone before. Of course, the German high command made psychological capital out of the achievement. Captain Haupt and Lieuten-ant Brandis of the 24th Brandenburg were both decorated with the "cross pour le mérite," the highest military decora-tion, for having advanced so fearlessly into what, for all they knew, was a situation of mortal danger. Pétain himself has written: "The courage of Lieutenant Brandis was exemplary. Many another man would have stopped short before this obstacle, which he had every reason to believe was bristling with defensive weapons."

On the afternoon of February 26th German General Headquarters released the following communiqué:

In the presence of His Majesty the Emperor we made considerable progress on the fighting front east of the Meuse River. Our valiant troops captured by force of arms the height southwest of Louvemont and the fortifications grouped on its east side. With all their old spirit the Brandenburg regiments fought their way to the village and fortress of Douaumont (south of the Paris-Metz highway) and took the latter by storm.

One of the military historians of whom we have spoken above claims that it was "fraudulent" for the Germans to talk of taking the fortress "by storm." But let us look at the official French communiqué for the same day:

In the region north of Verdun the bombardment remains continuous to both the east and west of the Meuse. The enemy's attacks on various targets have been met with vigorous counteraction. The German attempts to force their way ahead in the region of Champneuville and on the Côte du Poivre, where we are solidly dug in, have been repulsed. There is a raging battle around the fort of Douaumont, a forward post of the former Verdun complex. This post, captured at the cost of enormous losses by the enemy this morning, has now been retaken. In spite of repeated attempts, the enemy has been unable to make our troops retreat.

After the First World War it became a favorite game to sneer at propaganda of this kind. There was no such reaction after the Second World War. The systematic distortion of the truth has come to be considered a normal procedure, and the expression "brainwashing," which has replaced *"bourrage de crâne,"* has found a permanent place in the military vocabulary.

To return to the episode in which we have participated, let us note an estimate of it in numerical terms. "The loss of the fort of Douaumont," says General Rouquerol, "was tantamount, in the overall picture of the war, to the loss of a hundred thousand men."

6

THE MAN IN THE WOOL STOCKINGS

AT THE FOOT of the magnificent steps of the town hall of Souilly the two generals shook hands. It was cold and dark, with only an overhead gas lamp shining. An orderly held open the door of the big black limousine with the narrow tires. The general who was leaving, bundled in a heavy cloak, his cap pulled down over his eyes, signaled to the other not to linger outside; then he stepped quickly into the limousine and was driven away. The general who was to remain behind walked slowly back up the steps, a staff captain behind him. At the end of the corridor was a stairway leading to the second floor.

The reception room of the town hall of Souilly had nothing luxurious about it. Two soldiers were setting up some chairs and tables. When the general entered they drew themselves up to attention, but the captain motioned to them to keep on working. On one of the tables was a telephone worked by a hand crank.

"Get me the Twentieth Corps, please," the general said to the captain.

His clear voice echoed in the empty room. While the captain was putting through the call he paced up and down. He was a tall, well-built man, with a pale skin and remarkably light blue eyes, whose thinning hair and reddish moustache were starting to turn gray. The two soldiers could not help staring at his legs, the sturdy legs of a man who knew what it was to march. What fascinated them about his legs was that he wore neither boots nor puttees, but long wool stockings, the kind used by cyclists, with a diagonal band in the pattern, which made them look rather like puttees after all. They seemed an ingenious idea, since they kept his legs warm without putting any pressure on them. Puttees were one of the French soldiers' favorite topics of conversation.

"Sir, here is General Balfourier."

Without sitting down, the man in the stockings took the telephone.

"Balfourier? This is Pétain."

Making themselves as inconspicuous as possible, the soldiers pricked up their ears. The captain motioned to them to leave the room.

"Yes," Pétain went on, "I'm taking over the command. Please pass on the news. Hold fast. I have full confidence in you."

His face betrayed no emotion during his interlocutor's reply. Then, with a brief "Thank you," he brought the conversation to an end. "Hold fast. . . ." On the Verdun front this was nothing new.

"Now," said Pétain to his aide, "get me Bazelaire."

General Bazelaire was in command of the troops on the left bank of the Meuse. The general to whom Pétain had said goodbye at the foot of the steps was Castelnau, Major General of the Armies, sent by Joffre on the night between February 24th and 25th to take "urgent measures" to prevent the Verdun front from falling apart. Castelnau's first step had been to confirm the order sent by Joffre to Langle de Cary: the evacuation of the Woëvre Valley was all very well, but the right bank must be held. The second step was a telephone call to Joffre: "Pétain must be put in charge of the whole Verdun sector without delay." Once this had been done, Castelnau did not return to Chantilly, but went on a tour of inspection of the whole area.

"Sir, here is Seventh Corps Headquarters, and General Bazelaire."

This time Pétain sat down and talked at greater length. He had arrived; he had taken over the command. He had confirmed the order to hold the front north of Verdun on the right bank of the Meuse, but this would not be possible unless the position on the left bank were held as well and the firepower of the forts on the left bank supported the right-bank defenders. From time to time Pétain paused in order to listen to what was being said at the other end of the wire. He repeated that the firepower of the left-bank forts was essential, then listened again, holding the telephone receiver away from his ear. The captain could not catch Bazelaire's words, but he caught the mixture of respect and animation in his tone of voice, the goodwill and confidence in his manner.

Philippe Pétain was born at Cauchy-à-la-Tour, Pas-de-Calais, on April 24, 1856, a pupil of the Dominican Fathers of Arcueil, a lieutenant in the Chasseurs à pied, and a graduate of the War College. The head of the War College, General Bonnal, who asked for Pétain as an infantry instructor, described him as follows: *A remarkable captain, equally good as a staff officer or in the field. Has the proportions of vigor, good judgment, decisiveness and intelligence that go to make up a future leader. Exceptionally qualified.*

"Exceptionally qualified." Yet for twenty years Pétain remained with the rank of captain, and then was a lieutenant colonel for seven and a half years. Had it not been for the war, Pétain would never have risen above the rank of colonel. He was too outspoken, not enough of an intriguer, said some. The reasons are not important. What concerns us now is the fact that on the morning of February 25, 1916, Castelnau had telephoned Joffre to say that Pétain, commander of the Second Army, was the man needed at Verdun. Not with the limited task of holding the Meuse, which the

Grand Quartier Général had meant to assign to him, but as commander of the whole front, with complete freedom of movement and whatever means within reason he might request. Joffre's answer had been: *"D'accord"* (I agree), a phrase that, in those days, was used with discrimination and generally from a superior to a subordinate.

After General Pétain had finished talking to General Bazelaire, his aide told him that his room was ready in case he wanted to rest after the fatigue of the day. Pétain had left Chantilly early in the morning, after seeing Joffre. Traveling slowly over the icy roads, he had made his first stop at General Herr's headquarters at Dugny, where he was greeted by the news of the capture of Douaumont. Next he had come to Souilly, where Castelnau, as yet uninformed, was awaiting him. Castelnau made no comment. He jotted down something in a notebook, then tore out the page.

"No need to stand on ceremony. Here are your orders, to take effect immediately. Everything is in your hands."

Now, after his telephone conversations, Pétain found himself alone with his aide in the empty reception room of the town hall. From the mantelpiece a bust of the Republic seemed to be staring through him, into emptiness. It was, indeed, time to rest and to take stock.

Less than an hour later there was a stir in the empty room. Colonel de Barescut, chief of staff of the Second Army, and several other officers arrived. Orderlies shifted the tables and pinned a large-scale map on the wall. A few minutes later Pétain joined them. He shook hands affably enough, but his face was as emotionless as before. There were some sticks of charcoal on one of the tables and, picking one of them up, he scrutinized the map in silence. On the left bank, which the enemy had bombarded but not attacked, the front line was farther to the north than it was on the right. The difference was striking and perhaps significant. In any case, Pétain began to draw with his charcoal certain lines on the map.

"Look. It's like this. From Avocourt to the Meuse, Bazelaire, nothing new; from the Meuse to Douaumont, Guillaumat; from Douaumont to Eix, Balfourier; and from Eix to the Meuse, below Saint-Mihiel, Duchêne."

He spoke as calmly as if he were a professor in his classroom. Then he stood back, looking at the four lines, which ran together to form one, marked off in sections. Looking down at the area behind the front, to the south, his face took on a pensive expression. The four charcoal lines stood for definite responsibilities . . . all well and good; but uppermost in everyone's mind in the reception room was what had happened at Douaumont. The immediate necessity was to put things in order. In order? Was it possible, at this point, to have order on the French side of the front? And why could this particular general achieve it? By now it was one o'clock in the morning.

*   *   *

At this same hour, amid the ruins of the village of Douaumont, men looked up from their trenches at the flashes of light in the sky, and bent low when the ground trembled. The 95th, or what was left of it, was still hanging on. To these survivors the day and hour had no meaning; most of them did not even remember at what time they had dug the trenches in which they were now standing. In some places, in front of the village and to the east, old trenches had been pressed into use. The new trenches were comparatively dry; the old ones were filled with water. All along the front from one sector to another the trenches varied. The retention of rainwater was characteristic of the trenches along the Meuse and the Argonne. The men in the old trenches at Douaumont were standing in water halfway up to their knees, and unfortunately the water was changing into ice. Every now and then the sentries shuffled their feet in order to break the layer of ice forming round them. The others were so exhausted that they fell asleep on their feet, leaning against the trench wall. Eventually the ice round their feet woke them up. In the natural course of events, they could expect a new attack the following morning.

The soldiers knew that the fort had been captured and that consequently the front had broken. They had had nothing to eat or drink. At the end of the day they had detected, through the twilight, little groups of their fellows and a few isolated individuals walking or, in some cases, running toward the rear.

"What the devil are they up to, Lieutenant? Are they wounded, or just deserters?" The lieutenant made no reply. On every side the signal rockets, carrying a message to the German artillery, rose like comets above the overhanging smoke. The general effect was so confusing that it was hard to maintain any sense of direction. Men who were spending their second sleepless night, with empty stomachs and cold feet, could not but feel confused. And yet, against the icy trench wall, their hearts went on beating. With every explosion they beat momentarily faster, and their bodies, expecting to be buried, unconsciously hugged the earth into which they would be pulverized.

When casualties are so high, when men are dying where they stand, to order a front to hold at any cost has the quality of unreality. All through February 25th gray-uniformed, beetle-helmeted bodies fell on the battlefield, but the Germans knew that they had gained ground. By the end of the afternoon they had captured the Côte du Poivre and the heights of Haudromont. The general in command of the French 37th Division saw that he was in danger of being surrounded, and ordered his troops to withdraw to the last heights north of Verdun, only a mile and a half away from the city, Froideterre and Belleville. The order brought a quick reaction from Joffre, a telephone call in which he said: "Yesterday, the 24th, I gave orders to hold fast on the right bank of the Meuse, north of Verdun. Under these circumstances any commander who orders a retreat will be court-martialed." Of course, Joffre was quite free to make a telephone call of this kind and to cancel an order of retreat. But he could not force a regiment that had held its ground and been annihilated to halt the advancing gray lines. This was something beyond the power of Joffre or Pétain or anyone else.

The front was cracking; there was no other way to describe it. A mile and a half north of Verdun the civilian population had evacuated Belleville, leaving their unfinished meals on the tables. The retreating soldiers, weary and hungry, could smell disaster. They fell upon the unfinished meals, ripped open barrels of wine with their bayonets, and let what they could not drink flow down the streets.

The shadow of defeat was a long one; already it had reached the barracks north of the citadel, just outside the city limits, where there were stores of supplies that rumor had it the Germans might take over. Who inspired the free-for-all, nobody knows. But a whole regiment gave itself, with savage joy, to pillage; soldiers were soon staggering under loads of booty as they made their way, on their own initiative, to the rear.

All the bridges over the Meuse were mined; long strips of guncotton hung down from the spans, and in the river below engineers sat in small boats, ready to light them. Shivering with cold they listened to the voices and the footsteps of the pillaging deserters.

Soon night enveloped the area of disaster. Survivors of the 95th Infantry were still hanging on amid the ruins of Douaumont and on other small islands of resistance. In a headquarters close to the front, a general—witnesses charitably give him no name, but he had no reason to be ashamed, for events seemed to lend him reason—read, with lowered head, the fragmentary dispatches arriving from his sector. Finally he looked up and said, a distraught expression on his face, to the officers around him:

"Even if I were Napoleon, I could not halt the defeat of this army."

* * *

"This is the forest of Caures," said the driver. "Weren't you here?"

"No," answered the young soldier. "I was in Artois."

"Twenty-four hours ago this place was bristling with big guns, and we couldn't possibly have got through. They must have pushed farther on since then."

The wagon jolted along the deeply rutted, icy road. On either side an army of shattered tree trunks was outlined against the pale sky.

"It's lousy with corpses in there," said the driver. "If it weren't for the cold they'd be stinking."

His round military cap pulled down all the way to his eyes, the driver was the cartoonist's idea of a typical German. The soldier sitting beside him had an exceedingly youthful air. Underneath the heavy helmet his face was pale and thin, and he was holding his rifle between spindly knees. At first glance it might have seemed that the wagon was carrying the corpses of which the driver had just spoken, for there were damp, reddish-brown stains on the canvas stretched over the rear. Actually, it was loaded with beef and a few sacks of potatoes. The driver was talking now about his horse, a genuine Friesland, which he had picked up in an evacuated French village in the Artois region. The animal was so sensitive to danger that if he balked at going any farther, the safest thing was to stop. Just as his owner spoke, the horse shied, and two human forms appeared on the road.

"Military police," said the driver. "The horse has a nose for them too."

He came to a prudent halt and waited for the two men

wearing helmets and chinstraps to come closer. Then, in answer to their questions, he said:

"I'm coming from Damvillers and going to Beaumont, with supplies for the 73rd Infantry Regiment of the Third Army Corps. This boy is just out of the hospital. Not a single day of convalescence, and see the way he looks!"

But the M.P.'s had eyes only for the young soldier's papers. "All right," they said laconically as they handed them back. At once the driver urged on his horse.

"If we'd been going in the opposite direction," he muttered to his companion, "they'd have grilled you for a quarter of an hour. They can't bear to see anyone get out of this mess."

To the south could be heard the continuous roar of battle. The side road followed by the wagon ran into Route Nationale 405, which follows the ravine between the forest of Caures and the heights of the Wavrille. At the junction a cavalryman ordered the wagon to halt and give right of way to two convoys coming along the main road: a column of French prisoners and a line of horse-drawn ambulances.

"All the trucks are pressed into service to carry reinforcements and ammunition," said the wagon driver. "When you're wounded you lose your importance and have to travel more slowly. . . . Just look at those fellows there . . . if they don't look done in!"

He raised his chin in the direction of the French prisoners, who were marching three or four abreast, with mounted territorial guards riding beside them. They were walking very slowly, with bowed heads, covered by hoods and scarves that revealed no more than their eyes and a small part of their faces.

"They look even closer to giving up the ghost than you do," said the driver. "But they're lucky, at that. Our own fellows in the ambulances are dead or dying, plenty of them, you can be sure."

The cavalryman on his horse overheard these last words.

"This has been going on since the day before yesterday," he said. "This time it's the real thing. We've smashed them."

"I'll believe that when I get orders to go home," said the driver.

"It's true, though. They're running like rabbits. I think I see the last of the ambulances. You can get across now. But remember, where you're going keep out of everybody's way."

"That's crazy," said the driver. "If all our men starve to death without the supplies I'm bringing, what good will it do them to get fresh stores of ammunition?"

"You may have a point there," said the cavalryman. "But I have my orders. So long . . ."

For the next half-mile the road was free, and the driver never stopped talking. Not often did he find a hearer, and this one, because he was young, listened to him respectfully. Besides, they had common memories of Artois. The driver had been stationed for some time at Douchy, a camp that was exactly right, with movies, cafés, and canteens, and a bowling alley the officers had set up in the rectory garden. Everyone lived in barracks, since most of the village had been destroyed. The remnants of the local population were lodged in a few still intact houses; a miserable, frightened lot they were, and no one thought of maltreating them. The few young people among them were gathered together every morning to work in the fields with a sentry on guard. At regular intervals during the evenings rivers of beer were served free to soldiers of all ranks. A good life, in short, except for the lack of women. At Damvillers things were not nearly so easygoing. The commander was a martinet who demanded a salute from everyone, including the village housewives. Every now and then a local commander exercised a petty tyranny of this kind and made himself more feared and disliked than the toughest fighter.

"That gunfire's coming closer," the young soldier re-marked.

The intensity of the noise of battle varied considerably according to the windings of the road. Now the heavy artillery on the left, toward Herbebois, was distinctly audible. A few hundred yards short of Beaumont the road was suddenly jammed with new convoys of ambulances and prisoners. The prisoners were halted by the side of the road in order to let the ambulances go by. The other half of the road was taken up by a line of trucks, rolling slowly toward the front, in the opposite direction. Behind the trucks were horse-drawn wagons, and the driver asked what they were carrying.

"Hand grenades. The trucks are loaded with shells and have the right of way. No one knows why they're moving so slowly."

The jam had its center at Beaumont, where the mounted military police and traffic policemen were hoarse from shout-ing. At the entrance to the village the wagon was held up for ten minutes near a group of walking wounded waiting for transportation. The driver and his youthful companion learned from them that the French front had been broken wide open but that two or three positions were still holding, and also that the German artillery was complaining about the late arrival of ammunition.

"And what about you, you poor slobs from the infantry? What do you have to say?"

The men said simply that they had had it. They had been five days in the front line, suffering heavy losses, and still no one had come to relieve them. Reinforcements, yes, but no relief. What kind of system was that?

Finally the wagon entered what had once been the village of Beaumont. Engineers were trying to clear the debris in the middle of unbelievable confusion. After several times taking the wrong turning and cursing the fellows who had misdirected him, the driver found the mobile field kitchens, to which he was delivering the meat, a little to the east of the village. Here he was greeted by imprecations because of his lateness, but he was at no loss for an equally abusive reply. He held back the young soldier, who was ready to start off at once in search of his battalion.

"Have a bite of something hot to eat before you go," he insisted. "You won't be having anything of the sort very soon again."

As he himself ladled out a copious portion, he queried the cooks, "Is it the real thing up ahead?"

They shrugged their shoulders. Like their interlocutor, they were territorials of a certain age, not given to sudden enthusiasm, and indeed wedded to a war that was static. Efficient quartermastering requires stability. Settling down, mapping itineraries, delivering supplies to the front line— this they were ready and prepared to do, as long as they were given the time to organize them efficiently.

"Advance or retreat, it's a lousy business either way."

And yet they had some gossip to pass on that had come to them from headquarters of the Third Army Corps under the command of General von Lochow. The general had been visited by von Falkenhayn, in the course of a visit to Second Army Headquarters. "How are things going?" von Falkenhayn had asked, and von Lochow had replied: "Our men are exhausted. They can't push the attack any farther unless they are relieved." To which von Falkenhayn had answered: "We're expecting a push from the British at Arras, and we can't put everything we have into here. You have plenty of reserves, and you'll have to get along with them." An answer which threw both von Lochow and the Crown Prince, who was present, into consternation.

Of course, no one among the usual sources of soldiers' information—clerks or orderlies—was actually present at such a colloquy. And the colloquy itself is purely imaginary.

Yet the events that were to follow indicate that on February 26, 1916, the day when the French defeat seemed irrevocable, the German leaders had a certain preoccupation, and it is probable that rumors had reached the soldiers of the Quartermaster Corps at Beaumont. An army is a kind of enormous ear, and no secret, however well kept, escapes it. One of the men attached to the field kitchens had another episode to tell, which he swore had taken place at Beaumont twenty-four hours earlier. General von Lochow, on a tour of inspection with one of his divisional commanders, had paused to speak to a wounded man in the process of being evacuated to the rear.

"How goes it, young fellow?" he had inquired.

"Up my rear end," the wounded man had answered.

Of course, he had been quickly hustled from the scene, and the general had been assured that he was a simple case of shellshock. Such a thing might have taken place even in the German Army, and does not necessarily show that discipline was undermined. It is true, however, that many of the soldiers who had been nearly a week in the combat zone were in a state of high nervous tension.

Once he had had some hot food, the young soldier who had traveled with the meat to Beaumont asked the whereabouts of his regiment and was told that it must be fighting somewhere near the woods of Chaufour, before Douaumont. He was lucky enough to find another wagon—this one loaded with grenades—going in his direction. The driver was of his own age, and, like him, pale and drawn.

"No fighting for me," the driver explained. "I was mobilized for noncombatant duty. But even if I can't handle a gun, I'm good enough to bring up the grenades."

His older brother had been killed in Champagne; his mother and sister were working in a munitions factory near Saarbrücken. The downcast look on his face deepened when a military policeman forbade his wagon to enter the road

to Louvemont, branching off from the road between Beaumont and Vacherauville.

"But Louvemont is the place where I'm going!"

"This road is reserved for the artillery."

"Then how am I to get to Louvemont?"

"Just go down to the Meuse. You'll find a road to
Louvemont from there."

"But the French are down on the river."

"Not where I'm telling you to go. Vacherauville, that's
the place to look for; it's the starting-point of another road
to Louvemont."

"They told me at Beaumont that Vacherauville was under
fire. It's within the range of the French forts, that's what
they said. And I'm not carrying potatoes. I've got a load of
hand grenades."

"There's no other way for you to go. This is for the
artillery."

The horse, at any rate, did not object to taking the down-
hill road to the river. He was an old horse, indifferent to the
shelling, which now had slackened on the west and increased
in intensity toward the east and south. The two men saw
smoke rising into the wide-open sky above the ravine. Less
than a mile from the place where they had been stopped
they met an artillery ambulance filled with casualties. Some
of the more lightly wounded had bound up their hurts with
bandages from their own first-aid kits, but others lay deathly
still. The ambulance driver had a bloodstained handker-
chief round his forehead, and his horse was bleeding at the
neck and shoulder. What he wanted to know was whether
Beaumont was under bombardment.

"Not right now," answered the grenade carrier.

"At Louvemont we were hit by three shells. It wasn't
pretty, I can tell you."

"Shall I be able to get down to the river? I'm supposed to
go from there to Louvemont."

"Oh, you'll get there, all right, if you don't have the same luck as we did. What have you got in those bags?"

"Hand grenades."

There was an awkward silence. The grenade carrier shook his horse's reins. As he drove slowly on down the road, the wounded artillerymen looked pensively after him.

* * *

February 26th: 4:00 P.M. General von Schenck had just got through on the telephone to Fifth Army Headquarters.

"Your Highness, I've just called the commanders of the three other army corps. Here's my report in a nutshell. Just before noon the enemy tried to approach the fort of Douaumont, but was repulsed. Our infantry attacked between eleven o'clock and noon, all along the line. According to the most recent news, Hardaumont Wood, west of Douaumont, together with its fotified place, has been captured. The summit of the Côte du Poivre, where a few French soldiers are holding out, should soon be ours. I have given orders not to relax our pressure on the Douaumont-Hardaumont sector, because that is where the situation looks most promising. Toward the west we are being hurt by the fire from the French forts on the left bank of the Meuse. It seems that batteries have just been installed in the woods of Cumières and Les Corbeaux and the region of Mort-Homme. You have doubtless noticed, Your Highness, that most of the right-bank ravines go down toward the river and are thus exposed to fire from the opposite side."

"I made a point of saying that we should attack on both banks simultaneously," said the Crown Prince. "But other views prevailed. Please go on."

"That French fire is creating havoc. It is interrupting the flow of our ammunition, and the consumption of our big guns is insatiable. I know that the artillery parks are filled to capacity, but the shells have to be transported to the front. In the last few hours the front-line batteries have been told to economize. Verdun will be within our grasp, Your Highness, if we are able to slide our front over to the east, but we must have substantial reinforcements to consolidate our success. According to aerial photographs and to the most recently interrogated prisoners, reinforcements are beginning to arrive on the French side. The village of Douaumont is still in French hands, but we're plastering it with our artillery, and half an hour from now the infantry is scheduled to attack."

The German infantrymen who, at this same moment, north of the road between Bras and Douaumont were crouching, waiting for the order to attack, had no idea that the enemy on whom they were about to fall were the survivors of the 95th Infantry. We, of course, know very well what this number and this regiment represent, and we may add to our knowledge the fact that its remnants were not able to be relieved until the evening of February 26th. But the Germans waiting to attack the trenches of Douaumont imagined that they would come up against the fresh troops whose arrival had been rumored on their side. The Germans too were exhausted. They had not traveled twenty-five miles on foot, to find themselves the targets of an artillery barrage; indeed, they had set out from relatively comfortable trenches and found very few obstacles in their way. But, with the exception of a few latecomers, they had been in the thick of the battle, not for forty-eight hours but for five days and five nights, and some of them from February 12th to February 21st had been in the front-line trenches. The policy of the German command—which provided insufficient reinforcements and no periods of relief—was almost as cruel as that of the French, who insisted upon resistance at any cost whatsoever.

Pétain had taken over at eleven o'clock of the night before, and now the French artillery on the left bank of the Meuse, no longer content to answer the German fire from the north, was shooting across the river and playing its part in the battle. If we look at the map we shall see that these guns could not have intervened on the first, second, or third day, for the simple reason that the French troops on the right bank had not yet withdrawn from their positions. A single exception, the ill-conceived bombardment of French-occupied Samogneux, proved the validity of the rule. But the lack of response had continued through the fourth and fifth days, when it might have served some purpose. Now, upon Pétain's orders, the response was there.

At half-past four in the afternoon, the battle for the village of Douaumont was raging. Two equally exhausted adversaries were galvanized into an almost inexplicable energy. The two infantries pitted against each other were undoubtedly the best of their kind in the world, far superior in stamina and devotion to duty to the respective commands. Under a murderous crossfire each one gave proof of the highest qualities of its people. French accounts speak of the Germans' "fanatical" charges (a popular adjective of the time), full of self-assurance and confidence. Under the fire of the French machine guns, they fell in droves, but others took their places. And German accounts on their side, speak of "furious defense," "unparalleled courage," and "a fight to the death" on the part of the French defenders.

Some of the Germans came so close that the defenders could see their open mouths and hear them shout, above the explosions of the shells, *"Verdoon! Verdoon!"* No sooner was one attacking line mowed down than another took its place. Suddenly—at an hour that it is hard to pin down, but apparently not long after the start of the battle—two French 75's opened fire from the front line, at the edge of the village. "God only knows how they got there," is all that witnesses can say.

In any case, these two guns fired with precision and power, not on the first wave of the assailants but on the waves that followed it. The French soldiers could see with their own eyes the wide gaps made by the shells of the 75's.

The surviving Germans did not recoil; they continued to advance, but in such diminished numbers that the French were encouraged to make use of their machine guns, rifles, and hand grenades. Another German wave erupted just north of the road between Bras and Douaumont, and ran up against the same defenses: the 75's, the machine guns, the rifles, and the hand grenades.

No military historian has been able to discover how these two 75's arrived where they were. In the complex development of the battle it is no wonder that this small detail has never been unraveled. But detail though it was, it had its importance. The arrival of these two guns and their intervention in the infantry clash at the village of Douaumont seem just as significant, even if less impressive, than the artillery fire Pétain ordered on the left bank of the Meuse. Two field guns do not represent much firepower, but orders had brought them to the place where they were needed— along with their horses, gun carriages, and ammunition. In the midst of chaos they represented an element of stability. They continued to fire and to take their toll of advancing Germans until night began to fall. Then there took place a scene worthy of the pen of the poet Paul Déroulède, but which a historian can recount because it is true.

Major Compeyrot, commander of the third battalion of the 95th, gave orders to fix bayonets. Emerging from his trench, he held up his cane as if it were a sword. "En avant!" Beside him a bugler played "Sounding the Charge." Bugler Bruneau, 9th company, was his name. Fifteen seconds later he was dead, and the major had fallen to the ground with a wounded shoulder. But the impetus of the French counterattack swept the Germans back to a position behind their point of depature. The attack on the village of Douaumont was halted. At least for the moment.

*   *   *

Two boxers are in the ring. One has blitzed the other, with a left, right, right, left, and never a second of letup. His opponent has not even had time to raise his guard; he is pounded on the jaw, stomach, and liver, driven to the ropes, bent over double in the effort to protect his solar plexus with his elbows. From their seats the spectators are shouting, "We want our money back!" and no one can deny their right to consider themselves cheated. The seconds during which the loser bounces from place to place on the ropes seem never-ending. But he has not been sent to the floor, and connoisseurs take note that he has successfully staved off a number of blows, that he is still on his feet and trying to put distance between himself and his adversary. He has got away from the ropes, and at close quarters he manages to place a blow or two of his own, delivered from too close by but not altogether inefficacious. By degrees the assailant has slackened his pace; he is no longer bearing down uninterruptedly. There! The defender has placed a couple of good ones himself. Of course, there is a prompt reply, but he replies too, in his turn; he is no longer a helpless victim; he is beginning to spar, and the spectators make an appreciative noise, because they feel that something is changing. It is still impossible to say who is going to win. The starter has a strong chance because the rain of his preliminary blows has seriously handicapped his opponent. But at the same time it is obvious that the pace he set has run him down, and he actually needs to stop for breath.

This is how things went during the early part of the Battle of Verdun. Whether the respite would last for a matter of days or only hours (it actually lasted for days) the men in the trenches could not know. Meanwhile, the French command became aware of the fact that the tempo of the battle was slower. This was such good news that the first messages were overly optimistic. Castelnau sent a message to Joffre on the evening of February 26th which read:

The situation is not yet sufficiently clear for General Pétain and myself to size it up completely. But I believe that, if we can gain two or three days for the general in command of the Second Army to bring his action to bear and to put things back in order, then the risk of losing Verdun will be over.

Twenty-four hours later, Joffre wired to Pétain:

> *I should like to express my satisfaction for the rapidity with which you have organized a command on the field of battle. . . . At the present juncture you feel, as I do, that the best way of arresting the enemy's effort is to counter-attack. We must regain the ground that has been taken from us. Ammunition will not be lacking, and the flanking positions on the left bank will allow you to crush the enemy continually with fire.*

To crush the enemy continually with fire is a picturesque phrase. With his usual discretion Pétain merely hints that he read it with surprise. "This last statement, made at such a date," he says, "evidently reflects wishful thinking."

Actually, the village of Douaumont was to fall (on March 3rd) and the Germans to advance farther. We shall witness several more feverish moments and hear the situation described as dangerous to the highest degree. But the initial impulse of the German advance was, for the time being, spent. For the benefit of impatient readers, let us specify here and now when it was to be renewed, namely, on March 6th, when the Germans unleashed a fresh attack on both sides of the river.

Meanwhile, let us try to draw up a balance sheet of the first part of the battle. As far as distances are concerned, this is very simple. The Germans had advanced from three to five miles at various points along the front, and were less than six miles from the heart of Verdun. It has been established, with fair accuracy, that over 150 French cannons were captured or abandoned on the field. The losses of life are less easy to calculate. The Ministry of War enumerates them by divisions. But many divisions did not fight between February 21st and March 5th, and apparently no effort was made to establish a total. Here, for instance, is a partial count covering six days of battle (February 21–26) on the part of the Fifty-seventh and Seventy-second divisions, and three days (February 22–24) on the part of the Thirty-seventh: killed—681; wounded—3,186; missing—16,407. The disproportion between the numbers of "killed" and "missing" confirms what we noticed about the battle from the very beginning. The "killed" are the dead who were identified, or at least counted; the "missing" were those never seen again, whose bodies were mingled with dust or air.

And here is an unofficial figure of the total French casualties from February 21st to March 5th: killed—7,900; wounded—28,000; missing—33,000.

I have not been able to discover any reliable German figures for the same period. "Heavy" and "very heavy" are the words with which German historians refer to their losses. But it is generally agreed that they were not so heavy as those suffered by the French.

Sufficient suction had not yet been generated within the gigantic pump.

7

THE SACRED WAY

——————————————————

O N E I T H E R S I D E the fields were covered with snow. An uninterrupted line of trucks rolled down the road, skidding from one edge to the other. They had high, canvas-covered bodies, which were easily deflected by the wind, small motors, and tires narrower than those in use today, made out of solid hard rubber. Only from experience can anyone know what it was to ride on solid rubber for even as short a distance as twenty-five miles. It was forty-five miles from the station at Badonvilliers to Verdun, and the truck drivers shuttled back and forth without stopping. Some of them had not slept for more than twenty hours between February 23rd and 27th; one did not even take off his clothes or his shoes from February 22nd to March 8th. Their bloodshot eyes were dripping with tears and they could hardly feel their Vaseline-smeared, chilblained hands. Every now and then they raised one of these numb hands from the steering-wheel and nibbled at a piece of bread. But even under these conditions they were more comfortable than the soldiers they were transporting.

The route had its point of departure at Badonvilliers in order to avoid the traffic at Bar-le-Duc. It entered Verdun through the suburb of Glorieux, but most of the troops were dropped off before this because of the bombardment. Relief units had to be kept alive until they reached the battlefield.

And so they were put down at crossroads outside the city, where decimated units from the front climbed aboard to go to have a few days' rest before being sent back into combat.

The "conveyor belt," as it was called, had gone into operation before Pétain's arrival, and its manpower-supply service worked most efficiently. As early as August 1915 the road had been widened by twenty feet so that not only could it easily take two lines of trucks, but a fast vehicle could even maneuver between them.

This road from Bar-le-Duc to Verdun was the first express highway in history. At the very start of the battle the high command realized that to leave a single horse-drawn vehicle on this the only route untouched by enemy bombardment would be to court disaster. Pétain, as soon as he arrived upon the scene, made the rules even more severe. No trucks had the right to pass another, and no stops were allowed. If a truck halted on account of mechanical trouble, it was pushed off the road, which for this reason was lined in spots with discarded vehicles, some of them burning. Meanwhile, the double line of the conveyor belt functioned twenty-four hours a day. There was no blackout, because at this time night bombardments were rare. Even to fly a plane by night was a considerable exploit. And so the truck headlights formed a winding snake of bright dots along what the peasants called, quite simply, "the Road." Later on, the writer Maurice Barrès gave it a name with ancient Roman connotations, the "Sacred Way."

Matériel and munitions were transported to dumps on the near side of Verdun. The "Meusien," the narrow-gauge railway of which we have spoken before, served to carry quartermaster supplies, only eight hundred tons of them a day. A little later, another, regular-gauge, line (whose construction was begun on March 10, 1916) was opened up between Sommeilles-Nettancourt and Dugny.

The traffic along the icy road did not consist only of

trucks carrying matériel and munitions to the front and soldiers moving in both directions. There were ambulances, mail trucks, light trucks of the engineers, the artillery, the Air Force, the Signal Corps, and other services, besides heavier gun carriages and searchlights. A newly created traffic control board counted as many as six thousand vehicles a day, and, foreseeing that at least one out of every hundred would have an accident or breakdown of some kind during the twenty-four hours, kept thirty tow trucks on the road around the clock. The conveyor belt, in spite or perhaps because of the fact that it was a typical product of French improvisation, was a decided success.

During the morning of February 28th the color of the sky changed from gray to white, and soon afterward the sun came out. Less than two hours later two hundred telephone calls told the traffic board that this ray of sun might be as catastrophic as a ray of death. From one end to another the first express highway in history was a succession of mudholes, where it was not a sea of mud. Solid rubber tires were spinning in six inches of slime, stalled gun carriages blocked the way of lighter vehicles still able to inch their way along, and soldiers, unceremoniously unloaded from their carriers, were bending over double in their effort to get them free. When night fell the continued rise in temperature promised a continuance of the same state of affairs on the morrow. General Pétain could be sure that, unless immediate action were taken, Mud, the conqueror of so many great armies, would add this victory to its string.

Ever since the evening of February 26th things had been relatively calm. On February 27th and 28th the Germans had attacked on the eastern sector of the Verdun front, but with less vigor than the day before, so that it had been possible to contain them. But even a glimpse at the map made it plain that the Germans could not accept for long the attack of the French batteries on the flank and even their rear, from

The famous poster by Abel Faivre.

French infantry moving up to the front. Drawing by Georges Scott.

The fight for the fort. Drawing by J. Simont.

The Rations-Carrier. Drawing by Georges Scott.

In the full chaos of battle: French infantry attacking, June 1916.
Drawing by Georges Scott.

A lunar landscape: a calm night in front of Fort Douaumont.
Drawing by Georges Scott.

General Mangin at his headquarters, June 1916.

the left bank of the Meuse to the right. Renewed action on the part of the Germans was to be expected on both banks of the river, and the supply of men and munitions to meet it must not be interrupted.

The repair of a road in the condition of this one entails at the very least filling the holes with crushed stone and running over them with a steamroller. But no crushed stone had been provided, and there was no time to send for it. Pétain ordered the only possible solution. Quarries were to be opened up close to the road wherever rock was to be found. Forty-eight hours after the fatal thaw, thousands of bearded middle-aged territorials, in prehistoric uniforms and caps, were filling the holes with shovelfuls of crushed stone which other territorials, aided by civilians, were taking out of the nearest hillsides. The stone was not the type out of which to make macadam; it was a soft, local variety, which had, however, the advantage of not requiring a steamroller, whose bulk would have thrown the disrupted traffic into further confusion. Indeed, Pétain had issued a second, very simple order: "Regular Army trucks will serve as rollers. Their hard rubber tires will crush the soft stone."

Once more the conveyor belt was running. But obviously a road repaired in so primitive a fashion could not be expected to stand up under the passage of one automotive vehicle every five to fourteen seconds (depending on the density of the traffic) twenty-four hours a day. Pétain was aware of this fact. Hence his third order read: "Road repairs will be continuous, for as many days as necessary." And so the first express highway was also the first to be in a permanent state of destruction and reconstruction. Hard rubber tires rolled out the shovelful of stones a territorial had thrown into a hole, and a few hours later the passage of hundreds of tires left the hole once more gaping and ready to be filled all over again.

Sixteen work battalions, numbering 8,200 men, were

engaged in taking stone out of the quarries and patching up the 45-mile-long route. In the course of 10 months they handled from 700,000 to 900,000 tons of stone. Some 3,500 trucks chalked up a total of 600,000 miles a week, 25 times the circumference of the earth, transporting 90,000 men and 50,000 tons of matériel. No wonder the road was called a conveyor belt!

Every now and then a shell or, more rarely, a bomb from a plane fell on a moving vehicle. At once a tow truck and a squad of territorials went into action to pull it out of the way and keep the traffic moving. Many of the truck drivers were professionals in civilian life. In a humorous spirit they called upon their comrades who were specialists in camouflage—some of them famous artists—to decorate the sides of their trucks with painted mascots answering to the names of the Cock, the Ladybug, the Girl from Alsace, the Swan, the Comet, and so on. Motors roared night and day; indeed, the Second Army staff officers constantly listened for their reassuring sound. Like the passengers aboard a storm-tossed steamship, alert to the hum of the turbines, they said to themselves, "As long as it keeps up, all is well."

Just as had been foreseen, the Germans attacked the left bank on March 6th. The cold and fog had returned, and snow was falling. After a bombardment almost as intense as that of February 21st, the Twelfth and Twenty-second German reserve divisions threw themselves headlong into the assault, with flamethrowers in the advance. The staff officers in the town hall of Souilly, listening for the sound of the trucks, watched for the solid, reassuring figure of their new commander. But Pétain was laid low by a microscopic enemy; the wool stockings had not protected him against an attack of bronchitis, complicated by the threat of pneumonia, and during the first days of March he sent his orders from the Janvier house, to which the doctors had confined him. He came back, pale and wan, to headquarters, just in time to face new and unexpected danger. While at the front the battle was raging, just behind the lines there was a defeatist spirit. French soldiers had thrown down their arms and started for the rear, their silence more eloquent than a cry of panic. Territorials had halted these men on the road south of Cumières. Whole companies, according to rumor, had been rounded up and captured.

Pétain looked at the map, where the line marking the front had changed place and was studded with new names: Forges, Béthincourt, Cumières, Hill 304, and others, more picturesque, such as Côte de l'Oie (Goose Hill), Bois des Corbeaux (Crows' Wood), and Mort-Homme (Dead Man). The front was dented, also, at its eastern end, on the right bank of the Meuse, where the Germans were also attacking. A "battle of wings," military historians have called it. The human mind instinctively refers everything new to something already known, and it is true that, on the map, the two simultaneous German attacks, at the east and west extremities of the front, looked like a classical double-flanking movement. But the whole war apparatus was still bogged down, and attempts at strategy were hobbled, so that the only real movement was that of a series of sporadic forward pushes.

On the right bank parts of five different German army corps were advancing in force. They took the heights of Hardaumont, the railway station, and half the village of Vaux, and marched upon the fort of the same name, hoping perhaps for as spectacularly rapid a success, against a handful of territorials, as the one at Douaumont. The sappers of the Fifth Reserve Corps were already beginning to cut the barbed wire around the fort when they were mowed down by deadly accurate machine-gun fire from the parapet. No handful of territorials, but two skillfully commanded companies defended the fort. Pétain's orders had been carried out. The general commanding the Fifth Corps withdrew his infantry, and the furious long-distance bombardment resumed.

In a dormitory inside the fort, transformed into an infirmary, wounded men shivered with cold in spite of the blankets and sheepskins thrown over them. In one corner of the room lay the dead, covered by a piece of canvas. There was no question of venturing out to bury them, but fortunately the low temperature prevented their corpses from being unpleasant in other ways. Through the embrasures the defenders could see in the distance the clash between their own infantry and that of the Germans, the latter supported by field artillery. The fire of the guns melted the snow around them as it fell.

On March 8th the 401st Infantry, entrenched among the ruins of the village of Vaux, repulsed thirteen successive attacks. Companies of this regiment, along with some from the nearby 408th, were reduced to twenty, then to eight men, and in one case—that of the 1st Company of the 401st —to a single survivor.

March 9th. On the left bank crows circled above the Bois des Corbeaux, as if to stake a claim to the innumerable French and German corpses not completely covered by a twelve-inch fall of snow. The French line continued to give way toward the south, but more and more slowly, as again the shock of the initial attack was gradually contained.

Every evening the staff officers of the various army corps came to report to Pétain, and he interrupted each report with the question:

"What have your batteries been doing? We'll speak of the rest later."

The interruption was systematic. As a good teacher Pétain knew that he must make his point over and over again if he wanted to obtain from his generals something beside the conventional and elementary reaction, imposed to some extent by the immobility of the war, which consisted of filling up every gap by simply pushing a new mass of men into it. Here are a few of the answers I received from old soldiers whom I questioned about Pétain's popularity at the time:

"Whenever he stepped in, there was an end to confusion."

"He had a cold manner, but we liked him. He meant business, and that was reassuring."

"When he inspected us he had a fatherly air, severe, if you like, but above all watchful. In his eyes we had some individual existence."

"He had some regard for the life of an ordinary soldier. He wasn't a butcher."

This last opinion, expressed in different ways, was the one that recurred most frequently. Exactly what led to its formulation is hard to say. But it was widespread, long before the passage of time allowed History to pronounce a verdict, that Pétain was one of those military leaders who are careful of the lives of their men.

Until the present atomic age, which has opened entirely new perspectives, there was no way of saving soldiers' lives except by the expenditure of some mechanical means. A maximum economy was practiced by the Allies after the Normandy landings of June 1944, when aviation paved the way, crushing all resistance before it. In 1916 this was the function of the artillery. We shall listen now to a dialogue that began when Pétain first asked the question, "What have your batteries been doing?" For at the same time he was saying to General Headquarters:

"I want artillery and men. Men to accelerate the reliefs, and artillery to economize men."

JOFFRE: Since February 19th the army of Verdun has been built up from 150,000 to nearly 500,000 men. You have been given heavy artillery besides. This is all I can do. You know that I'm preparing an offensive on the Somme. That's going to be the big blow, and nothing can distract me from concentrating all my strength upon it.

PÉTAIN: The Germans are striking their big blow at Verdun. That's where *they*'ve put their concentration.

JOFFRE: Exactly. And you're wearing them down. I shall unleash my offensive upon a weakened foe. When the Germans have to meet my drive on another front, you'll see them give way on yours.

PÉTAIN: You sent word to me by Castelnau less than three weeks ago: "Save Verdun. Ask for what you need, and we'll try to give it to you."

JOFFRE: But I tell you I've done all I can. You'll see that my attack on the Somme will cause the pressure on you to lighten instantly.

PÉTAIN: If I don't get more artillery, I shan't last long enough to see it.

JOFFRE: You'll last, Pétain. You're holding on perfectly well, already. It may be tough going for a while, but there's no longer any danger of a breakthrough.

PÉTAIN: I don't know whether you realize that we're losing three thousand men a day.

JOFFRE: Of course I know. Manpower is one of my responsibilities.

PÉTAIN: These are the worst losses since the beginning of the war. If I had more guns I could limit them.

JOFFRE: My dear Pétain, we've got to win the war!

The above is a reconstruction, stripped of conventional phraseology, of the messages that went back and forth between General Headquarters and Pétain after the German attack on the left bank of the river. As to the last words of Joffre, I should not be surprised if in this conversation between himself and his subordinate he had not been more explicit: "If we win the war, no one's going to quibble about two or three hundred thousand casualties." Although Joffre may well have been affected by the slaughter at Verdun, it is quite true that the winning of the war was a responsibility that his own country and its Allies had laid upon him. From a historical point of view he would have been justified in recalling the words inadvertently pronounced by Napoleon over the dead of the Battle of Wagram: "One night in Paris will make up for all this."

Joffre and Pétain did meet face-to-face, with no witnesses present, on March 10th, when the commander-in-chief, disquieted by the German advance, came to Souilly to find out whether the Second Army leader could not really get along without artillery reinforcements. The German drive had been halted, at this point in the battle, on a line running from Béthincourt, through Mort-Homme and the southern part of the Bois des Corbeaux to just south of Cumières. This permitted Joffre to write the first of the famous orders of the day, which I shall quote in full because, unlike most of the official texts, it shows a certain regard for reality:

Soldiers of the army of Verdun! For three weeks you have been bearing the brunt of the most formidable assault which the enemy has yet attempted upon us. The Germans believed that this attack would be irresistible, and assigned to it the cream of their troops and their most powerful artillery. They hoped that the capture of Verdun would bolster their allies and convince the neutrals that they were sure to win the war. But they did not reckon with you. Night and day, in spite of an unprecedented bombardment, you have staved off the attack and held your positions. The struggle is not yet over, for the Germans need a victory. But you will snatch it from them. There are plenty of men and munitions behind you. But you have, above all, your indomitable courage and your faith in the Republic. The nation's eyes are upon you. You are those of whom it will one day be said: "They barred the road to Verdun!"

Only one phrase, "faith in the Republic," really annoyed the soldiers in the front line. Most of them had nothing against the government, but in March 1916 their political convictions were a minor consideration. Here is a glimpse of the conditions, by no means exceptional, undergone by a group of soldiers of the Sixty-seventh Division, in front of Mort-Homme, twenty-four hours after the publication of Joffre's order of the day.

*   *   *

Journalists, official historians, and writers of military manuals called it an "improved shellhole." "Improvement" was hardly the word to apply to the hurried and even terrified digging, by the light of rockets, from both sides of the night before. Nor were the occupants at all sure that the shellhole in which seven of them—a captain and six soldiers—had taken refuge was originally made by a shell. At certain moments the gas released by the exploding shells had been suffocating, the earth had trembled under their feet, and the violence of the bombardment had cut off any chance of talking to each other. Now there prevailed a strange calm. The earth still trembled, but at regular intervals. The German barrage was falling some two hundred yards behind the shellhole; the French barrage was falling some three hundred yards behind the German shellholes. The artillery on both sides was concentrating beyond the front lines, and in between isolated groups of men of both armies were caught, face-to-face, in holes in the ground. The situation was not uncommon.

The calm, then, was strictly relative, and confined to a narrow area. It is easy to imagine the caption which the magazine *L'Illustration* would have used under a photograph of the scene: *French infantrymen on the alert in an improved shellhole in the sector of Mort-Homme. The third man from the right is wearing a revolver holster, which shows that he is a captain. But he is holding a rifle as well, in order to join his poilus in taking a potshot at the Boches.* A little wall of dirt, eleven or twelve inches high, had been thrown up on three sides of the hole, and the occupants took turns, two by two, in keeping watch. On either side, some distance away, other Frenchmen occupied the same sort of hole. For the moment the Germans were not shooting. About midway between the opposing groups of holes was a shallow pond, some thirty feet long, and around it a dozen corpses.

The captain was leaning against the parapet, peering out through a rudimentary periscope. What the photograph might well have failed to show were the furrows left on his blackened face by tears. The captain had wept a short time before, not out of despair but because the stench of the hole had caused him not once but several times to vomit. For four days he and his men had eaten nothing but tinned rations and they had had nothing to drink for forty-eight hours. All of them were suffering from diarrhea.

Even in full battle the soup carriers, with huge cans strapped to their backs, left the field kitchens and made their way, sometimes walking, bent over double, sometimes crawling, to the most forward shellholes. Their bodies were strewn over the battlefield among many others, except that the soup cans lying beside them gave them a special interest. Their loaded silhouettes were easily recognizable, and sharpshooters took particular delight in picking them off.

The holed-up soldiers suffered not only from diarrhea but, in spite of the cold, from thirst as well. All over the battlefield thirst was the principal enemy on both sides. Civilized men had acquired the habit of kneeling down and lapping up water from a puddle.

Certain details are not very pleasant to recount. A man may want to leave the shellhole and go off on his own in order to relieve himself. That of course means exposing himself to enemy fire. Because of this understandable craving for privacy, thousands of men met their death during the First World War. Another solution is to dig a small hole at the bottom of the big one into which your comrades are crowded. That is what brings on vomiting. But most often, when a man has diarrhea, there is no time to do anything at all. Not only the captain but his six men as well would have had plenty of reason to weep had they not been distracted by thirst and the wish to survive.

Who fired the first shot to keep the enemy away from the pond would be difficult to ascertain. French or German, he must have been soft in the head. At twilight of the first day a tacit truce had been established. Men from both sides approached the pond, first on all fours and then, under cover of darkness, walking upright, although their figures were visible in the glare of the rockets. No one fired at them. The officers on both sides looked the other way. After all, the men in the shellholes could do nothing but maintain their positions. So what harm was there in going for a drink of water? Only at night, of course; by day it would have looked too much like fraternization.

The body of water in question was probably a duck pond in the middle of a green field. At present there was no trace of grass. The snow had melted, and spring was just around the corner, but on this blackened, uptorn land it seemed as if no grass would ever grow again. The water in the pond was gray-green, or at least so it appeared in the light of day. When it was brought back in a can, at night, it had a strange odor, but one that was, at least, different from that of the hole. It was better not to try too hard to imagine what was at the bottom of the pond.

Toward the end of the second night there was a sudden burst of gunfire, and men fell, groaning, to the ground. The fool who was the first to shoot may well have killed his own comrades. In any case, the tacit truce was over. Now anyone who went to the pond for water knew what was waiting for him. The corpses all around it told the story.

"Captain, sir, last year, in Champagne, there were three of us in a hole very much like this. We pissed into a can and then drank out of it. More fellows did that than you have any idea. But just now I couldn't. This whole place is too smelly. I can't stand being so thirsty, though. Tonight I'm going to crawl out to the pond, no matter what happens."

"You'll get yourself killed."

"What do I care? It's going to happen to us anyway."

It is possible to go without water for several days. These men would have been able to stand their thirst better had they not been dehydrated by diarrhea. Their tongues felt like thick pieces of blotting paper, and toward the middle of the day, when the captain vomited again, there were no more tears in his eyes. Because he had had nothing to eat, he vomited only bile. Mechanically he patted the wallet in his pocket. Hundreds of thousands of soldiers, French and German, British, Russian, Serbian, Bulgarian, and Italian, made the same gesture several times a day. It was a way of verifying the fact that they still had some identity and were still alive.

In the captain's wallet were snapshots of his wife and family, one of them of a row of smiling faces, taken in front of a country house, beside a De Dion-Bouton car. The other men in the hole had similar snapshots, and so did the Germans in the holes across the way. If the wallets had been emptied and all the snapshots shaken up together, it would have taken only a moment to separate them and return them to their owners. Now these same men, face to face in evil-smelling holes, who the night before had drunk water such as even a farmyard animal would have refused, increased the hardness of their lot by cutting one another off from the source of supply. But in fact they had passed the stage when they were surprised by this return to savagery. They had accepted it as one of the phenomena of war. The thing that occasionally occurred to them and that was peculiar to this war was that only ten miles behind them, other men were leading an almost normal existence, eating fresh food, drinking wine and fresh water, relieving themselves in privacy, and not vomiting because of the odor of their own excretions. The abomination that was never reported in the newspapers, of which the soldiers themselves were too ashamed to speak, was endured only by those in the most advanced combat positions, in a narrow space only a few miles from the everyday life of the rear. To them hell was no far-away or hypothetical place; it was close to the ordinary life of every day.

"Captain, sir, the Germans are shooting! They're throwing hand grenades! Over there on the right some of them are coming out of their holes!"

"Captain, sir, the range of their artillery has shifted. That means they're about to attack."

"Well, it won't be the first time, will it?"

There was no need to turn around in order to be sure that the range of the German artillery had lengthened. The ground was trembling in a different way. The French barrage was still falling in the same place. It was impossible to know whether the Germans would drive through it for the sake of making a major attack. In any event their infantry who had been always on the near side could now advance, as some of those on the right were already doing. The Germans in their shellholes directly opposite were less quick to move, because they were afraid of the French rifles. No one fired at random, but whoever did shoot was obliged to show himself, no matter how little, and in so doing he became a target. In the area between the rows of shellholes the crossfire made a hum like that of a gigantic hive of bees. In the "improved" shellhole a soldier suddenly threw down his rifle.

"Shit! I'm out of ammunition!"

There was no chance for his comrades to give him some of theirs. The only question was: Which side would run out first? The soldiers in the shellholes felt sure that the Germans had hand grenades; they themselves had none.

The silence that descends when on both sides ammunition

is exhausted is not tragic in character. There is a feeling of astonishment, as if something totally unexpected had happened. The Germans continued to fire for a few minutes; then they stopped. Were they out of ammunition too?

"This is it, sir! They're coming out. They've got grenades. We're done for! There's nothing we can do but raise our hands. They're coming close! . . . Sir, what are you doing? What good is that revolver? It's just going to make them shoot us! Don't do it! Oh! you bastard!"

8

VERDUN AND
THE SERGEANT-PILOT

THE ENGINE of the Nieuport single-seater was running quite satisfactorily at an altitude of 4,500 feet. From this height the scene was charged with poetry. The earth was a succession of frozen waves, or the surface of a suddenly solidified pot of boiling grease, with wisps of smoke rising and floating above it. There was no indication of anything like a battle. The hum of the plane's engine drowned out the roar of the guns, and every shell explosion was the opening of a dark flower, out of which unrolled a white scarf, an airy veil, impelled with other veils, all of them slightly curved, in the direction of the wind. The procession of veils had a strange beauty, like that of an assembly of nuns, or of girls making their first communion, or perhaps of Ophelias; there was something feminine and pure about these images, which rose out of the pilot's unconscious memories of childhood or perhaps of another world. The pilot was moved to genuine emotion, but he would have died rather than reveal it. At the squadron's canteen the airmen—no matter how sensitive they might be as individuals—affected an attitude of virile cynicism.

Many airmen were beginning to say, "The war's getting to be no joke." They reminisced about the first year, when they had been given a leave after every mission and had gone four or five times a month to enjoy the night spots of Paris. Now discipline was more strict. The roll was called every morning, and the pilots had definite hours of duty. The very idea caused the young pilot in the Nieuport to smile. Two days after his arrival at the camp, as soon as his crate was in good order, he had taken to the air without asking anyone's permission, and brought down a German. To be sure, a slightly choleric captain was awaiting his return.

"What's this? You went up without orders? Where do you think you are? You weren't even supposed to be on duty!"

"I don't give a damn about being 'on duty.' I fly when I please. I brought down a German, didn't I? And as soon as I can get gassed up I'm going to bring down another."

Hardly any sooner said than done. *Brought down two German planes by machine-gun fire,* ran the captain's report, *making a total of five to his credit.* This was the first time that an aviator had been mentioned in an official communiqué. The captain had to hold his tongue while the champagne corks popped that evening in the canteen.

The Air Force was a problem child, unconsciously taking its revenge for the disbelief, the scorn, and sheer stupidity, with which it had been officially treated. In February 1914 André Faure, a graduate of the famous Ecole Polytechnique, who had gone from the artillery into aviation, wrote a report to the Ministry of War asking for consideration of his project for an airplane gun. The reply, dated July 2nd, ran as follows: *An interesting piece of work, demonstrative of a spirit of scientific inquiry that deserves encouragement. Unfortunately, the project is closer to Jules Verne than to reality. The sort of aerial warfare which it presupposes is not at all likely to take place in the near future.* Three months later a highly placed official of the same Ministry wrote a magazine article containing this sentence: "If our Air Force officers, who after all are soldiers, were to realize that their spectacular feats may lead people to believe that the war can be won elsewhere than on the ground, they would be the first to correct this erroneous impression, even if it meant discarding their planes altogether." There were some grounds for such an impression, especially after the first air battle, which took place on October 5, 1914, when the French aviators Frantz and Quenault brought down an Aviatik with a machine gun. The only reason they were able to carry so heavy a weapon was that they were flying a heavy but slow Voisin (capable of making fifty to sixty miles an hour in horizontal flight), which had room enough to house it. Most other planes of this period carried no such gun. They were largely two-seaters, with the pilot in the rear and in front of him the combined navigator, observer, and gunner, whose gun was . . . a rifle.

Young people of today, whose heads are filled with jets and rockets, can hardly imagine such prehistoric combats. The opposing planes came within thirty or forty feet of one another, flying in the same direction, like passengers in parallel railway trains. Their rifles against their shoulders the gunners took aim. . . . But they had to be good marksmen, because the speed of the planes was apt to vary, and the wind made for sudden differences in altitude. Such gun battles were called, even in those days, à l'américaine. When one gunner took the other by surprise, either sneaking up on him from the rear or from above, he felt almost guilty, as if he were committing murder. Even later, when all planes carried one or two machine guns, fired through the propellers, fliers had this same sense of murder. The French ace René Fonck entitled the story of one of his victories "An Aerial Assassination." But in most cases the adversaries had each other in plain view, and the two planes performed a dance of death, which was often watched by thousands of spectators below. The secret of success was to be in a position the adversary's machine guns could not reach, and then to let him have it.

Now the pilot of the Nieuport was flying at 5,100 feet. The procession of veils reformed over and over above the frozen waves, and drifted, one melting with indescribable grace into another, in a southwesterly direction. The pilot felt that he was entitled to enjoy the beauty of the sight, since he was risking his life to watch it. Besides risking his life he was suffering from the cold, although not so intensely as on February 26th, the day when he had brought down two German planes. His flying clothes were the following: a sweater and jacket, a fur-lined waterproof coverall, a hood (parka), a helmet, paper gloves, fur gloves, paper socks, and fleece-lined boots. The helmet was not obligatory. In this particular case the pilot was wearing on his head a woman's stocking, dyed bright red.

He was a pilot of very special skill. On February 21st he had taken off amid ice and snow and shot down a German observation plane engaged in finding the artillery range. No weather was bad enough to deter him, and he seemed to have a bird's instinct for direction. He had obtained permission to spend every night at Bar-le-Duc, but this did not prevent him from taking off early in the morning. After a while he had come to the conclusion that his airfield was too far behind the lines to allow for quick action, and he had another, very small field staked out near the town closest to the front, which he took under his special protection. In the afternoon he went to gas up at squadron headquarters and then took off again, returning only at night, as silently as an owl, in order that the enemy should not locate his landing field. Once, over a period of three days, he had spent a total of thirty-one hours in the air. On March 2nd he brought down an Aviatik, his sixth German plane; and this duly recorded feat was, once more, an item in the official communiqué.

The High Command was beginning, little by little, to acknowledge the importance of aviation, chiefly because of the prowess of the Germans, whose observation planes so effectively regulated the range of their artillery and, when the necessity arose, shot down their less numerous French counterparts. And when it came to the daily bulletin from Head-quarters, the account of an air battle was a welcome variation in the ill-disguised monotony of ground operations.

After Joffre's order of the day, there was a feeling of victory in the air at Chantilly, in Paris, and indeed all over the country, in the front-line canteens and in the Air Force squadrons. But the news from the front was already less reassuring. The Germans had attacked in the woods of Malancourt-Avocourt, on the left bank of the Meuse, and a brigade of the Twenty-ninth Division had given way. Among the staff officers there was talk of "lack of vigilance," "doubtful elements," and even "intelligence with the enemy." A telephone call from the brigade's command post had announced, "The Germans have surrounded us," and nothing more. Almost the entire brigade had been made prisoner, and the general morale was adversely affected.

From the air the ground gained by the Germans did not seem to be so very considerable, but one thing was plain: the increasingly clear outline of the trenches. The Germans had a gift for digging, deepening, enlarging, and outfitting the trenches as they advanced. The pilot of the Nieuport had no experience of trench life, but he had read something about it. The mud-covered infantrymen inspired him with real compassion, which he displayed in a curious but convincing way. Often, when he came back from his forays, he made an almost vertical dive over the front lines and then, as he pulled up out of the dive, at a dangerously low altitude he would pause and put on what the delighted spectators called a "show," a series of acrobatics, repeated several times, greeted by applause that he could not hear. He was a bird of the air, far removed from their earthbound servitude, but this was his salute to their endurance. Even the Germans, whose trenches were not so very far away, enjoyed this display, and refrained from shooting.

These acrobatics were not only dangerous in themselves:

they were performed in the face of the strength and ability of the German aviation. All the best German planes (especially the twin-motor Fokkers and LVG's) and pilots (except for Immelmann, who was still operating in the Artois region) had been assembled for the attack on Verdun. There was nothing improvised about the German air operations. The planes took to the air according to carefully elaborated tactical plans, in groups of ten and sometimes twenty. On the French side, in spite of the exploits of such famous pilots as Louis Blériot, Henri and Maurice Farman, Léon Morane, Louis Breguet, Adolphe Pégoud, Jules Védrines, Roland Garros, and Brindejone des Moulinais, all of whom had made a name for themselves before the war, everything was on a strictly amateur basis.

The aviation training school at Avord welcomed candidates from every branch of the service, who were subsequently distributed here and there according to the unforeseeable demands of local army commanders. The airmen wore their old army uniforms. The majority, stemming from the cavalry, wore red riding breeches with a black stripe, leather leggings, and a short black jacket with a collar of various colors, white in the case of Dragoons. The first pursuit squadron was made up of men from the Fifth Army, and commanded by Tricornot de Rose, a forty-year-old former cavalry officer, a magnificent specimen, bull-necked, gray-haired, aristocratic, winner of competitions in civil aviation before the war, and a technician who, together with Garros and the inventor Alkan, had worked out the method of firing a machine gun between the blades of the propeller.

"Gentlemen," he had said to his pilots, "the sagacity, foresightedness, and imagination of the General Staff are well known. Army discipline demands that we have confidence in whatever it has to say. Nevertheless we are not forbidden to second its Olympian meditations. It may be useful to contribute some factual data to its theorizing."

In other words, military aviation had to prove itself regardless of what aid it was given. This was obviously the personal philosophy of the Nieuport pilot, pursuing his prey over the battlefield of Verdun. He wore the newly established dark uniform of the Air Corps, since he was one of its few original members. In order to be accepted he had lied about his age and diplomas and flying hours, all this because he was a brilliant, unstable young man to whom the job of pilot offered possibilities of escape from everyday life. Major de Rose understood the potential value of pilots of this kind and knew how to train them and how to make use of them. In April of 1916 Pétain had given him the command of eight squadrons of single-seaters, a formidable aggregation for this period in the war, based at Bar-le-Duc and assembled for the sole purpose of challenging the German air superiority. Such French aces as Georges Guynemer, Charles Nungesser, Jean Navarre, Captain Auger, Captain Boillot, and Raoul Lufbery, who were the first to arrive in the Verdun sector, were certainly the equals of the Germans Oswald Boelke and Ferdinand von Richthofen. Unfortunately, Guynemer was wounded before his arrival, and Nungesser and Navarre were deadly rivals. Rose encouraged such competitive feeling, but at the same time he fostered and taught the team spirit that was necessary to ensure the Germans' defeat. Pétain had given him not only full powers but also the simple order: "Clear the sky above Verdun."

*   *   *

Pétain had quite enough worries on the ground, both at the front and behind it. Joffre, who was still concentrating on preparations for the Somme offensive, sent him reinforcements only in dribbles. To Pétain's latest request he received, on April 2nd, the following reply:

You know the general situation of the enemy and our own. . . . Hence you must do all you can to relieve me of the necessity of calling upon the last fresh army corps at my disposal.

Poincaré had paid him a visit, in his odd military outfit whose most striking component was a chauffeur's cap. He seemed surprised to hear Pétain give orders to hold out, to resist, and asked why no counterattack was in order. Actually, a counterattack was under way. On April 3rd the Fifth Infantry Division, which had arrived on April 1st from the region of the Somme, had partially recaptured the woods of La Caillette, which the Germans had occupied the day before. The name of the Fifth Division's commander was considerably discussed at various headquarters, command posts and canteens, as were the names of all the other military leaders newly arrived on the scene. "Where does he come from? What's he going to do?" men asked, with a feeling of anticipation. The name of this particular general was Charles Mangin.

Poincaré could not take much interest in the recapture of a single trench or of areas that were small to begin with. When he spoke of a "counterattack" what he really meant was a counteroffensive. Pétain explained that he was in favor of the same thing. Only a counteroffensive could bring victory—that was obvious—since the Germans were occupying French ground. But this was a major and decisive project, which could not be launched without the accumulation of large forces and the definite support of our British Allies. Such a project was what Joffre was planning for the Somme.

"Meanwhile, here at Verdun, we are engaged in a holding operation, which includes a certain amount of reasonable enterprise. I have ordered General Nivelle to study and to work out the recapture of Fort Douaumont. There will be nothing small about this operation."

Poincaré glanced at the map and saw that Douaumont was no more than four hundred yards from the most advanced point of the French front lines. The recapture of the fort would, indeed, raise the general morale, but were such lengthy preparations necessary? Was Pétain after all the defeatist that some of his enemies called him?

I have not been able to ascertain whether Poincaré, the other members of the government, and the Minister for War (the insignificant Roques, who had succeeded Gallieni) knew that, ever since the beginning of March, Pétain's chief of staff, Colonel de Barescut, had been studying the possibility of a withdrawal to the left bank of the Meuse. Pétain did not intend to be taken by surprise in case of a German breakthrough before Verdun, and if a withdrawal became necessary careful preparations would make it less catastrophic. Barescut had been ordered to keep this plan completely secret, even inside Pétain's staff, with the exception of the artillery commander, whose foreknowledge was indispensable. But complete secrecy is impossible, and a leak of some kind must have originated the later false rumor that Pétain had ordered an "abandonment" of the right bank. It is unlikely that, in April, Poincaré would have heard a rumor of this kind. But he was irritated by the didactic manner in which Pétain insisted upon the spadework necessary for the success of a counteroffensive. This man, who was as cold as he, but in a different way, irritated him. The deputies who made official visits to the front were right in saying that Pétain was anything but agreeable; he treated them with icy politeness and gave them as little information as possible. Could he not see that such behavior was doing him no good? His report to General Headquarters of December 1915, showing the slim final results of the "glorious" Champagne offensive, had already given him a bad name. And now this temporizing on the matter of Verdun . . . On the way back, Poincaré reflected on the makeup of Pétain and also on that of another general, the one whom Pétain had ordered to work out the recapture of Douaumont. The painstaking President had read the service records of all the front-line commanders, and now he said to himself that he would look again at that of Nivelle.

Robert Nivelle, artilleryman and corps commander, was a graduate of the École Polytechnique and the War College, an officer full of dash. "On maneuvers, always galloping in the lead," one of his early instructors noted. Nivelle had been in the lead in China, Korea, and North Africa, but colonial service did not mean rapid advancement, and in 1914 Nivelle, like Pétain, was only a colonel. They were the same age—fifty-eight—and Nivelle was promoted to the rank of general only two months after his present commander, in October. Meanwhile, upon two occasions, he had given a conspicuous display of his ability. In Alsace, in August 1914, the fire of his batteries had nailed down and captured twenty-four enemy guns. Then, on the Aisne, in September, with the Seventh Corps, at a moment when the French infantry was retreating, he had boldly galloped his artillery to a position in front of the infantry and had slaughtered the Germans, advancing in close ranks, as was their custom at this early stage of the war.

In January 1915, at Soissons, and in February at Quennevières, Nivelle had handled himself creditably. Moreover, when Poincaré returned from Souilly, he found that everyone had a good word to say for him. The deputies who had been turned over to him by Pétain were enchanted with the welcome they had received. Thus Nivelle had what might be called a "lobby" in his favor, which few front-line commanders enjoyed.

On April 8th a telegram reached Pétain's headquarters, ordering "a vigorous offensive to be undertaken with the least possible delay." Unfortunately, the Germans were the first to attack, both the next day and the day after, on either bank of the river, with five divisions on the left bank alone. Once more a worried Joffre hastened to the scene, just in time to find that the enemy had been contained. Pétain had released an order of the day:

> *April 9 is, for us, a glorious day. The furious attacks of the Crown Prince's soldiers have been broken. Infantrymen, artillerymen, engineers, and aviators of the Second Army outdid one another in bravery. Honor to them all! Without a doubt the Germans will attack again. Let every one of us work and watch to obtain the same success as yesterday. Courage! We shall have them yet!*

"We shall have them!" (*On les aura!*) was a popular slogan, and one that was to become even more popular later on. But Paris and Chantilly were not satisfied with containment. On April 11th Joffre sent another telegram:

> *In the course of my inspection of General Nivelle's sector I was happy to see that your instructions to take an aggressive attitude had borne fruit and that this local commander was planning to pursue the advantages already gained on both sides of Douaumont.*

Even a corporal could have read between the lines. Pétain was being told that an "aggressive attitude" was definitely expected of him.

At this very moment, on the left bank, the German bombardment rose to an intensity almost as great as on the first day. The counterattack (there *was* a counterattack) of the 227th Infantry, which was ordered to recapture the woods of Avocourt, was such a butchery that Major Piccard, the man who led it, with a cigar between his lips and a swagger stick in his hand, was to write: "Oh, the hideous face of war! When you're walking in blood, on the firing line, that's when you see it! The colonel's command post is part of the rear." Nevertheless it was this battle that made him a colonel himself. On April 10th his men had charged under machine-gun fire, the second line stepping over the dead bodies of the first. That night, under a heavy sleet, their store of hand grenades caught fire, and the soldiers passed the burning boxes from hand to hand, smothering the flames with their greatcoats. They had attained their objective, but seven hundred out of the original thousand were casualties.

With variations in intensity the bombardment went on uninterruptedly, day and night. General Headquarters was afraid that the Germans might capture the crest of Souville-Saint-Michel, hardly more than a mile from the northeast of Verdun, from which they could have fired directly into the city. Pétain was informed, more explicitly, that he was to adopt "counteroffensive tactics." Even the names of the two who should initiate these tactics were spelled out for him. They were Nivelle and Mangin.

Here we see the historic conflict, between military doctrine and human feeling, that pitted Pétain against the French High Command during and even after the war. He continued to order the organization and execution of whatever counterattacks he thought had a chance of success, but at the same time, with exasperating obstinacy, he kept on asking for the reinforcements that were being held in readiness for the summer offensive. He insisted upon being sent fresh units, formations that had not previously been in the Verdun sector. He had noticed that those that were sent back a second time were filled up by conscripts of the class of 1916. Here are his exact words; they are of historical importance:

My heart failed, I must admit, when I saw twenty-year-old boys going into the firing line at Verdun. I thought to myself how, at their age, they would soon lose the enthusiasm of their first battle and fall into suffering and perhaps discouragement over the enormity of the task before us. From the porch of the town hall of Souilly—this headquarters of mine which is so fortunately located at the junction of all the roads leading to the front—I looked at them with affectionate attentiveness as they passed by, either jolting along in a truck or weighed down, if they happened to be on foot, by their combat equipment. They

sang and joked in an effort to appear nonchalant, and I
appreciated the trusting way in which they looked at me.
But what a disheartening change when they came back,
either as maimed or wounded or marching in decimated
company ranks! Now the look in their eyes was a stare of
terror, their stance and gait reflected complete exhaustion;
they were stooped under the weight of horrifying mem-
ories. They no more than mumbled an answer to my ques-
tions, and the jeering comments of their older comrades
did not even seem to reach their ears.

This text should have pleaded for Pétain when he was on
trial thirty years later. It has literary quality and evocative
power and testifies at the same time to the depth of the writer's feelings. But for a general it is utterly damning. A military leader is entitled to have imagination of an abstract,
geometrical kind or to have no imagination at all. But this
poetical expression, this way of calling up the faces, lives,
sufferings, and deaths of human beings, belongs to the artist
alone; to a commander it can cause only trouble. History
reserves its accolade for leaders who treat their soldiers as if
they were strictly expendable. "One night in Paris will make
up for all this."

*   *   *

The pilot was flying over the never-varying sea of smoke.
The ground, when he could see it, was still gray-brown, and
showed no sign of turning green. The fort of Douaumont
was a six-pointed star embedded in the earth, with two of its
sides slightly indented. When the pilot flew lower he could
see the geysers of dirt raised by exploding shells and the
smoke that opened up like a flower into the air. From lower
still he could make out the slow movement of men no larger
than insects, the soldiers of Mangin's division in the ravine
of La Caillette, between Souville and Douaumont. They
were climbing, day by day, from one spur to the other of the
cliffs leading up to the fort; every twenty-four hours their
trenches were dug a little closer. But at intervals there were

sudden dark excrescences on the advancing tentacles; these represented the impact of the fire of mortars and *Minnen-werfer*. When the gunfire ceased, the Germans would make an infantry attack, and a fierce local combat ensued.

Suddenly the sergeant saw a Fokker, heading west, above him. He accelerated and rose in pursuit. The German described a wide curve to the right; the pilot knew that the enemy had seen him and accepted the challenge. Rapidly the distance between them narrowed. The configuration of the earth and the drift of the cannon smoke ceased to exist. The pilot had eyes only for the rectangle of the biplane in front of him, growing larger every second.

Quite distinctly he saw the flashes of light. The German had begun to shoot. The magazine of the German machine gun had a thousand rounds of ammunition, the French, forty-seven. As a result, the German pilots could afford to be wasteful, to start shooting at a distance as great as three hundred yards. The sergeant knew that he must wait for a distance of thirty.

Now the dance of death had begun, with its alternate movements of ascent, descent, and passing, first on one side, then on the other. Because both planes were moving at approximately the same speed the pilots sometimes had the impression that they were floating motionless in space. Every time that he thought he was at a favorable angle the pilot fired his machine gun, and at frequent intervals he saw the German gun flashes. The favored targets were the plane's gasoline tank and the exposed part of the pilot's body. The pilot could see the fair skin of his enemy's face under his glasses, a face as immobile as if it were sleeping. No matter how well he knew that glasses mask all expression, the effect was disquieting. To kill a man who is practicing the same exciting sport as oneself, how absolutely insane! This sort of feeling was the origin of certain customs of the period, of the military honors paid to enemy aviators killed in combat.

Thus a German swooped low over the grave of Pégoud and threw down a wreath inscribed, "His adversary pays tribute to the aviator Pégoud, who died fighting for his country." Later, the British honored the German ace von Richtofen. Chivalry was not yet dead. Among airmen, at least.

The pilot swore under his breath as he instinctively leaned on the stick. His machine-gun charger had to be re-loaded, and this was the process: Holding the stick between his knees and endeavoring to maintain a straight line of flight, he grasped the machine gun with one hand and the ring that held it in place with the other, opened up the gun, took out the empty circular magazine, threw it on the floor, and slipped in another, then clipped the gun back in the ring. All this he had to do, if he could, within thirty seconds. He did not have to look over his shoulder to know that the German was shooting at him, and at a moment when he was not free to maneuver. There was something else on his mind. He was heading south over the French lines, in order not to be caught over the German positions and attacked by other planes while he was temporarily defenseless. But he did not like to be seen in this attitude of flight; also, he was afraid that his enemy, fearful in his turn of being drawn too far away from his own base, might turn back and give up the battle. As soon as the machine gun was in place he pulled the stick and wheeled over on one wing.

The German had turned northward just a second before, but now he too began to describe a curve, and the pilot realized that he was once more accepting the challenge. A good fellow, he thought to himself. No beginner, either, since until this moment he had never allowed the pilot to get above him. Now or never, the sergeant thought as he rose. Suddenly the gray-brown ground and the puffs of smoke were over his head. As the German involuntarily raised his eyes, the sergeant could not help smiling. Nine times out of ten this maneuver—attack from an overhead upside-down position—provoked surprise and indecision. A moment later the sergeant saw red and yellow flames shooting out of the gas tank, and the German's jaw dropping. One more volley and the entire upper part of his body crumpled. Well, wasn't that better than burning alive? The German plane was a blazing mass, hurtling toward the earth. Jean Navarre had brought down his ninth enemy plane.

9

THE FLARES OF MANGIN

You will reshape your thinned lines, your scattered ranks. Many of you will have occasion to go home and tell your families of your soldierly ardor and desire to avenge the dead. No Frenchman can rest as long as a savage enemy treads the sacred soil of our country; there can be no peace for the world until the monster of Prussian militarism is overthrown. So you will ready yourselves for new combats, to which you will bring conviction of your superiority, having seen the enemy raise his hands or flee before your bayonets and your grenades. Now you know it: Any German who reaches a trench held by the Fifth Division is killed or captured; every position which the Fifth Division methodically attacks is a captured position. You are marching under the wings of victory!

General Mangin's order of the day was dated April 21st, when all the French press had reproduced it. Now it was half-past eleven o'clock in the morning of May 22nd; the sun stood high in the blue sky and it was warm. The general stood on the parapet of a trench in front of Souville, looking through his field glasses at the smoking fort of Douaumont, which was scheduled for attack twenty minutes later. The trench was old and wide, with broken-down walls. Two officers stood on its sloping side, behind their chief. A cane hung from his left forearm, with which he was holding up his glasses, and his massive silhouette gave an impression of energy and power. At dawn he had remarked to Lieutenant Brunet, one of his liaison officers:

"Let's go along and watch the bombardment."

The two of them had arrived at the trench, where three other staff officers soon joined them. The bombardment was so violent that it seemed as if the fort must surely be blasted to bits. The German reply was no less massive. Huge clumps of earth were blown into the air all along the French front line, while the heavy shells fell continuously in the rear. The sun rose in the northeast, and the smoke of the bombardment was outlined against its pale pink and yellow light. Suddenly there was a crackling sound in the air nearby, a roar, and a draft of air. A mound of earth rose in the air; the general staggered but did not fall. Turning around he saw that two of his companions had fallen to the ground; the others were deathly pale. All of them were wounded; only the general was untouched.

After his wounded aides had been removed, he had decided to stay and watch. For a man with no fear whatsoever this artillery duel was infinitely exciting. Six German observation balloons were straining at their cables just behind the enemy front lines. At seven o'clock a squadron of French planes passed over the general's head, flying at sixty miles an hour in a northerly direction. A few seconds later there was a sudden flash where the balloons had been; all six of them had exploded. The general turned bright eyes and a smiling face on the two officers who had come to take the places of those previously standing behind him.

"Well done, wasn't it?"

This exploit was some consolation for the partial failure of the day before, when the Lafayette Squadron, commanded by Captain Thénault, had made its first appearance in the Verdun sky. The young American volunteers were skillful and daring pilots and did not hesitate to join combat with twelve German planes they met over Étain. Unfortunately, most of their machine guns had jammed, and they were lucky to get home with only two of their number wounded.

French aviation was not even yet properly organized, and

the Germans seemed to be as strong as ever. But they were not invulnerable—witness the loss of these six observation balloons. The thing to do on the ground was to push boldly ahead, as the planes had done. Scrutinizing his own front line, the general could imagine the men's impatience to start forward. If he had listened to his natural impulse, he would have been in the first wave with them, at their head, as he had done with his Spahis on the Niger against the Sudanese or at Nzala Adem in Morocco against the white burnouses:

> *Lieutenant Mangin of the infantry has performed with particular brilliance in cavalry service. With his robust build, good health, energy and courage, he has never lost a chance to charge, heedless of danger, but at the same time with the certitude of exactly how much he could do without forfeiting success.*

Now there was no question of charging on horseback, waving his sword over his head. But for a man who loved to fight, the prospect of attacking a visible enemy with a bayonet or a hand grenade was almost as exciting. Mangin honestly regretted that field glasses were his only weapon. No other general was so often seen in the front line.

The moment of attack was always intoxicating; but not so what went before and came after. On his visits to the trenches he did not overlook the filth and stench in which the soldiers lived. But he too had had his share of discomfort and pain. The Congo-Nile mission, under Jean-Baptiste Marchand, had provided plenty of those. The blazing sun, the mosquitoes more dangerous than wild beasts, the process of cutting through the jungle at the rate of a mile a day, the navigation of rain-swollen rivers and snake-infested marshes, where the water was poisoned by dead animals, the bouts of fever, the loneliness, the natives' betrayals, and finally the striking of the French colors and the evacuation of Fashoda. The campaign of southern Morocco had been no joke either; the same heat (even if here it was dry), the sand continually blown by the desert wind into the tent, the constant thirst. As for his wounds, Mangin never stopped to count them; he was so strong that they made no more effect upon him than scratches. Yes, he had done his share, never backing down in the face of any effort that was required of him. Of course, there had been compensations: honors, citations, the tribute of the natives, the elaborate entertainment offered by conquered sultans. And something that was, to Mangin, still more precious, once the conquest was accomplished, the inebriating task of pacification, the service with Lyautey, the building of roads and sanitary facilities, the transformation of cities and, most satisfying of all, the gratitude of the former foe. Mangin could still hear the toast which Louis-Hubert Lyautey had proposed when he decorated him after the capture of Marrakesh: "I raise my glass to Colonel Mangin, who has caused the French cock to crow louder than we have heard him in a long time."

Now, on the morning of May 22, 1916, shortly after the destruction of the German observation balloons, the general repaired to his command post. Immediately an orderly proceeded to brush the mud from his uniform. He was meticulous in his dress, to the point of being somewhat of a dandy, as only a leader completely unafraid—even of death—could afford to be. The mud-stained infantrymen stared incredulously, but without resentment, at his prewar-style red trousers. "The Boches are going to see red, all right!" was their comment. Among the higher echelons, there was much talk about the size of his entourage, and the luxury of his headquarters. In 1915, when he moved into a requisitioned château near Neuville-Saint-Vaast, the population was left goggle-eyed by the sight of twenty soldiers working for half a day unpacking furniture and rugs and tableware.

"Does he think he's turning it into a palace?"

A man to whom sultans had bowed could not very well do without Oriental rugs. At the head of his housekeeping staff was Baba, the devoted black giant who had followed him all over Africa, originally a kitchen orderly, but now a major-domo, master of ceremonies, and the man one had to talk to if one wanted to see the general—Baba, the Mameluke of Mangin-Napoleon. The general to whom Arab chiefs had offered thoroughbred horses could not very well do without a car, and Mangin had more cars at his disposal than Joffre, most luxurious among them a captured Opel, not military gray but of a highly polished bright red. German airmen could spot it on the roads and signal its whereabouts to their artillery. But Mangin relished this mark of the enemy's special attention.

Toward eleven o'clock he went back to the trench that served as his post of observation.

"Sir," said one of the officers standing respectfully behind him, "our bombardment's getting heavier. We're more than matching their fire."

This was true, not only in the immediate neighborhood of the fort but beyond it and to the west as well, where shells tore up the earth so consistently that the whole area seemed to rise in successive waves, like a brown sea. The Germans in the front-line could not have been happy. The fact was— this was one of the lessons of this war—that there could not be too much softening up before an attack. Officially artillery preparations had started on May 17th, with what could be more accurately called an intensification of fire, which was to develop into the real thing on the 20th. At once the Germans had opened up in reply, using heavier shells and on a broader front. To know what destruction had been effected by the French guns was not easy. Aerial photographs were all alike, showing a blistered but uninformative surface like that of the moon, with trenches like threads—light or dark, depending on the lighting—and the fort a hexagon traced by a pencil, of which no one could guess the actual condition. The day before, however, Lieutenant Brunet, one of the officers wounded that morning, was told by the colonel in command of the artillery of the Third Corps:

"You can report to your general that the fort of Douaumont is no more than a sieve."

This was a professional artilleryman speaking, and it seemed as if he must be able to judge what effect a given concentration of shells would have on a target. Granting that the French barrage did not cover a sufficient area— (What barrage ever did? How broad is to be the swath of destruction?)—no one could fail to admire, even without benefit of field glasses, its precision. All the high-ranking officers agreed that nothing like it had been done for a very long time, perhaps not since the beginning of the war. These officers, too, were in a position to know.

The commander of the attack group (Mangin's Fifth Division and Lestoquoi's Thirty-sixth) was General Lebrun, but Mangin had organized the attack and his division was to lead it. Originally he had asked for four divisions, but as soon as this request had traveled through the usual channels to General Headquarters it met with the immediate reply:

"You're forgetting the offensive on the Somme! It's impossible to use four divisions for a local objective."

A local objective indeed! Everyone in both Paris and Chantilly could give a dozen reasons (the chief one psychological, because civilian morale was low) for the recapture of Douaumont. Mangin had been warmly encouraged when he proposed that he take charge of the preparations. But as soon as there was a mention of "more men," anything in the neighborhood of Verdun was a "local objective" and first place went to the Somme. Disappointed, Mangin remade his plan.

"Three divisions, then. Two to make the attack, side by side, and one to relieve them."

"Out of the question. You will have to get along with two, one behind the other."

This was really stretching things. A whole division of engineers was necessary to dig the departure and communication trenches. The original trenches had caved in, and those that had been rebuilt had been almost immediately rendered useless by the counterfire of the German batteries. A large part of the front-line troops were in shellholes, and for twenty-four hours they had suffered considerable losses. Of course, the Germans had suffered too, so that numerically the opposing forces were not unequal.

The final plan of attack had been approved by both Nivelle—enthusiastically—and Pétain—with reservations. Pétain wanted stronger artillery support and four divisions; at the back of his mind there was always a fear of falling short of the necessary strength. Mangin wondered what lay behind the older man's impenetrable reserve. Pétain had made no comment on May 2nd, when he had turned over the Second Army to Nivelle and himself assumed command of the Central Armies Group; he was as impassive and courteous as ever. But there was a hint of sadness in his expression, because this promotion was obviously a way of kicking him upstairs. He was officially charged with maintaining the inviolability of all the armies' front-line positions, but local initiative had passed into other and bolder hands.

"Five minutes to go, sir."

The stakes were high. Mangin remembered clearly the words he had publicly pronounced after the fall of Douaumont. "The Germans intend to take full advantage of this unhoped-for success. The recapture of the fort would be a feat to arouse general admiration. It is an absolute necessity!"

Now the task had fallen upon his shoulders, with only two divisions—his own in the lead—to accomplish it. But he felt sure that the men of the Fifth would not let him down. They would stage a "forward retreat," like that of Neuville-Saint-Vaast.

"Two minutes, sir."

The officer's voice was drowned out by a shrieking sound followed by an outburst of thunder. The French 75's were laying down a barrage just in front of the departure trenches, as if to give the waiting soldiers last-minute reassurance. Who could stand up against such an iron fist?

"Eleven-fifty, sir."

All the officers and men who took part in the May 22nd attack on the fort have spoken admiringly of the accurately timed progression of the barrage of the 75's which covered just the right area and moved, like a protective curtain, at exactly the correct speed to stay in front of the advancing infantry.

From close up the advance was terrible to see, for the German artillery had not slackened its fire: quite the contrary. The French infantry bounded from shellhole to shellhole, crouching for a moment before they leaped up again to go on. Some of them, of course, did not leap up, but died in these illusory shelters. General Mangin was too far away to follow every movement of the infantry, but he saw the barrage going steadily forward, and knew that all was well. Men were dying, of course, but in the general's philosophy to be afraid of death meant to be unworthy of life, and he ardently wished that he could share their danger. Now the barrage had reached the fort; it was impossible to see whether it was actually in front or behind it. For several seconds Mangin stared through his field glasses. Then he lowered them and said to the two officers behind him:

"There! Did you see?"

"Yes, General; the Bengal light!"

The Bengal light was the signal by which the first wave of attackers were to convey the news that they had reached the fort. The time was one minute past twelve. This meant that within only eleven minutes the men of the 129th Infantry had overrun three lines of enemy trenches and reached their objective. It was too good to be true. Mangin and his officers looked at one another almost in anguish. Just then two runners came, literally running, from the command post. The one who spoke was quite breathless.

"General, we've had a message from the observation plane. A flare has been sent up from the top of the fort."

Mangin nodded to show that he had understood, and went on peering through his glasses. Actually, he could not see any more than he had seen before and was merely trying to mask his emotion. Eleven minutes! Once more he lowered his glasses and looked at his officers.

"What do you say to that? That's covering ground in a hurry!"

His broad face was wreathed in smiles. The French Army was a formidable instrument. One had only to know how to use it, how to use it with audacity. He stepped down onto the floor of the old trench and walked, followed by his two aides, toward the command post. At twenty minutes to one a runner arrived to say that two German officers, several non-coms, and a hundred or more disarmed soldiers had been brought in to the command post of the 10th Brigade. Fifty minutes after the onset of the attack, prisoners had been taken.

*　　*　　*

The limousine of the general commanding the German Tenth Reserve Corps passed through the village without stopping. The headquarters of General von Lochow, commander of the Eastern Group, was in a stone-and-brick manor house. To the right and left, in long rectangular fields, men and women were weeding. The age of the men, who were either white-haired or very young, and the large number of women were the only indications that there was such a thing as a war. Yet the estate was only a few minutes by car from the front. The Battle of Verdun had begun five or six miles to the south; here there had been no fighting

since 1914. What thoughts crossed the minds of the French
peasants as they looked up to see the limousine go by? Did
they hope that their countrymen would take the offensive
and advance, even at the cost of the destruction of their
houses and their fields? The limousine came to a stop at the
bottom of a broad flight of steps.

"I'm here to listen," General von Lochow said simply.

The clock on the mantelpiece marked five o'clock in the
afternoon of May 22nd. At once the commander of the
Tenth Reserve Corps launched into his story:

"Our information was correct. The first attack was led by
four battalions, five if you count their wing support. The
French artillery preparation was quite effective on our right;
less so elsewhere. The rolling barrage just before the attack
was well aimed and extremely destructive, so that our men
in positions south and west of the fort were either killed or
completely stunned, and the French had no trouble captur-
ing the survivors. Small French detachments have penetrated
the moat on the west side and climbed up on the central
platform of the ramparts. Fortunately, on the east side, our
positions held, and the French battalion attacking on that
side was wiped out. Both the superstructure and the underground parts of the fort on this side are still in our hands.
The French detachments still in the west ditch and one of
the casemates are isolated."

"Why haven't we made efforts from within the fort or
from the east side to dislodge them?"

"Because of the bombardment, sir—I mean our own. As
soon as the French broke through, the colonel of the Twelfth
Grenadiers asked for a saturation bombardment with delayed fuses. The whole outside of the fort was plastered with
them.

This is how the action appeared to German eyes, and their
view of it was substantially correct. The men of the 129th
Infantry had fought their way ferociously through the ditch

on the west side of the fort and reached the roof. Meanwhile, the Germans still preserved their communication from the east, and when they sent word to their artillery to intensify its fire directly on the fort, the French suffered tremendous losses.

"What is the situation at this moment?" von Lochow asked.

"The French, as I have just said, are isolated. They received some reinforcements at about half-past two, but not much. Our artillery commands the fort from three sides. Locally, the situation is under control. I am willing to assume full responsibility for what may happen as long as I continue to get artillery support."

"You shall have it."

That evening von Lochow telephoned the commander of the Tenth Reserve Corps, now back at his headquarters.

"The French are telling the whole world that they have retaken the fort of Douaumont. Berlin has rung me up with the news-agency information. His Imperial Highness is upset."

"I can't understand it, your Excellency. If you will send me an officer I'll take him myself to the interior of the fort, where he will see for himself that everything is going on as usual. Food, ammunition, and replacements of matériel have been arriving continuously. Of course, there are still some French soldiers on the west side; they have even tried to dig a trench in the platform of the ramparts. But their situation is quite hopeless—that is, just as long as our artillery prevents them from receiving reinforcements."

"It will continue to prevent them."

In fact, it was all a question of artillery. The army of Verdun possessed, at this time, 1,770 guns, of which 1,200 were fieldpieces and 570 heavies. The Germans had 2,200 guns, of which 1,730 were heavy. The German superiority—particularly in mortars—meant, in this particular case, that the

French had been unable to prevent the German reply to their barrage or a German envelopment of the fort.

At six o'clock in the morning of May 23rd the colonel of the French 34th Infantry received orders "to advance upon the fort, occupy it, defend it at any cost against attack and clean out the casemates of any lingering Germans." One man out of five managed to cross the German barrage and join their comrades isolated on the west side of the fort. At nine o'clock the German fire became even more intense, and no more reinforcements could get through. French officers who were taken prisoner and led to the interior of the fort found the occupants going about their business as if they were in peacetime barracks. Through the slits in the armored walls they witnessed the slaughter of the men being sent to reinforce them. At the same time, sixty feet above their heads, a group of soldiers of the 36th Infantry, under the leadership of a second lieutenant, were still defending the trench they had dug during the night before to protect themselves from the German grenadiers attacking them from the east side of the fort. It was an impossible situation.

At half-past two Mangin was still ordering a "ceaseless" continuation of the struggle, but there was no reasonable prospect of success. At seven o'clock of May 24th the French soldiers in the moat withdrew to the south and, under a hail of shells, rejoined the last group of reinforcements, which had never been able to reach them. Soon they were all encircled together. For thirty hours they had held a hopeless position; now they were a little island doomed to destruction. Finally the survivors surrendered to some Germans from the fort, who attacked them with grenades and machine guns.

A dramatic event summons up our most elementary emotions. General Mangin looked at his telephone with disgust. When a man has led cavalry charges, saber in hand, he cannot but be disgusted to find himself fighting a telephone.

Mangin was not a mere crude fighter. He had enjoyed working out the details of the attack, but now, face to face with
the telephone, he had a feeling of impotence. He said nothing, but because of his position of leadership his broad face
was under constant scrutiny on the part of those around him,
and its vertical creases were indicative of both disappointment and irritation. When the telephone finally rang he
waved his aide aside and picked it up himself.

"Mangin speaking."

His interlocutor, General Lebrun, spoke at once of a
fresh attack, or rather, ordered it, repeatedly and insistently,
like a man in a hurry.

"An attack?" said Mangin. "What with?"

His manner was as dry and to the point as when he voiced
his favorite phrase, "There'll be time for rest when you're
dead." Around him there was absolute silence.

"We simply cannot withdraw," Lebrun was saying. "We
must keep the fort. Attack!"

Two seconds elapsed. Mangin's face muscles had contracted; the onlookers could see that he had something to
say. He spoke slowly and distinctly.

"I'm not making a second attack, an attack that pretends
to being an attack when it cannot possibly be one."

No answer. Lebrun must have been choking with anger.
The mouthpiece of the telephone vibrated with his shouting.

"So you don't want to attack, is that it? Well, I'm relieving you of your command. Start right back to the rear and
turn over your command to General Lestoquoi. . . ."

Mangin made no answer. He put down the telephone and
stalked across the heavy carpet to the door. For the first time
in his life he had been accused of not wanting to attack. A
few days later the entire Fifth Division was relieved. From
the 18th to the 25th of May it had lost 130 officers and 5,507
men—half its total number.

10

THE CROWN PRINCE
PRESENTS A SWORD

A LITTLE over a mile southeast of Douaumont, slightly behind it, on the far side of a ravine, was the fort of Vaux. By the end of May 1916, the communication trench leading to the fort was a veritable charnelhouse. Corpses, their helmets still on their heads and their blackened fingers grasping the handle of a shovel or the trigger of a rifle, stared from wide-open eyes, soon to be reduced by the crows to empty sockets. The late spring heat did not make things any prettier. The presence of a passerby caused clouds of flies to rise into the air.

For several days the fort had been the target of eight thousand shells every twenty-four hours. Every five seconds a shell loaded with poison gas fell. In order to prevent the fumes from penetrating the interior, many of the slits had been stuffed with sandbags. Inside, kerosene lamps barely lighted up the hot, dusty gloom. The fort was built to be occupied by two hundred and fifty men; there were now over six hundred. Amid an ocean of destruction it was like a giant lifeboat, crowded with survivors, men wounded or lost or cut off from their units. For a while, during moments of calm at night, small groups had been evacuated, but others had arrived to take their place. Now there was no question of being able either to enter or to leave the fort. Some of the men were looking at the cage which contained a diminishing group of carrier pigeons.

"They're drinking, the little devils!"

The mysterious birds drank from the cup, then turned their necks to stare out of their beady eyes at the men standing around them. They seemed to be quite unaffected by the heat and dustiness of the air and the crash of the falling shells.

"That one there doesn't seem to give a damn. No wonder! Let him go, and in twenty minutes he's in Verdun."

"What do you mean, twenty minutes? Seven minutes!"

The soldier in charge of the pigeons was always bombarded with the same questions. Why did the pigeons never get lost? How did they know in which direction to go? The answers were always the same. The pigeons came from the citadel, and instinctively they returned there. Nobody knew whether or not they recognized and were guided by the landscape. In any event they had been known to return from much farther away.

"Just because that's their nest, eh?" was the inevitable reaction. "They're brighter than we are, to make straight for home. If the Germans and we did the same, the war would soon be over. . . ."

The men flattened themselves against the stone walls, in the hope of feeling cooler, but the walls were repositories of heat. The air would have been easier to breathe had it not been filled with cigarette smoke. But smokers said their cigarettes prevented them from feeling thirsty.

"The saturation point can't be much higher than this. We'll all be asphyxiated together."

The fort had two cisterns, which had been empty long before the bombardment had made them incapable of holding anything. Water was brought, in theory, from Tavannes, a mile away, but for several days none had come through.

Eight thousand shells a day. The big ones were so earth-shaking that they made a man's stomach turn over. Every one raised a cloud of dust, and often the dust did not have time to settle before another shell fell. At times the soldiers said to themselves: "This is it. This is going to bury us, for sure." Men were injured, and died not only on the parapets and in the casemates but in the concrete boxes that defended the moat as well. The 320's and 420's had made a hollow in the flat, central portion of the roof, a seven-foot-deep slab of special concrete. And yet a misguided instinct of self-preservation made the defenders wish, more than anything, to remain in the illusory safety of the inside of the fort.

Six hundred of them there were in all. Among them were some deserters, who hardly improved either discipline or morale. They were the ones that had managed to remain the longest.

*   *   *

There is no end to what can be said about forts; a whole literature exists on the subject. To the layman a fort is a solid piece of construction, a sort of land battleship whose numerous guns, spitting flames and smoke, forbid any enemy advance. But specialists do not agree. They explain that a fort cannot have a large number of guns, because it is a fixed target rather than a moving battleship, and the larger its size, the greater weakness it exposes. The ideal fort, in their opinion, is a single turret, but this unfortunately provides no space for the defenders, for their supplies and ammunition. So every fort is bigger than the experts want it. Every fort seems doomed to fall, but meanwhile it constitutes an annoyance and even an obstacle in the enemy's way. That is, if it is defended, and not from the inside alone. But no matter how strong the defenses, a fort cannot hold off the enemy forever; it is bound eventually to be crippled by continuous bombardment.

*   *   *

June 1, 1916. For several days the surrounding German artillery had pounded the fort for twenty-two hours out of every twenty-four; during the two remaining hours the German infantry attacked. The phrase "heaps of corpses" recurs in the accounts of both French and German survivors. To describe the attacks in detail would only confuse the picture. On several occasions the Germans made small advances and took prisoners, then retired, for safety, to the positions from which they had started. On the French side there were the same orders as on the first day of the battle: every square foot captured or recaptured was to be defended to the death.

To the French, obviously, the defense of the fort meant not to yield ground. And yet it was hard for a veteran infantryman to understand why, having left a perfectly comfortable trench (he was not too hard to please) in order to advance as little as twenty-five yards, he should have to crouch in a shellhole for hours instead of going quietly back to his point of departure. Another thing that impaired morale was the fact that the fire of the French artillery was not only intermittent but often short.

Once more the artillerymen were the objects of curses. But actually their lot was anything but happy. Their guns were huddled together in a salient the Germans pounded from three sides; they had no observation planes or balloons to guide their fire; signal flags and flares were often invisible because of the heavy smoke and the irregularity of the terrain; and the runners who came through alive on an average of one out of three brought information that was no longer new.

Sporadic, hand-to-hand infantry encounters took place between two hundred and six hundred feet from the fort. A hand grenade pierced the kidneys and shattered the legs of the captain of the 7th company of the 142nd Infantry. "Continue the defense! Fire!" he called out to his men. Then he dragged himself on his shattered legs to an opening in the fort, where he was pulled in and taken to the infirmary.

* * *

June 2nd. Lieutenant Ranckow looked at the luminous dial on his newly acquired wristwatch. It was a novel and attractive feature, but just now it was of no help to him in reading the hour, because daylight was coming on. Three minutes to four. The fort, a few hundred feet away, looked like an irregular hump. He could see the surrounding moat and beyond it the counterscarp. Reconnaissance missions had brought back word that the thirty-foot wide, fifteen-foot-deep outer ditch was partly filled with huge blocks of concrete, displaced by some of the daily eight thousand shells. Now the German barrage carried south of the fort; it had been decided to use the fallen blocks in the ditch as stepping-stones for scaling the wall. This was just as it had been at Douaumont, but with one important difference: here the ditch would be sprayed by French machine guns and mortars. But orders were orders, and an Iron Cross might reward success. An Iron Cross or a wooden cross, one or the other.

Four o'clock. Forward! The four attacking companies, disposed in a semicircle, threw themselves forward as one. Men carrying flamethrowers, axes, and wirecutters could not advance very fast; and yet, as at Douaumont, theirs was the first job to be done. The first volleys of machine-gun fire came from just the place where the concrete blocks had fallen. This was natural enough. The defenders had had no respite in which to clear the ditch or mend the wall, but it was elementary tactics to place machine guns in the breaches. Nevertheless the Germans got the impression that only one machine gun was actually firing.

"First and second section, forward!" shouted Ranckow.

The pioneers did not charge like the Light Brigade. They crept on their knees over the ground on both sides of the escarpment, while their comrades tried to blanket the fire of the machine gun. Ranckow had mentally rehearsed the scene a hundred times. Now he went through an anxious moment when he saw flashes of fire from the two pillboxes that guarded the inner moat. But he was reassured when he heard the explosion of hand grenades above the escarpment. A few seconds later the machine gun was silent, and the escarpment was overrun by his men. The first part of the plan had been faithfully executed.

Ranckow was eager to join his men, but it was his duty not to expose himself until the operation was further under way. The two pillboxes were still firing, and it was obvious that the ditch could not be crossed until they were silenced. This was the task of the pioneers, or such of them as had got through, carrying their heavy equipment. After climbing up to the top of the counterscarp, they had hoisted themselves onto the roof of the west pillbox.

You are on the roof of a house. The people who are shooting from inside it cannot hit you, but they can hit your friends on the street below. What are you going to do? The pioneers were working like ditchdiggers, at top speed. Ranckow could see them fitting curved sections of tubing together. Perhaps you can imagine by now the correct strategy of an attack from a roof. The tubing was introduced into a pillbox embrasure, and out of the end of the tubing spurted a flame six feet long. Soon the interior of the pillbox was filled with suffocating black smoke, and its machine guns were silenced. In the calm that followed, Ranckow sent thirty more pioneers across the ditch.

Ranckow looked at his watch; the minute hand seemed to have advanced by leaps and bounds. Six o'clock already; he could hardly believe it. Fortunately, the French artillery could not plaster the fort or even the ditches for fear of hitting the defenders. He felt that the operation had progressed far enough for him to take certain risks. He jumped down into the ditch, leaving the rest of his company behind.

Meanwhile, the pioneers of the second wave had climbed up on top of the roof of the other pillbox. They were lucky, for they found that the roof had been damaged—probably by a 380 shell—and repaired. Tossing their tubing and flamethrowers aside, they set to work with picks and axes.

The French opened fire from the apertures in the central part of the fort. It was very warm, and the feverishly working pioneers spat white saliva. Ranckow looked at his watch again. Seven o'clock. He heard grenades explode nearby. The hole in the roof of the second pillbox had been reopened, and the pioneers were throwing their grenades down into it. Ranckow signaled to the lieutenant he had left in command behind him to bring the rest of the company across the outer moat.

About an hour later a noncommissioned officer came to tell him that the pioneers had penetrated the second pillbox and taken thirty prisoners and two machine guns. "Good!" said Ranckow. "I'm going to join them." At just this moment there was shooting from the embrasures of the first pillbox, the first to have been attacked. After they had recovered from the flames and smoke, the French had returned to the defense. Did this mean that everything must begin all over again? This had been foreseen, but Ranckow was distressed by the delay. What if the French changed their minds and began to bombard?

Already the next phase of the operation was under way. Men with sandbags on their shoulders ran across the hundred yards that separated the first German positions from the fort, disappeared into the ditch, and then, with their comrades' help, clambered up the counterscarp and onto the roof of the west pillbox, all this under intermittent but well-aimed French fire. The Germans were sweating, and with reason. The sandbags contained not sand but hand grenades. Two of the carriers had been blown to bits along the way.

The next step was to attach the bags to ropes and lower them down the side of the pillbox to the level of the embrasures, where one of the grenades with a special timing mechanism exploded. (This antiquated system was used as late as 1940 on certain forts of the Maginot Line.) The exploding grenades wrecked the embrasures, killed the occupants of the pillbox, and put it definitely out of action. At five o'clock in the afternoon the German sappers penetrated the interior, in complete possession. Thirteen hours had elapsed since the beginning of the attack, and neither Ranckow nor his men had had anything to eat since three o'clock in the morning.

Once the first two pillboxes had been taken, other Germans penetrated the inner ditch, most of which was filled with fallen blocks of concrete, and attacked the next pillboxes they found in their way. Apparently these were captured without too much difficulty.

* * *

The gallery was so filled with smoke that the beam of the flashlight revealed nothing more than eighteen inches ahead. There was danger of asphyxiation, but a gas mask would have diminished the visibility even further. Lieutenant Ruberg knew something about the construction of forts and their subterranean galleries, and he had taken part in all sorts of difficult and dangerous expeditions, but this smoke-filled burrow utterly disgusted him. It was all he could do to hide his feelings from the soldiers who followed, in single file, behind him.

The gallery opened out of the pillbox and obviously led to the interior of the fort; it was three feet wide and almost five feet high. First came a flight of descending stairs, then a corridor slightly wider, slightly higher. Ruberg held his flashlight in front of him, but it did not prevent him from stubbing his toe against the first of another flight of steps, eight in all, and very steep, leading upward. Just ahead of him the beam thrown by the flashlight became a solid circle. A door stood in the way; to the touch it seemed like wood. Obviously it was very heavy, and there was no use wasting time in trying to force the lock. Ruberg waved the flashlight behind him.

"Easy there. Give me some grenades."

They relayed the grenades to him, four at a time. Ruberg strung them together and leaned them against the door.

"The fuse."

The fuse was timed to burn in twenty seconds. Ruberg ordered his men to go back to the top of the other stair. As soon as he had lighted the fuse he would run to join them. Then, the minute the door exploded, they would all rush forward, as quickly as the narrowness of the gallery permitted.

The man who was helping Ruberg adjust the fuse jogged his elbow. Voices were audible behind the door. The voices were whispering, in unmistakable French. Obviously the speakers had heard the Germans coming and were making some sort of plan to circumvent them. They were like one group of rats, threatened by another. Suddenly Ruberg heard the fizzling sound of a Bickford fuse. The French must have imagined that the Germans were clustered in front of the door, and they meant to kill some of them and perhaps counterattack. Various possibilities swept in rapid succession through Ruberg's mind, but meanwhile he took action.

"Get out of the way," he whispered to the man with the fuse. "Quick!"

Then he took the pin out of a grenade. He was going to set off the charge and kill as many Frenchmen as possible; then his men would grapple with the rest. A hand grenade goes off in five seconds. Ruberg leaned the one he had just prepared against the door and ran back toward the steps. The French and German charges went off simultaneously, when Ruberg was halfway down the staircase. He was thrown several yards away, and felt the burning sensation of splinters in his back. A back wound; that's no fun, he had time to think to himself. Already his men were charging down the smoke-filled gallery; a moment later they had passed through the exploded door.

Ra-ta-ta-ta-ta. Ra-ta-ta-ta-ta.

The staccato sound of the machine gun echoed with un-accustomed loudness. There were two machine guns, actu-ally, one of them on either side of a second, transverse gal-lery. The Germans could advance no farther.

At midnight of June 2nd the fort of Vaux was, to all in-tents and purposes, divided between two owners. Inside were the besieged Frenchmen, who could not stick their noses outside the walls; outside were the Germans.

* * *

The inside of any fort is a maze, and it would take a stranger several days to find his way around it. Nevertheless it is not hard to picture the battle fought for the possession of Fort Vaux. The German aim was to penetrate the entrails and at the same time to cut off the head. For several days in the bowels of the fort a series of frightful hand-to-hand com-bats ensued. From behind a pile of sandbags the defenders would peer into the darkness, pricking up their ears at the least sound. Both sides threw out occasional hand grenades (a dangerous business because of the close quarters of the fighting) and even fired machine guns, with an aim so wild that as often as not the bullets ricocheted from the walls. Sometimes there was a sudden burst of flame as the Germans tried out their flamethrowers and forced the defenders to withdraw to another barricade, fifteen feet farther back. The winding, intersecting passageways facilitated this stalling operation. But the Germans had other means of exerting pressure.

"You won't let us reach the heart of your fort, is that it? Then suffocate!"

Outside the fort they fired every time a sandbag was removed from an aperture in order to gain a breath of air. Wherever a shell made a breach in the wall the Germans filled it with dirt. If the defenders were determined to hold, they would be buried alive.

Inside, the earth-shaking detonations of the heavy artillery were no longer heard, for the German bombardment had been suspended. The silence of the French artillery was quite inexplicable. Every now and then, at night, one of the defenders slipped out, armed with a powerful flashlight, and signaled a message from Major Raynal, the commander, to Souville: "I ask for artillery fire on the fort. . . . Confirming my request for artillery fire on the fort." Perhaps, at Souville, they found this message disconcerting; they failed to understand that the defenders were faced with a choice between being bombarded and being buried alive. A French plane flew over several times, at an altitude of no more than three hundred feet, braving German machine-gun fire. Ten minutes later a few desultory French shells wiped out some of the attackers. But these were quickly replaced, and the bombardment was not repeated. On June 4th Major Raynal saw some sign of French activity outside. A battalion of infantry was counterattacking. In the distance waves of men advanced under a stepped-up German barrage. Then, apparently, the attempt was abandoned.

Inside the fort the ventilators were no longer working. Water was rationed to one cup per day. No one thought about food; men filled with toxins have no appetite. For lack of oxygen the kerosene lamps went out, and the only light was provided by a few candles. Here and there men fainted; often, amid the darkness, no one saw them fall. In the galleries "a handful of brave men" (as the official communiqué called them, in apparent contrast to the inert majority) continued to fight. Major Raynal sent a message, by carrier-pigeon, his last, to the citadel of Verdun:

> *We are still holding out, but we are under a very dangerous attack by poison gas. Absolute necessity of disengagement. Arrange for us to have communications with Souville, which has not answered our signals. This is our last pigeon.*

Day after day, night after night had gone by. To the defenders of the galleries and the weakened majority in the central rooms of the fort, there was not much difference between them. Outside, however, they were not at all the same. Major Raynal decided to evacuate, under cover of darkness, all the uselessly dying men who did not belong, strictly speaking, to the garrison.

The first contingent seems to have numbered about a hundred men, preceded by a group of four to act as guides— Second Lieutenant Buffet, two corporals, and a runner. The plan was to cross the German lines to the south, where there was a gap, which, however, was always under fire, then to cross no-man's-land and, once at the French front lines, to make themselves known before being shot.

*　　*　　*

June 5th: half-past one in the morning. As the guides emerged from the fort, they drank deep drafts of the June night air. Even if it was gas-polluted and smoky, it was like a breath of paradise after the unbearable stuffiness in which they had been living. The four climbed down into the ditch and up the other side. Four men should not have been conspicuous in the enveloping darkness. But the watchful Germans had lynx eyes. A flare shot up, then another; machine guns went off, and then were silent. Two hundred yards farther on there was almost certain to be a barrage. But they must keep going. There was no use denying they felt shaky, no matter how many battles they had survived. But these phantom figures firing machine guns, these bursts of flame, this freezing consciousness of danger, this stabbing fear at every step had their compensations. They made them forget their thirst and fatigue and the special sickening odor of no-man's-land. Civilians may pronounce the words "war" and "battlefield," but the most important single feature, of which they are totally ignorant, is the sickly-sweet stench of the dead.

The rest of the contingent followed, in small groups, with varying degrees of boldness and good fortune. When the stench of the dead became slightly less strong, it was time to be on the alert.

"Halt!"

"France!"

Of course, this single word did not suffice. It was necessary to give an explanation, to shout it in a tone of extreme urgency, because the sentries' fingers were nervous on their triggers.

"Good! Come on over!"

*   *   *

Benevolently the general motioned to Second Lieutenant Buffet to stand at ease.

"Have you been taken care of? Have you had something to eat and drink and a bit of a rest?"

"Yes, sir."

And Second Lieutenant Buffet proceeded to tell his story for the third time. With due regard for rank, he had told it first to the colonel in command of the brigade, then to the general in command of the division, and now to the general in command of the sector. Each time he was warmly commended.

"Now then," the general was saying, "are you willing to return to the fort with an urgent message for Major Raynal?"

"Yes, sir."

What other reply can a second lieutenant make to a general's "Are you willing?" And yet Second Lieutenant Buffet had every reason to hesitate. It is hard to go over the top, especially if you are the first one to go over. It is hard to cling to an impossible position, to stick it out rather than to turn tail and run. It is hard to go back to the front after a furlough. You can ask any old soldier about that, and he will tell you he would almost rather not have any furlough at all.

But the idea of returning, after only a few hours of fresh air
and a life worth living, to the exact same horrible place you
have just escaped from at such risk and peril—this was almost more than the second lieutenant could bear. His whole
body seemed to revolt against it.

"Thank you, Buffet!" the general was saying. "You'll get
complete instructions at Brigade Headquarters. A car will
take you there."

Brigade Headquarters was the fort of Tavannes, where
Buffet had arrived in the first place. The instructions were
there, and he had only to commit them to memory.

"You'd better not go back all alone. There's another es-
capee here, a sergeant. Ask him if he's willing to go along.
Sergeant Fretté, that's his name. A young chap . . ."

Fretté . . . Buffet remembered him perfectly well, a fellow with a perpetual smile on his face. There might be
some satisfaction in erasing that smile. . . . Why didn't the
colonel ask the question directly, as the general had done before him? Perhaps because he imagined that it was a good
deal easier to say "Will you come along with me?" than
"Are you willing to go?"

"Will you come along with me, Fretté?"

"Of course."

The smile refused to be erased. Fretté frowned only when
he read the instructions, with a view to memorizing them.
Buffet agreed that the message left a good deal to be de-
sired. It was the usual: "Hold out; we're going to counterattack," with a few details of the projected action, which was
to take place the next morning. But neither a second lieutenant nor a sergeant has any right to comment on the word-
ing of an order from Headquarters. Besides, darkness had
fallen, and it was time to go.

The German barrage was still relatively far away. The
large number of identical shellholes might have caused the
two men to lose their way, had not Buffet brought a com-

pass. A brave young man, he never denied that there was a moment of frightful despair on the way back. It was, as he frankly admitted, when they first became aware of the stench, the stench that was unlike anything in the world of the living, the stench that men's and animals' instinct for self-preservation made absolutely unendurable to them. Then, once more, the presence of danger made the two men forget the awful smell. German 210 shells were falling with the regularity of rain; to make their way through the barrage required all their attention.

"Fretté, we must be getting close. Can you see the fort?"

"I can feel it, yes."

The orders were quite definite: in the vicinity of the fort they were to separate, each was to try his luck independently of the other.

"God help us!" said Buffet, by way of farewell.

The barrage was behind them, and the irregular outline of the fort lay ahead. The fallen blocks of concrete stood out most clearly of all, lighter than the black earth or the black sky. A flare mounted in the air, but Buffet had already thrown himself flat on the ground. The Germans had a way of sending up flares at regular intervals, whether or not they saw or heard anything stir. In the flare's glow Buffet saw the fort distinctly, surging up as if from the depths of a dream. All the apertures were sealed off with boards or sandbags, and the general aspect was that of a tomb. What if the garrison were all dead? Or if it were occupied by the Germans? Buffet climbed down into the ditch and started up the counterscarp. Another flare made him hug the ground. Who would be the first to shoot at him?

After several seconds of silence, a French voice said: "Come on up! This way!"

Buffet clambered onto a piece of masonry; a makeshift door swung just wide enough open for him to be pulled inside, then closed.

"Splendid work!" said Major Raynal, embracing him.

Buffet was taken aback not so much by the warmth of the welcome as by the fact that conditions seemed so much worse than less than twenty-four hours before. Or had he, in this short time, forgotten how small and dark and smoky and dirty the fort was? Do I look like these men? he wondered.

Raynal and his officers listened in silence to the message. As seen in the candlelight, their bearded faces and sunken eyes expressed nothing more than their pitiful physical state, but their complete immobility spoke eloquently of disappointment and dejection. So they were to hold on until the new counterattack. A counterattack of what kind? Four companies . . . Not what you could call a large number of men. But there was something more: "Four companies, together with squads of engineers carrying special ladders." Ladders with which to scale the walls? It sounded like the Middle Ages! What idiot on the staff could have imagined that the Germans would passively allow squads of ladder-bearers to reach the walls? What about artillery preparation? There was no mention of that. And what was most needed was a protracted bombardment, a duplicate of what the Germans had done.

"Well, gentlemen," said Major Raynal, "we shall do the best we can."

A little later Buffet found out that Sergeant Fretté, too, had reached the fort.

*   *   *

June 6th. The counterattack was a fiasco, in spite of the "special ladders." Not that the idea of using ladders was intrinsically wrong. Twenty-eight years later, to the day, when the Allies landed in Normandy, Canadian troops used ladders (rope ladders, rocket-fired) to scale the cliff of Hoc, twenty times higher than the walls of the fort of Vaux, but this was after a massive air attack supported by a bombardment from heavy ships lying just offshore. At Verdun there was no such thing as bombardment from the air. As for artillery, it was in vain that from his Central Armies Group Headquarters Pétain tried to acquire for his battle what Joffre was stubbornly holding in reserve for the Somme. The only result was that his insistence irritated Joffre and G.Q.G. How many guns did Pétain want, anyhow? Why didn't he use his infantry? Didn't he know that the reason he had been relieved of the direct command of the Verdun sector was that he had failed to show sufficient aggressiveness, sufficient "punch"? "Punch," that was the word currently in style. Nivelle had it, and that was why he had been put in Pétain's place. Nivelle was not one to hedge and say, "A counteroffensive requires careful preparation." Not Nivelle. "A counterattack? Splendid! And if the first isn't successful, then a second." The survivors (one out of four) of the counterattack of June 6th were lying low in their shellholes that ringed the fort, unable even to raise their heads, but this was no reason for not trying again.

"It has become a question of honor. The fort must be recaptured, whatever the cost. We will counterattack again on the morning of the day after tomorrow."

This is what Nivelle said to his chief of staff on June 6th at nine o'clock. In my brief account of the prelude to the counterattack of June 8th I must, to my regret, indicate three names (including one place name) by their initials. This is exactly as they are recorded. Apparently the officers involved did not wish to be designated in any other way. But we are not preparing an indictment; we are more modestly (or perhaps more ambitiously) searching for the human factors with which the official records cannot supply us. If, like Arab women showing only one eye, these officers reveal nothing of themselves but an initial, we have no reason to be disturbed. Let us return to the conversation between Nivelle and his chief of staff.

"To recapture the fort, General, is no easy matter," the

chief of staff observed. "It means heavy artillery preparation. And besides, we are short of men."

"We will shift some troops from the left bank of the river. I'm going over to R., where I have called all the group and division leaders together."

"Very good, General. Major P. will go along. If you give him an idea of what you're going to say, then, when the time comes, he can draw up your orders."

Before the general was ready to leave, the chief of staff took his fellow officer, Major P., aside and begged him to do everything he could to dissuade Nivelle from ordering a second counterattack."

"Of course," said P. "I agree with you completely."

The car started, then rolled along. Nivelle was silent, and the silence of top brass has something mandatory about it. Finally Major P. made up his mind to speak.

"Sir, the chief of staff told me to remind you that you were to give me an idea of what you are going to say."

"Yes," said Nivelle, looking straight ahead, "but I haven't yet made up my mind. The chief of staff suggested that we counterattack with a brigade made up of elements taken from the left bank."

P. was nonplussed, and wondered whether he had understood the chief of staff correctly. Was this some Machiavellian maneuver on the part of his immediate superior? In the high echelons it is not always possible to follow a straight line. But thinking, like the good fellow he was, of the casualty lists of the last few days, and believing himself to be covered by the chief of staff's personal plea, he took the initiative and argued against the whole idea of a counterattack. Nivelle seemed impassive. At R., where twenty generals were waiting, he explained his plan of attack, which on this occasion he did not credit to his chief of staff. P. could not believe his ears.

After Nivelle had finished talking, General N. "vigorously protested." Then a corps leader, after saying that if the order for an attack were given it would be obeyed, made clear his opinion that, in its projected form, it was doomed to be as unsuccessful as its predecessor. The recapture of the fort required long preparation. Others nodded their assent.

"Consider the order given," said Nivelle. "General Savy will command the brigade. The troops will be taken from the left bank's second line; they will march down to the river, then travel by truck to the front in the sector of Souville-Tavannes during the night between June 7th and 8th, in order to attack early in the morning of the 8th."

"Immediately after a long march and a truck journey?" asked one of those present.

"Write out the order," Nivelle said to Major P. "I will sign it."

*　　*　　*

The last carrier pigeon of Fort Vaux was dead. It had died of the toxic effect of gas fumes a few seconds after flying into the pigeon cote of the citadel. At Souville men peered through their field glasses to catch the signal flashes: *The enemy is working on the west side of the fort, building a mine chamber in which to set off enough explosives to blow the roof off. . . . We cannot hear your artillery. They are attacking us with liquid flame and gas. Conditions are almost untenable. . . . I must be relieved this evening and supplied at once with water. I am at the end of my rope. Officers and men have all done their duty to the end.* The ship of stone was perishing: that much was clear. Yet from the outside no one could guess the full extent of its agony.

In the dark passageways a few diehards continued to defend the sandbag barricades, which they had thrown up a dozen times over. In five days the Germans had advanced only twenty-five yards. But many of the defenders were beginning to lose consciousness, and their comrades did not have sufficient strength to drag them away. Elsewhere there was not enough oxygen for the candles. In the infirmary there were no more bandages or medicine for the hundred or so men in need of attention. There was a foul smell in the air; the stench of corpses mingled with the smell from those who had been gassed or had fainted, and there was no prospect of separating and burying them. And—the clearest and direst sign that the limit of endurance had been reached —both inside and outside the infirmary men were drinking their own urine.

It was three-thirty in the morning. Souville continued to receive fragmentary messages. "Stand by . . ." Major Raynal (who a few hours before had been raised to the rank of Commander of the Legion of Honor, perhaps because it was presumed that he had not much time left in which to enjoy it) had sent an emissary to treat with the enemy. In the game of hide-and-seek with Death that had been going on in the galleries of the fort, it was difficult to make contact except with a machine gun or a hand grenade. But finally the Germans understood that there was an offer of surrender, and sent an officer to receive it. As soon as the surrender was signed, all the blocked apertures were reopened.

> *There was complete silence, except for the sound of their boots when the Germans came in. They walked in single file up the stone stair, with the truce officer at their head. Along the central passageway the French were lined up on either side. The General saluted as they passed between them.*

Shortly after this a door swung open and a column of specters, flanked by German guards, walked out of the fort. At the bottom of the slope some of them gave a hoarse shout, and the guards fingered their guns. Then suddenly they understood that the prisoners were not revolting or trying to run away. Around the fort there were shellholes, half filled with muddy water. The specters rushed toward the shell-holes, threw themselves flat on their stomachs, and began gulping it down.

* * *

"Admirable, Major. The tenacity and courage of yourself and your men are admirable."

The Crown Prince, at attention, looked at his ranking French prisoner. The week's siege of the fort of Vaux had left its mark on Major Raynal's face, with its high forehead, widespread eyes, and strong chin. The Crown Prince was given to studying French faces. A curious mixture of racial strains seemed to have produced them; no one physical characteristic stood out above the rest. A hardy mixture, on the whole, since these loquacious and in their appearance widely differing Frenchmen were holding the superbly organized German Army at bay. No matter what Falkenhayn, Knobelsdorf, and the others might say, the French front was not going to be broken, at least not at Verdun. The idea of a breakthrough might as well be discarded; it looked as if a new phase of attrition were setting in. Of course, I shall not admit it to the troops, the Crown Prince said to himself, but perhaps I'll put it in writing someday. The French have scored a defensive victory by holding out against us, thanks to the incredible endurance of men like this.

Major Raynal submitted the Crown Prince to something like the same scrutiny. He's not so ugly after all, he reflected, not at all like the monkey portrayed by our cartoonists. . . . There is nothing of the notorious German stiffness about him. The Crown Prince was, indeed, slender in build and aristocratic in manner. Of course, German cartoonists, in their turn, endowed Joffre with a potbelly. Such exchanges make up one of the more foolish and trivial aspects of war. At this point an aide-de-camp stepped forward, and the Crown Prince took something from him.

"Major," he said, "I meant to pay tribute to your valor by giving you back your sword. Unfortunately, no one can seem to find it. I can offer you nothing but this modest weapon belonging to a simple soldier, which I hope you will accept at my hands."

A modest weapon, indeed: a wire cutter. Raynal raised his eyebrows, and a hard look came over his face.

"Modest, yes, but glorious," the Crown Prince went on. "I look upon it as just as much of a symbol of French valor as the proudest sword."

Raynal's expression softened.

"I accept the weapon in the spirit in which it is offered. And I thank Your Highness for the tribute to my humble comrades' valor."

A gallant-enough reply. Raynal saluted, made an about-face, and it was all over, except for the long journey into captivity that lay before him. But he had not gone more than a few hundred feet beyond the fort when the aide-de-camp caught up with him.

"Sir, His Imperial Highness requests your presence."

What, again? This time the Crown Prince held a French officer's sword in his hands.

"I have found it, Major," he said. "Please take it in place of the unworthy substitute I was forced to offer you before."

* * *

Just after the Crown Prince had treated the French major with such courtesy, such chivalry (what a beautiful French word, and how descriptive of the attitude a prince can afford to maintain, even in war!), the rescue brigade put together by General Nivelle—the Second Regiment of Zouaves and Moroccans—was trudging under a pelting rain and a barrage of 210's toward the fort of Vaux. The men were tired long before they moved to the attack, but would things have gone very differently even if they had been in the pink of condition? The Zouaves fell like lead soldiers, swept off a tabletop by a child's capricious hand, and the Moroccans after them. Only one Zouave officer survived to lead the eventual withdrawal. Eighty-five percent of the Moroccans were left on the field of battle.

11

A BALCONY
OVERHANGING HELL

THE OFFICER raised his arm and moved backward, one step after another, while the elderly soldiers of the *Landsturm* advanced toward him, each one of them holding a rope attached to the *Drachen* (literally, "sausage"), or observation balloon, which at twelve feet above the ground looked like a ridiculous old elephant with a wrinkled hide. The rudder hung like a limp tail behind it.

The officer halted at the point of ascent, where an extralong and heavy armored truck, carrying the winch, was waiting. The men busied themselves under the quivering elephant's belly; the mechanic and the telephone tester signified that they were ready. Then the observer, Feldwebel Otto Schmitt, stepped over the side of the basket.

Schmitt had stayed aloft on occasion for as long as fifteen hours, prey on his first flights to acute seasickness. There is nothing like an observation balloon for this; planes are eminently stable by comparison. Some people say that the sensation is caused by the sight of the cable plunging toward the ground, but an equally important factor is the recurrence of wide elliptical swings in the face of a high wind. Otto Schmitt had passed the written test for airplane observers but had failed the physical examination. This was how he had found himself in the Balloon Service. There were risks, to be sure, but it was a neat and clean way of taking part in the war. Anything was preferable to the infantry.

Schmitt tried out the telephone and checked his maps, sketches, and notebook. In the basket there were three pairs of prismatic field glasses, a light machine gun, a knapsack filled with food, and a Thermos bottle. The officer in charge gave him final instructions.

"Ready, Captain."

"Let her go!"

The winch began to turn, releasing the cable, and the balloon rose in the air. Soon it had lost its grotesque shape, and the rudder had assumed its normal proportions. Schmitt fitted the parachute belt between his thighs and around his shoulders. Below him the retreating surface of the earth seemed to take the shape of a hollow, while a powerful wind pushed the balloon, still held by its slanting cable, in a southerly direction. The basket was a balcony overhanging the theater of war operations. The balloon shook and then oscillated. On the ground the winch had stopped turning. Schmitt spoke into the telephone.

"Altitude?"

"Fifteen hundred meters. How is the visibility?"

"Good."

There were no clouds, no fog. Clouds made for a fairyland far above the tragic earth, but they interfered with efficient observation. Schmitt knew this region of the Heights of the Meuse by heart. Under his eyes it had turned into a landscape like the moon. Schmitt was aware of the meaning of even the most imperceptible change. With the naked eye he could guess, almost infallibly, at what his field glasses were about to confirm.

It was four o'clock in the afternoon of June 22nd, and the Germans were bombarding. Beyond the front line, almost directly below the balloon, a constantly surging wave of smoke rolled over the ground, punctuated by geysers of dirt thrown up from the pockmarked lunar terrain. Through his glasses Schmitt could even make out shattered pieces of wood, splintered stakes of barbed-wire fences, and fragments of ripped sandbags flying into the air. These objects spoke well for the German aim; it meant that the shells were hitting the trenches, dugouts, shelters, and shellholes where the harassed French soldiers were trying to save their miserable lives. The first time that, through his glasses, Schmitt had seen human arms and legs tossed up with the other débris, he had vomited over the side of his basket. But by now he was hardened.

Yes, the balloon was an unmatched place for observation. Besides the white smoke and the dark upheavals of earth there were thin ribbons of blue tulle, which floated at the bottom of ravines and valleys. These were the waves of poison gas, fired from shells marked with a green cross. Schmitt studied the square-sectioned map, tacked to a piece of board in front of him.

"Good," he said aloud. "Corner of wood on the left, concealing a battery of 75's. At least, according to the latest photographs. Let's see."

Schmitt had got into the habit of talking to himself as he floated in the air, and he knew that many of his comrades talked in the same way, even when they were on the ground, and everyone laughed at them for it. "Corner of a wood" was rather a grandiose description of the collection of charred stumps he actually saw; the wood hardly existed except on the map. Just then his telephone buzzed, and the battery commander questioned him about the velocity of the wind. Schmitt had to report that it was twenty miles an hour, although he knew that the artillerymen would not be pleased with this kind of wind that deflected their shells.

In order to see better through his glasses, Schmitt knelt down in the basket. This seemed at times to be plunging forward toward the ground; at others it shot straight up like a lift in motion. To keep the objective within his rim of vision was difficult. For the moment, at least, the French 75's were not shooting. Schmitt could identify the camouflage, but of course the guns might by now have been shifted. He looked again at the square-sectioned map, marked on the tracing the apparent position of the 75's, then telephoned his own artillery to give the coordinates. As long as the 75's were not heard from they would not be a target, for the massive German bombardment of the French lines was rarely wasteful. The balloon continued to bump from one side to the other, and the balancing ailerons never stopped flapping. But Schmitt was accustomed to both the movement and the noise. The men of the Balloon Service enjoyed none of the prestige of fighting aviators. Perhaps it was the unwieldy awkwardness of their craft that made them the objects of good-humored needling. Few people understood the discomforts of a balloon basket, but Schmitt reassured himself that they were nothing compared to those of the trenches. He had been scrutinizing his objective for some time when suddenly he saw two pale sparks and two trails of pale blue smoke. There could be no mistake about their source.

"Battery 204–417 in action," he spoke into the telephone.

"Wind?" queried the ground.

"Same as before."

Now he had to relocate the objective and wait to see the fall of the first German shell as it tested the range. Usually there was an interval of twenty seconds. But after ten seconds had elapsed Schmitt heard the roar of a motor overhead.

"Have your fun!" he said to himself. "I know your tricks. Only, I don't see what you find so amusing."

This was not the first time that a pilot, returning from a mission, had in good clean fun buzzed an observation balloon. For a second the plane's wing appeared in Schmitt's field glasses, but he did not lower them from his eyes until the plane buzzed him again. Then he looked up, and his heart started pounding.

"It had to happen someday."

For a long time the German balloonists had had a feeling of complete safety. Their air patrols controlled the skies. But lately French planes had appeared in increasing numbers. Nine times out of ten a balloon observer was too intent upon his scrutiny of the battlefield to notice the presence of an enemy. And if he did notice, what could he do? The machine gun in his basket was a farce; everyone knew it. The balloon observer was an animal with far-seeing eyes but no defenses.

Words came through Schmitt's telephone, but he could not hear them because of the noise made once more by the swooping enemy plane. He did not need to consult his book of diagrams; the shape of the French Nieuport fighter plane was perfectly familiar to him. He saw the pilot's head and shoulders, and for a second he felt almost as if, through the Frenchman's rubber-rimmed goggles, he had met his eyes. In any case he saw that the pilot was waving his arm in a gesture which meant "Hurry up and jump!" The Nieuport circled the balloon, its wings almost vertical, disregarding the white smoke of the battery firing impotently from the ground. They had no hope of making a hit. As the plane disappeared above, the pilot fired a departing machine-gun volley, a warning, no doubt, since nothing happened.

"I have no choice," Schmitt said to himself; "but I can't say I like it."

The gaping space below was not at all attractive, but he had to jump. He disengaged the telephone from his helmet and threw one leg over the edge of the basket.

His parachute had just spread out when he heard an explosion above him. The great red and yellow rag, which was all that was left of the balloon, rose, as if drawn by suction, into the air before it fell. Schmitt was actually relieved by its destruction. No one could accuse him of having jumped to safety while the balloon was still whole.

The ground was in no hurry to draw near. Schmitt felt almost as if he were traveling horizontally. Then he remembered his own estimate of the direction and velocity of the wind. The wind was driving him toward the French lines, where the German shells were raining down in profusion.

*   *   *

The twenty-five vehicles of the American ambulance corps were lined up in front of the Saint-Paul barracks at Verdun. Every morning the drivers drew lots to see who would be the first to go out on a mission. The group had two commanders: an American called Lovering Hill and a French supervisory doctor. These two were stationed alternately at Verdun and at Bras three miles away, which served as a pickup station for the wounded.

The ambulances left Verdun at ten-minute intervals during the night, so that no more than one of them would be loaded at a time in Bras, which was under fire by the Germans. The Americans drove at top speed, blowing whistles to announce their passage, as if they were firemen. The lights of the arriving and departing ambulances were as bright as magnesium flares. The road followed the course of the valley, at some distance from the lateral canal. After Belleville, half a mile beyond Verdun, there was an ugly smell that came from unburied dead horses. Every now and then a wagon filled with supplies or ammunition ran over a dead horse's neck or leg, and the live horses whinnied.

At frequent intervals the road was shelled. The quarter-mile stretch before Bras was in such condition that ambulances and trucks merely bumped from one hole to another. The village itself was in ruins and as silent as if it had been totally abandoned. The ambulance left the main street, where enemy shells frequently fell, and came to a halt in an alley where, in the darkness, a group of wounded was waiting. Most of them came from the field hospital of Quatre-Cheminées, two miles as the crow flies in the direction of

Fleury. The driver opened the rear door of the ambulance, and the doctor gave right of way to the most serious cases. The others crowded around in the hope of being taken, and the doctor harangued them, always in approximately the same words:

"Those of you that can walk must go to Verdun on foot. You have only to follow the towpath along the canal, which is not a target like the road. Get started as soon as you can, while there is darkness to protect you. The ambulance is for those that cannot possibly walk. If we don't take them to-night, they'll have to wait twenty-four hours longer."

The walking wounded protested, insisting that they too were entitled to transportation. They refused to travel on foot, insisting that they would not until someone picked them up in a car. They had their "rights," they repeated, and they were not accepting the excuses handed out to them. The doctor often feared an outbreak of violence, and the ambulance was followed by a volley of curses as it finally pulled away.

*   *   *

Feldwebel Otto Schmitt could feel the flies crawling over his cheeks, and opened his eyes. There was no sun in the pale white sky; perhaps it had not yet had time to rise. Schmitt wanted to pull the parachute over his face, but he could not find it. He fingered his chest and found that the straps were intact, but there was nothing attached to them. Apparently the parachute had been cut away. "They've stripped me as if I were a corpse," he said to himself. Everyone knew that to French and Germans alike, parachute silk was very much in demand. A man's shirt or woman's blouse made of parachute silk was a highly prized memento of the war. What bothered Schmitt was the fact that he did not know who had plundered him or when. "I must have fainted," he concluded; "perhaps more than once."

The first time was when he struck the ground, moving at a speed of about twenty-five miles an hour. He had had just time enough to think: I've broken my right leg and knee. Toward evening a pain in his right wrist brought him back to consciousness. With his left hand he ascertained that his watch was smashed and that the strap was digging into his wrist. After loosening the strap he concentrated upon changing his position, for he knew now that he had fallen on a hill and that his head was lower than his feet. With every movement he was aware of the fact that his right leg and knee were broken. "But apparently they aren't bleeding, or else I'd feel a trickle and I'd be much weaker, or even dead." The roar of the bombardment filled the air. Though at times the ground around him trembled, no shells fell nearby. "There's no smell of gas, either. I must be right in the middle of no-man's-land, and that means there's a chance of my coming out of this alive."

An indefinable length of time went by. "Have I been asleep? I feel as if I'd been dreaming an interminable and tiring dream." Now, in the pale daylight, Otto Schmitt knew that his parachute had been taken from him. Who could have been plundering by night in no-man's-land? He was very thirsty, but not to the point that he might have imagined, doubtless because he had no open wound. With his left hand he unbuttoned his tunic; then he pulled his left arm out of the sleeve and spread the sleeve across his face to protect him from the flies.

The earth was trembling less furiously as the bombardment moved forward. "That means the infantry's about to attack. God help me, I hope I'm not within the French lines. No . . . if I were I'd have had a whiff of gas." At intervals he repeated this last phrase: "I'd have had a whiff of gas," for the sake of reassurance. Minutes, quarters of an hour, hours went by. It was strange to be unable to measure the exact time. Schmitt had heard battle-tired veterans speak of this strangeness. But hearing and experiencing are two quite different propositions.

Flies kept trying to crawl under the sleeve he had draped

over his face. Beside his cheek he could see an expanse of dried mud, with cracks that ran in every direction. Fortunately there were no dead bodies near him.

The German infantry charged over the summit of the slope where Schmitt was lying; he saw first their heads and shoulders, then their legs and feet descending upon him. Tears of relief welled up in his eyes. He was saved! Within a few minutes . . . an hour . . . two or three hours . . . surely before night, stretcher-bearers would pick him up. The stretcher-bearers were extraordinary fellows, perhaps the real heroes of the war.

A second wave of infantry followed the first. Before he actually saw them Schmitt heard their footsteps and voices, a little farther away than those who had already passed him by. They did not run; they moved at a fast walk, occasionally breaking into a trot, with their gas masks swinging at their waists and, if they were machine gunners, their weapons on their shoulders. After a certain number of groups had gone by there was a pause. "When the next group arrives I'll ask them to send me a stretcher-bearer," Schmitt said to himself. Just then some shells began to fall. They were not heavy German 210's, tearing up the ground. Apparently the French 75's had come into play.

At intervals, other German units came over the hill; Schmitt waved his left hand and cried out, "Stretcher-bearers!" One soldier did shoot him a glance before continuing on his way. Then others came along, and again Schmitt waved his hand. Several of them turned their heads, but none of them halted. Below their helmets their eyes darted from one side to the other, watching for exploding shells or for holes in which to take refuge if the French bombardment became any heavier. A man lying on the ground and calling for a stretcher-bearer could not hope to engage their full attention.

The advancing soldiers talked among themselves, and occasionally Schmitt caught an expletive, or an officer's shouted order. The voices were tantalizingly close, but their owners walked or trotted on as if Otto Schmitt did not exist. An icy hand seemed to pluck at his heart, and shells continued to fall around him.

Sometimes wounded men lay on the ground for days before anyone was able to look after them. Either the enemy bombardment was too heavy or a counterattack was under way; the first-aid posts were overcrowded, the stretcher-bearers had more work than they could handle, or perhaps they were dead. All these negative possibilities swept through Schmitt's mind, a hundred fragments of stories that in the days when he was unmarked he had heard and dismissed from his mind:

A wounded man could lie dying in a shellhole only twenty feet away from another shellhole where unwounded soldiers had taken shelter. But because the slightest movement made a target for enemy machine-gun fire, none of them would stir to help him. The wounded man could overhear their conversation and try to interrupt it; he could beg them for a cup of water or even for a shot in the head to put him out of his misery. For hours on end he might call upon them by the names he had heard them use among themselves. But all they did was to plug their ears and hope that he would give up and die.

From one shellhole to another the wounded communicated among themselves as well. Night and day they alternated their moans and groans with nightmarish conversations. Blinded men, for instance, repeated over and over that they were blind. Some of the wounded went mad and staggered or dragged themselves over the ground stark naked. "Water! Water!" was the most frequent cry. Soldiers with full flasks passed by, heedless of the cry "Water!" or the abusive "Bastards!" that greeted their indifference. And yet their indifference was only human. The unscathed soldiers knew that the chances were one to three that they too would find themselves wounded and thirsty. Even if they suffered no wounds, two or three days might go by before they had a chance to refill their canteens with water. On the battlefield thirst was the sister of death.

I'm not too badly hurt, Otto Schmitt reflected, and yet I'm in danger of suffering the pains of hell and dying the same dog's death I've heard tell about so often. Any man who was flat on the ground and unable to move had already lost 80 percent of his chances of survival. Under certain circumstances he was as abandoned as a shipwrecked sailor on a raft in the middle of the ocean.

Shells fell at varying distances, and growing thirst and rising fever caused Schmitt's thoughts to wander. The sun must have been hiding behind a cloud, for the pale, glimmering sky did not change color. Schmitt heard the sound of running feet, but he saw no one pass by. His field of vision was limited, and every movement was painful. A little later there was a sound of machine-gun fire and shouts as of men quarreling. The quarrel had pauses, but the machine guns went on firing, interrupted only by the louder sound of a trench mortar. Occasionally Schmitt heard a shouted order or another wounded soldier's cry. A balloon, not unlike his own, passed overhead, and he was tempted to cry: "Stay up in the air, my friend; whatever you do, don't drop to the ground!" For the ground had something monstrous and cursed about it.

A man stricken by fever mingles bits of nightmare with the reality around him. Sometimes Schmitt thought that the noises he heard came from a village fair or from some Homeric drinking party among his comrades. Later there was silence: no more machine guns, no more voices. Then a sudden crackle. Firecrackers? No, hand grenades. Then silence again, until in the midst of it he heard the footsteps and the hard breathing of men climbing the slope, directly behind him. He called out and made a superhuman effort to turn his head, but it was too late. He could see only their helmets disappearing over the top of the hill.

Soon after this, another group went up the hill at a run. From their puttees, blue uniforms, and the shape of their helmets Schmitt knew that they were French; more and more French soldiers followed. He fell into a mood of despair and self-pity, and began to cry. At this point he felt that he would never get out of it alive. The French were not going to waste their time picking up German wounded; and besides, the ground where he lay might be disputed for days, passing from one hand to another, while Death carried away the unfortunates who had fallen in its area.

But, in his own case at least, Schmitt's forebodings were not fulfilled. The next day, on June 24th, some French stretcher-bearers picked him up and took him to the field hospital at Quatre-Cheminées, whence he was taken twenty-four hours later to the village of Bras and then, in one of the American ambulances, to Verdun.

* * *

Horses and wagons brought the stretcher-bearers from Bras to the ravine of Pied du Gravier; after that they had to walk half a mile, within range of enemy fire, to Quatre-Cheminées, a subterranean shelter in the side of the hill between the ravine of Les Vignes and Froideterre, dating from before the war, which belonged to the system of outlying defenses of Verdun. Four chimneys emerging from the ground gave the place its name.

Inside Quatre-Cheminées there were two brigade headquarters and two regimental command posts, but the atmosphere was not one of spit and polish. In addition there was the field hospital. Every newcomer to it was the bearer of some fragment of bad news, whether he was wounded, badly wounded, or simply a refugee. After June 15th the new arrivals included German deserters, who said they had had enough of war and did not want to take part in the next attack, which they described as of mammoth proportions, with a barrage of gas shells preceding the advance of several fresh Bavarian divisions. The Bavarians, they said, were complete savages. The wounded and the refugees listened somberly to these dire predictions, made to the accompaniment of falling shells.

The wounded who had been brought in from the first-aid posts complained about the lack of care and comfort and the strict food rationing. Yet some of them refused to leave the shelter and brave the gunfire outside when a new crew of stretcher-bearers came to take them away. They were simply at the end of their rope, and got their only satisfaction from telling over and over the same terrible stories of the things they had seen and heard and endured.

"Boys, I saw Lieutenants Herduin and Milan of the 347th go before a firing squad. Have you heard that one?"

The storyteller had not always seen the drama with his own eyes, but it had actually taken place and was a favorite story among soldiers when there was no officer around. The regiment to which these two officers belonged, which had occupied the front line before Fleury, had been reduced from 3,000 men to 350, with only six officers to lead them. For forty-eight hours Herduin and Milan had held out, at the head of their seventeenth company. When they found themselves with only 35 survivors out of 200 men, their ammunition exhausted, and in danger of encirclement, they had ordered a withdrawal. Had they not done so, what remained of the company would, like so many others, have been taken prisoner. Unfortunately for them, another order, all-embracing and imperative, had been sent out by General Nivelle, in the moment of dismay that followed the fall of Fort Vaux, an order that read; "Do not surrender. Die on the spot rather than yield an inch." It was now an old story. No one could run after the prisoners of Vaux and lead them back to execution. But it was easy to make an example of the officers who had ordered the withdrawal.

"The firing squad was made up of men from their own company. Can you imagine that? They had to be threatened with death themselves to do it. Herduin and Milan had guts, and everyone knew it. One of them was married and had written a letter to his wife, which no one could read without crying."

"These swine on the staff!" said those listening to the story. Others told of the shock suffered by a staff officer when he went down into a second-line shelter on the left bank, near Chattancourt. Twenty men lay there, eyes staring out of their stony faces; in their midst, hanging from a beam, a corpse that no one had even thought of taking down. They had just been ordered back to the front line without a promised furlough. It was more than they could endure.

Some men spoke with curses and hate of those who were safe and sound in the citadel of Verdun. The city was under bombardment, but in the citadel, a hundred feet below-ground, there was underground paradise, with cooperatives and officers' bars. Old territorials were not the only ones who were sitting it out. One day a rifleman saw a young, pink-cheeked sergeant of the Quartermaster Corps coming out of the citadel, and trailed him down the street, shouting insults at his back, because the other did not dare to turn around. Finally the sharpshooter came close to him and struck him across the face.

"You haven't the nerve to fight it out with me like a man, have you? You're looking for the military police—admit it!"

Pale-faced, the sergeant accepted the challenge. Stripped to their waists the two men dueled with knives at the foot of the ramparts, while two hundred soldiers gathered round. Some of them had put out a barrel of wine and were drinking copiously, although not far away the shells were falling.

The sergeant of the Quartermaster Corps had one lung punctured before the police reached the scene.

The military-police would not let anyone enter the city of Verdun without special orders. To the soldiers the police were sheep dogs, always pushing them back into the battle, to the slaughter. Obviously their job did not build up a great deal of goodwill for them. A young rifleman, with his arm in a sling, told how his regiment, on its way to the front, met four battle police on the road called Pied du Gravier. The soldiers spat on the ground without speaking, because there were severe penalties for insulting a gendarme. Suddenly a cheery voice arose from their ranks:

"Greetings, military police!"

Everyone was amazed, especially the police, who wondered why they were the recipients of such courtesy and whether they ought to reply. But they did not have to wonder long, for soon the cheery voice rang out again:

"Heavy losses among you?"

This innocent question was an enormous success. But the fighting man's feelings toward the police were not always expressed in so light a vein. There was a rumor—a legend perhaps—that in a butcher's shop on the Rue Mazel of Verdun police meat had been put on sale, the flesh of assassinated policemen. Exactly how and when it was not easy to ascertain, because the details of the story did not quite fit together. But the story as a whole was accorded respect, and it was wiser not to doubt it. After it was told there came an inevitable moment of silence, or an exclamation like *Merde!* which might or might not have indicated reprobation.

In the mouths of certain narrators the loss of lives took on epic proportions and became even more appalling than the frightful reality. Sometimes the most extraordinary details were added. On the night between June 12th and 13th the lieutenant of a machine-gun unit on his way to the command post of his battalion commander took a communi-

cation trench leading along the north slope of the Ravin de
la Dame, near the farm of Thiaumont. What did he see
there? Soldiers, with fixed bayonets, leaning against the
parapet of the trench, except for one man, who was sitting
on the ground. The lieutenant had called out to the seated
man, but received no reply. He was dead. The standing
soldiers did not reply, either; they were dead, too. There
were more than fifty men in all, stone dead, their rifles
beside them. What destroying angel had passed over them?

This was the origin of the story of the "Trench of
Bayonets," in which legend and reality were to mingle, in
the classical tradition. In 1919 Colonel Collet, former commander of the 137th Infantry, a regiment that had suffered
particularly heavy losses, ordered a search made of that part
of the battlefield where his men had fought. This led to the
discovery of a line of rifles protruding from the grass. Their
owners had been buried alive by the explosion of a shell
before going over the top or while bracing themselves to
resist an attack. At once the "dead men's trench," was remembered, described by the lieutenant in 1916, at almost
the same location. But the "buried alive" story, perhaps because it was so macabre, persisted.

Eventually a comparison of various fragments of testimony made it possible to reconstruct what had really happened. On June 2nd, the third company of the 137th, after
a heavy pounding from the German artillery, was attacked
from both sides, and hung on only as an island of resistance
until it had no more ammunition. The captured survivors
left their rifles sticking in the air, and they were partially
covered when the Germans threw dirt over the dead bodies
in the trench. The inaccuracies and exaggerations of the
story goes to prove simply that men who have lived for weeks
under nightmare conditions can no longer discriminate between what they saw with their own eyes and the figments of
their imagination.

The name of "Fantomas," taken from a famous series of mystery stories by Souvestre and Allain, was frequently mentioned in the feverish conversations that went on around Quatre-Cheminées. "Fantomas" was the name given by the French to a German aviator who used to swoop down and machine-gun the front-line trenches. The plane was always the same, so rumor had it, and so was the pilot, recognizable by his "black leather helmet." In reality several German planes raked the front line with machine-gun fire. The creators of the "Fantomas" myth finally had to admit that he was more and more seldom in evidence, and their listeners saw for themselves that French planes were flying in ever greater numbers overhead.

Flyers, unlike military policemen, were not looked upon as cowards. They could be seen being shot down in combat too often for that (no infantryman would have wished to be in their place), and there was a romantic aura about them besides. They were commonly imagined to spend their time between missions drinking and whoring, but this actually gave their mud-stained comrades on the ground a vicarious satisfaction.

Shells fell all around the subterranean shelter of Quatre-Cheminées and even directly on it, causing the thick, protective earth roof to change shape and the interior to tremble. Every night a new lot of wounded was brought in. Simple people may not have much storytelling ability, but when they have been involved in the dramatic events of war they seem to find their tongues and even, strangely enough, to enjoy describing in detail their vicissitudes. This was the case with many of those brought in from the first-aid posts. The official designation of "first-aid post" gives a misleadingly reassuring picture. Often enough it was no more than two medical corpsmen crouching in a shellhole or behind a pile of sandbags with a stretcher beside them. At best, it was a low-ceilinged shelter, at the bottom of two or three steps.

Postwar visitors to the battlefields were amazed at the close quarters in which first-aid was administered.

Stretchers were lined up side by side or sometimes one above the other along the walls. In the center there was just room enough for the doctor and his assistant and a table. The two men's jackets were literally saturated with blood, and the flesh with which they had to deal was frequently dirtier than that of a slaughterhouse. Often there was no time to throw out the bloody bandages, and they formed a stack on the floor which the doctor had to step over to get around the table.

The horrors of the first-aid post have been frequently described: the men holding their intestines in both hands, the broken bones tearing the flesh, the arteries spurting blood as a clot gave way, bared brains ("Why didn't the fellow die long ago?"), the maimed hands ("What were you in civilian life?" "A sculptor."), the empty eyesockets, the pierced chests, the skin hanging down in tatters from the burned face, the missing lower jaws. . . . All these things have been seen in later wars as well, but we must remember that in 1916 there were no adequate antiseptics and no tranquillizers.

In the First World War morphine (which was often in short supply) was given only to the seriously wounded on the operating table. Those who had not progressed thus far were left to moan in their agony, as the case might be. For lack of D.D.T. the doctor constantly had to brush away flies gorged on decomposed débris; the only light was provided by acetylene lamps, flashlights, or candles, and sometimes it was necessary to work in the dark. Doctors have told of groping to wind or unwind a bandage. Their hands were soiled with blood, mud, and pus. The "nice little wound," which every soldier dreamed of as just serious enough to ensure his being sent home, was often the prelude to death from infection.

The doctors at Quatre-Cheminées, to whom their patients told these grim stories, in the hope of getting more to eat or drink, of being evacuated to the rear, or at least of remaining where they were in relative comfort and safety, had already a clear picture of conditions in the field. They had served themselves at similar first-aid posts, or under circumstances even more difficult, such as those which prevailed at the Château d'Esnes on the left bank of the Meuse.

This was no molehill. The cellar of the castle (a mile from the front and destroyed aboveground by bombardment) had been reinforced by army engineers and was provided with acetylene lamps. Two doctors operated continuously, twenty-four hours a day, attended by a chaplain. To this first-aid station came most of the wounded from the decimated regiments that between March and August 1916 defended Hill 304 and Mort-Homme.

The place was desperately overcrowded. New arrivals were left on their stretchers outside, in the former "great court" of the château. Gradually they were transfered to the cellar, where the doctors made a pitiless selection. There was no use wasting time and medicines on the hopeless cases. The rejected stretchers were, for this reason, taken back up to the courtyard and put down a short distance away from the new arrivals. Night and day the courtyard was crowded with these two groups—the condemned and the newcomers—both of them groaning with pain when they were not protesting.

Orderlies, holding sticks in their hands, stood by, ready to fight off the rats that, not content with the corpses stacked in the barn, made bold to attack the dying men in the courtyard. As soon as a man died his body was taken over to the barn, where in one corner there was a great stack of wooden crosses. Until there was a lull in the battle there was no chance of burying the dead. When the nearby village was bombed by the Germans, some of the shells fell in the court-

yard of the château. At such times the wounded men instinctively tried to get up from their stretchers and make
their way to the safety of the cellar, and the orderlies had
to restrain them. Formal historians are apt to pass over
details of this kind.

*   *   *

"No, gas was not a feature of Verdun, and many men who
served there at different times will tell you that they never
had a whiff of it. But I do remember, quite clearly, the night
between June 22nd and 23rd, at Quatre-Cheminées, when
gas was one of the worst things with which we had to cope.

"Sentries gave the alarm before dusk, at around eight
o'clock (the longest nights of the year are in June). Immediately we lighted fires in front of every opening; in those
days we were sure that the outward draft created by the
fires would be effective in driving the gas away. Of course,
we had put on our masks, although we were not at all used
to them and found ourselves decidedly ridiculous in these
grotesque protuberances with their goggle eyes. A few of us
tried to be funny and started wagging our heads and doing
a sort of bear dance. You know how unpleasant it is to
breathe with a mask on, and a lot of men pushed it up over
their foreheads or took it off altogether. They had just begun
to cough when four smothered, screaming soldiers came to
take refuge in the cellar.

"They weren't exactly screaming. They made a noise like
the crowing of an old rooster or a child with whooping
cough, only louder, and without being able to stop. Most of
them had been caught by surprise at the bottom of a ravine.
We laid them out on stretchers, but there was nothing much
we could do for them. A sort of pink foam was oozing out of
their mouths. You can't imagine how terrible it looked,
especially to those who had just begun to cough and were
unable to put on their masks.

"The rest of us kept the fires going through the night.

From time to time we looked over at the four men caught by surprise, who were now in the last stages. Each of them made the same gesture of clutching his chest.

"At dawn the gas alarm was over. We opened up everything and went outside for a breath of fresh air. But before we'd been out very long the 210's began to come down on us. Bits of the roof fell, and we had a feeling that everything might crumble. I remember looking out of a window and seeing a pigeon released, because the telephone lines were cut. The blast of the German shells through the air was so violent the pigeon couldn't fly in a straight line.

"When the bombardment was over we looked at one another, knowing what the end of it meant. Finally someone put it into words: 'They're at Thiaumont!' A minute later some of our men came plunging down the steps, crying, 'They're here!'"

*   *   *

"They're here!" a cry that has come down through the ages, always followed by an interval of time longer than is expected. At Quatre-Cheminées men huddled together, some of them wounded, others dead, who could not have reacted even if they had wanted to. Others went up on the platform and shot at the Germans, at the little groups of field-gray-uniformed men who were moving up toward Fleury. The picture might have come out of *War and Peace,* had it not been for the airplanes with black crosses on their undersides passing overhead and the red and yellow flames from the mouths of the flamethrowers. The waves of German assault troops were coming closer. On the platform above Quatre-Cheminées a staff captain watched them through his field glasses. Suddenly he dropped his glasses, staggered, flailed the air with his arms, and fell flat on his face.

"For the love of God, get inside!"

The feathery brown smoke of the machine-gun bullets traveled up the sides of the shelter, probing for the openings.

Anyone that showed himself was as good as dead; on the platform there were only corpses.

Behind the rattle of the machine guns was the deafening roar of the heavy and medium artillery. Inside the shelter the gas victims were still dying of convulsions. Some of the soldiers grumbled, first to themselves and then aloud, that they had been bloody fools not to clear out the day before, instead of waiting to die like so many rats. Shit: there was no other word for it; their resentment could find an outlet in no other word.

Now the rattle of the machine guns was accompanied by orders shouted in German. At one of the underground regimental command posts, where death or capture was expected momentarily, officers were burning the codes and smashing the already dead telephones. The air was almost unbearably close.

Suddenly there was an explosion, the blast of a grenade thrown through an opening. This time the Germans were really there, and they seemed in no mood for quarter. There was a second explosion, followed by loud cries. Men lay writhing on the floor or else flat, with their heads buried in their arms, while others stood against the walls, their eyes staring. "To clean out a shelter with hand grenades" is a good military phrase. But it is a different matter to be caught inside.

Seconds ticked by. More grenades exploded, but outside. A machine gun rattled at the door; sandbags were ripped open; the cloth caught fire, and a bitter, black smoke poured in. No one moved. Minutes passed. No more grenades, no more maching-gunning. In the distance there was still the sound of the 75's and 210's, but that was all. The men on the floor and along the walls began to stir.

*　　*　　*

This was the battle of June 23rd, the last great German assault on the Verdun front. Feldwebel Otto Schmitt, the bird who fell out of the sky, saw no more than a dozen pairs of boots and then of puttees cross his limited field of vision. The besieged soldiers of Quatre-Cheminées saw only a few gray waves of attackers moving up toward Fleury. But, all in all, 70,000 German soldiers were thrown into the assault on the front of Thiaumont-Fleury-Vaux.

It is useless to study a map of the battlefield of Verdun in order to locate individual actions. But by observing the fluctuations of the front day by day, up to the beginning of July, we may understand the general progress of the battle. It is simple enough to follow: first the Germans made an assault, and then it was halted; then they made another assault, and it was halted in its turn. To understand how the German assaults were halted is equally simple. It is reflected in the phrases that recur again and again in the pages of this book: last-ditch resistance, desperate local counterattacks, and the annihilation of the participating units. The 121st Chasseurs on the slopes of Froideterre, the 114th Battalion of Chasseurs in the Vignes ravine, the 39th Infantry at Fleury and the 407th at Souville are only a few examples. Only once since the battle had begun was there a variation in the pattern: under the most favorable circumstances, Pétain launched a simultaneous flank and rear artillery barrage from the left bank upon the Germans advancing on the right. Otherwise, the refrain was the same: "Die rather than yield a single inch of ground!" Perhaps this was the only thing to do, since the counterattack on Douaumont had so dismally failed.

Why not let the Germans take Verdun, in the expectation of dislodging them as soon as the Allied armies were the stronger? Strategically, this was a viable idea, and all the generals knew it. Time was working in the Allies' favor, even on a short-range basis, for within exactly a week the opening of the Somme offensive would draw off the German concentrations. Yet the Germans could not be allowed to

take and hold Verdun, even for a single month, a single
week. For France and the whole world the name had become a symbol. The capture of Verdun would not mean the
loss of the war from a strategic point of view, but it might
bring on, first, a serious loss of morale, then a demand for a
change of government, perhaps even revolution. This was
what happened a little later in Russia, where there was no
military defeat. And at the same time it might cause the
United States to reverse its stand, to decide to bargain with
Germany. The factor of "Verdun" could not be isolated
and stripped of its wider significance.

On the evening of June 23rd Pétain telephoned to Castelnau:

"Our present lines run from Fort Saint-Michel to Fort
Souville. If that were to be lost, Verdun would be at the
bottom of a basin whose rim would be held by the enemy,
leaving it indefensible. I must have reinforcements. The
troops of the Second Army are too tired to launch the
counterattacks that will certainly be called for in the next
few days. I ask, also, that the date of the Somme offensive
be advanced."

Castelnau took notes, and called up half an hour later to
say:

"Tomorrow you are to have four fresh divisions."

*   *   *

Fresh divisions. Fresh men. Fresh flesh. Now the invisible
Monster was devouring French flesh and German flesh in
equal measure. The total loss of human life at Verdun has
never been calculated in figures more precise than hundreds
of thousands. In 1919 there was talk of 400,000 men killed
on either side; later on, of between 400,000 and 500,000,
and the same number of wounded, most of them crippled
for life. I have before me a photograph of July 1916, which
shows a German burial squad in front of an overflowing
mass grave. The members of the squad have a totally dif-

ferent air. At the same period some French reserves on their way to the front passed a group of territorials in helmets and overalls, digging ditches thirty feet back from the road.

"We're getting ready for you!" one of the territorials called out.

To which one of the marching column indulgently replied, "Don't hurry, old man!"

There was a general hardening of feeling, not confined to the general staffs. Yet consider the injustice of History. At just this time a voice spoke out, not once but several times, to cut the losses, since the result did not balance any worthwhile military advantage. The voice was that of the nominal commander of the German Fifth Army, the Crown Prince, who after the war was branded by German journalists as the "smiling assassin of Verdun." (Equally intemperate language, as we shall see, was used on the French side.) The Crown Prince's protest was drowned out by the unanimous clamor of the real German military leaders. The imminent French offensive on the Somme (of which the German command was so well informed that French soldiers moving into the line found signboards on the battlefield announcing the exact time and place of their next attack) did not seem to the German generals a reason for cutting losses at Verdun. On the contrary, they reasoned that to break through the French lines, and to capture Verdun as they had originally intended, would offset any defeat they might suffer on the Somme. Thus they continued to attack, regardless of the cost.

On the French side there was Mangin, who had the four fresh divisions to use as he wished. His prestige had not suffered from his failure to recapture Douaumont or the quarrel he had had over the telephone with Lebrun, and he was now in command of the Thiaumont-Fleury sector. In his superbly tailored uniform and his highly polished leather boots, he strode up and down on the thick rug on his office floor. Deep furrows marked his face even when it was at rest, but in his eyes there was a constant sparkle of animation. Two officers stood by, waiting for his orders. Orders to counterattack, naturally.

Counterattack is a commonly used expression that, in military parlance, may have a variety of meanings. You are in command of a section; you see the enemy coming and, instead of waiting, you throw your men forward: this is a counterattack. You have been surprised by a sudden assault; you have hastily evacuated, not without losses, your trenches and shellholes, and fallen back into other holes, twenty yards away; a few minutes later you regroup your men and dash forward to recapture your original positions: this is a counterattack. But there are other meanings of the word. The enemy has won a real advantage and you have made a considerable retreat. Several days later, after a softening up on the part of your artillery, you throw fresh or rested or reinforced troops into an attempt to regain the lost ground: this, according to the number of men involved and the interval between your retreat and your reaction, may be termed either a "counterattack" or a "counteroffensive."

Another pattern, however, was more frequently followed during the First World War. After a forced withdrawal, you throw your troops, reinforced or not, with or without artillery support (more often without it), back into a counterattack the next day or the day after, when the enemy has had time to dig the holes which we have seen to be so all-important and to place his machine guns effectively. Nine times out of ten this kind of counterattack turns out to be a useless slaughter.

On June 24th and 25th Mangin organized (it would be more exact to say that he simply ordered) five such costly operations. They should be described in detail in order to justify the description.

June 24th. Counterattack on both sides of the road between Froideterre and Thiaumont, by two battalions of the 63rd and one of the 297th Infantry, supported on the north by three companies of the 106th Light Infantry. Result: heavy losses, and no gain of ground.

On the same day, counterattack by the 19th Chasseurs in the Fontaines ravine and the thinned portion of the woods of Vaux-Chapitre. Result: heavy losses, and no gain of ground.

On the same day, counterattack by the 171st Infantry at La Voux-Régnier. Heavy losses, and no gain of ground.

On the same day, counterattack (I have not been able to ascertain by what units) on the village of Fleury. Result: recapture of the ruins of three houses.

June 25th. Counterattack at dawn by the 129th and 340th Infantry divisions on the whole Thiaumont-Fleury front (a little less than a mile long). Result: the fortified entrenchment Z, near Fort Thiaumont, was captured at four o'clock in the morning, when the impetus of the advance was strongest, and "some prisoners" were taken. Elsewhere on the line no progress. At eight o'clock an order from Mangin: "Advance at all costs, having no regard for individual fortified works." Result: heavy losses, and no gain of ground.

"The butcher of Verdun." The name was added to the four stars of the new corps commander, Charles Mangin. To speak of it is to tread on dangerous ground. To touch upon it at all is to incur a double danger, to shock the readers of our history books and to revive cruel memories on the part of the veterans of the battle.

During the whole period of late June and early July, Mangin ordered (let me say once more that the verb "organize" cannot be properly applied to such improvisations, which consisted simply of putting the finger on whatever units were unlucky enough to be close by) these murderous counterattacks, in which the gain of ground was infinitely small in proportion to their cost in human lives. The question is: What else could he do?

At this particular moment of the war, Verdun had to be defended, at whatever cost. "At whatever cost" is a trite phrase, but let us consider its terrifying implications. On June 23rd the German battering ram made a new and furious assault in the direction of Verdun, which was halted on the evening of the same day by what even official accounts admit was "the total sacrifice of several units." Was it not possible, we may ask, at this point, to dig in and bring up fresh troops to hold this last line of defense instead of launching the series of murderous counterattacks described above?

It was possible, yes, but there were two things against it. First, there was too little space between this last line of defense and Verdun itself. The area of movement was too narrow and it seemed necessary to enlarge it; second, the counterattacks, however costly, inflicted almost equal losses on the Germans and weakened their thrust toward their final objective. This monstrous "war of attrition," of which historians speak so lightly that we do not pause to consider its real meaning, found at Verdun a sort of terrible justification. The name of "butcher" can appropriately be pinned on almost all the military commanders of the time. Many of them ordered attacks and offensives, or counterattacks and counteroffensives, not in order to obtain a tactical or strategic advantage, but simply, at the cost of calculated losses, to whittle down their enemy's manpower. Few battles of the First World War were anything but butcheries. At the beginning of this book it has been shown that the commanders were not themselves responsible for this decline in military science.

* * *

July 1st. This was the day of the opening of the Anglo-French offensive on the Somme. For a whole week, along a twenty-mile front, from Foucaucourt to the Ancre River, there had been a deafening cannonade. The Allied artillery gave the German positions the same pounding as the Germans had inflicted upon the positions before Verdun nearly five months earlier. At half-past ten on the morning of July 1st, the Allied artillery lengthened its range, while French and British troops made their way over the pitted, smoking ground. The first and second German lines were crushed, at least at the French end of the salient; the British were not nearly so successful. A new front was open, a new slaughter-house, for eventually the Battle of the Somme turned into another chapter of the war of attrition. The German trains carrying men, munitions, and supplies were for the most part diverted toward a front different from Verdun.

And yet the German thrust in the Verdun sector continued. "Thrust" is not the right word; it was more a bloody give-and-take, where local attacks and counterattacks followed one upon another so fast that it is difficult to keep track of them. Because of the obstinacy of the French resistance things went as they had gone in February. The reaction was a purely physical phenomenon, quite outside the general staffs' calculations. Every day the German forward position narrowed, and the troops found themselves in a sort of funnel, a shrinking terrain, with no more trenches, permanently overhung by a cloud of dust, smoke, and the fumes of poison gas.

On both sides the losses were staggering, 70 percent and 80 percent, even more. French and Germans alike were deafened, suffocated, stunned, aware only of what was going on within their own small circle, their physical resistance bolstered up by alcohol. "The corpse of an infantryman in his blue tunic emerged from a heap of earth, stones, and unmentionable débris. A few hours later he had disappeared, and in his place there was a khaki-clad *tirailleur,* replaced later by other corpses and other uniforms. The shell that buried one corpse uncovered another." The stench of gas was mingled with that of decaying human flesh.

On July 11th the Germans made another all-out attack. This time there was a certain desperation about it. The opening of a new front on the Somme called for either this type of attack or a calling off of the offensive. At four o'clock in the morning, after an incredibly heavy bombardment on a two-mile front, the élite Alpine Corps, reinforced by three infantry divisions, drove toward Verdun. The order to break through, regardless of losses, was so imperative that, twenty minutes after the launching of the attack, the "funnel" had reproduced itself, squeezing the attackers into a narrow area face to face with the half-mile French defense line between Souville and Fleury. Nevertheless, at dawn on July 12th the Germans had not only reached but were holding the cross-road of the Chapelle Sainte-Fine, a quarter of a mile north of Fort Souville.

* * *

The outcome of a major battle, fought by large masses of men, is sometimes determined, in the space of a few minutes, by a group so small that every member of it is remembered by name. We are speaking now not of the generals but of the actual participants. At the moment when the opposing forces attain the limit of balance, this small group can tip the scales.

The third company of the 7th Infantry had received orders, at dawn on July 11th, to report to a place called The Quarries. Long before it had reached this destination, before it had drawn level with Fort Souville, the third company numbered no more than sixty out of its original two hundred men and two officers. Its captain, who was drunk, had turned over the command to one of these two officers, Lieutenant Dupuy. The other officer was Second Lieutenant d'Orgemont. The German artillery preparation was at its height, and even the most optimistic of calculations indicated that the remnant of the company would be destroyed within ten to twenty minutes if it pushed on toward its assigned destination. Lieutenant Dupuy decided to seek shelter in Fort Souville.

This fort, built between 1875 and 1879, that is, earlier than either Douaumont or Vaux, and only superficially strengthened later on, was a superannuated structure to which army manuals tried to lend some prestige by calling it a "valuable observation point," a description warranted by the view over the slopes of Douaumont, the Cote du Poivre, and the whole Fleury-Vaux region. This view was presently enjoyed by a company of territorials, together with a few *tirailleurs,* engineers, and artillerymen. The commander was a lieutenant colonel, wounded earlier in the war and now in a state of collapse after several consecutive weeks of bombardment, who refused, however, to be evacuated. The reader should have some idea of the state of the fort when Lieutenant Dupuy together with the sixty survivors of his company arrived on July 11, 1916, at five o'clock in the morning.

From the outside it looked like a heap of stones without a roof, open to the sky. The 38,000 shells which had fallen between April 21st and June 21st, when the bombardment became even heavier, had flattened the escarpment and counterescarpment and filled in the ditches. The lieutenant colonel and his two lieutenants were lying on mattresses among a crowd of men who had been either wounded or gassed. Among those still on their feet the highest rank was that of a sergeant.

At six o'clock in the morning Lieutenant Dupuy sent by runner a report describing the situation to his colonel, ending with the words: "Unless orders to the contrary, I shall stay at the fort and defend it." "The remains of the fort" might have been a more accurate description. The entrances to the underground part were obstructed, and such territorials as had not collapsed had taken refuge in the safest place, the storeroom, where, with no one to give them orders, they waited to be taken prisoner or asphyxiated.

Lieutenant Dupuy was a man of amazingly quick decision.

He ordered the entrances cleared, stationed men armed with hand grenades at each one, posted sentinels to watch over the approaches, assigned the territorials to combat posts, with definite instructions for each post as to their area of fire, and evacuated as many as possible of the gassed and the wounded. At nine o'clock Captain Decap, aide-de-camp of the colonel of the 7th Infantry, arrived upon the scene. He gave blanket approval to all the measures taken by Dupuy, insisting only that he concentrate on the defense of the northwest side of the fort, which seemed the place where the first attack would logically fall.

Had not Lieutenant Dupuy, on his own initiative, chosen to provide shelter for his men at Souville instead of making a suicidal march to The Quarries, the fort would have remained what it was, a useless skeleton. If we ask why the High Command had let it fall into such condition when the last-ditch defense of Verdun was so vital, we can choose one of three answers: the High Command was still skeptical of the value of forts; it did not believe that the German advance would reach as far as Fort Souville; it was not informed of the situation as it should have been.

At six o'clock the next morning, July 12th, messengers from the forward posts arrived breathless at the fort with the familiar news, "They're here!" And indeed the Germans, as anticipated, from the northwest starting from the crossroads of La Chapelle Sainte-Fine, were advancing toward the fort, a hundred and fifty strong. They moved deliberately, some of them with fixed bayonets, some carrying hand grenades. To the combat soldier it must be a strange moment, when the enemy is seen so clearly; and in a few minutes he will know the answer, either "we or they." The attackers had no trouble crossing the filled-in ditches; already they were reaching the superstructure. But Dupuy held back his machine gunners:

"Not yet . . . Wait. All right, now. Fire!"

Two of the slow "coffee grinders," the most efficient weapons, perhaps, of the whole war, went into action. The advancing field-gray figures hesitated; men were falling on all sides.

"Cease fire! Charge!"

An immediate counterattack, with grenades. The Germans fell flat or took refuge in shellholes, from which at intervals they emerged, grenades in their hands. This was their spearhead, perhaps not more than twenty picked men. The rest of them could not advance because of a battery providentially placed a short distance east of the fort. The consolation in writing history is to be able to report the occasional combination of courage and intelligence that reaps its own reward.

Dupuy sent out more of his men and kept his two machine guns trained on both sides so as to stave off any possible German encroachment. We must remember that this defense of the fort of Souville, a small-scale operation but a model of its kind, did not take place in an atmosphere of silence and immobility, but in the middle of a furious bombardment, with other attacks going on all around. This was the spearhead of the German advance, and the Germans knew that if Souville fell they could drive straight through to Verdun. The hours went by, and on the stone-littered ground in front of the fort sky-blue and field-gray uniformed figures ran to and fro, throwing themselves on the ground, getting up again and tossing their grenades. Captain Decap and Lieutenants Dupuy and d'Orgemont directed the movements of their miniature army with perfect coordination.

"At a certain moment the assault weakened. Three Germans, close to the fort, surrendered, and the others fell back."

This was the turning point, on July 12, 1916, at somewhere around half-past eight in the morning, when the fate of Verdun hung in the balance. A sculptured lion, outstretched as if he were wounded to the death, marks, at La Chapelle Sainte-Fine, "the farthest point reached by the Germans before Verdun." It is hard to understand why this monument was not placed in front of the fort, where a handful of brave men, led by three quick-witted young officers, forced Fate's hand. History books say: "The Germans gained a toehold at the fort, but were thrown back by the counter-attacks of Generals Mangin and Paulinier." The readers of this book have seen things closer at hand, and more exactly.

On the evening of July 12th the Crown Prince, commander of the German Fifth Army, received from General Headquarters the following order:

> *As the objectives of today's attack have not been reached, the Crown Prince's Group of Armies will henceforth adopt a defensive attitude.*

Germany had lost the Battle of Verdun.

12

RECONQUEST

BEFORE raising the curtain on the last act, I made a last trip to the battleground. The ineffaceable sadness is still there, all the deeper, perhaps, on a sunny day. Except in the tourist season there are few visitors, and those chiefly Americans, because of the nearby cemeteries, or Germans. "Silence. Silence. Silence. Silence," say the signs in the ossuary of Douaumont. But long before visitors arrive they feel the silence descend on them. After reading the interminable lists of regiments, they leave the icy passageway, pass behind the monument, and stoop to see, behind thick glass panes, the heaps of whitened bones, of skeletons and staring skulls, only a small part of what the battlefield has swallowed up. Silence almost like a command emanates from these bones, and indeed nowhere on the battlefield do visitors have the heart to talk. On the monstrously dented summit of the fort of Douaumont, at Vaux, Mort-Homme, everywhere people come and go without speaking. Even the noisiest children seem to follow, quite naturally, their example.

The ground itself is mute, shut up, as it were, in a refusal to disclose its secret. Veterans say: "What you see now doesn't give any idea of what it was then." But I think that it does, unless the spectator is totally lacking in imagination. Beneath the rachitic underbrush and sparse grass I can visualize the hammered ground, which thousands of separate filled-in shellholes have left permanently uneven and so obviously untillable that there is no need to call it poisoned ground, soaked with human blood instead of productive of God's bounty. In my mind's eye I push away the under-brush and grass and see it furrowed and torn as it was in 1916, with the thin assault lines of the French infantry moving to the attack.

*   *   *

At eight o'clock on the morning of July 15th Mangin ordered a counterattack, by the 37th Division, for the purpose of disengaging Souville and recapturing Fleury. Souville and Fleury are two localities frequently mentioned in this narrative. The time was sixty hours after the French stand that saved Verdun. The faded blue figures advanced, slipping and stumbling, for it had rained during the last two days, the ground was wet, and the shells raised huge geysers of mud. A French barrage preceded the infantry advance, but German artillery fire continued to cover the sloping terrain. Advance was irregular. The men of the 37th Division walked or trotted, holding their rifles or their grenades in their hands, throwing themselves into shellholes, then advancing again. With every leap forward there were a few less of them. The advancing lines grew thinner and thinner. And every following wave was thinned out in the same way. How many times has this scene repeated itself! So many that it is hardly necessary to record the result of the attack: heavy losses; almost no gain of ground. "The attackers melted away under the heavy enemy fire." The upshot is overwhelmingly discouraging. We know, of course, that on the evening of July 12th the Crown Prince had received orders to maintain a strictly defensive position. Were the French counterattacks at Verdun doomed to perpetual failure? In grim jest the men of certain units moving up to the front marched through the last villages bleating like sheep, and the military police furtively tore down posted signs which read "Road to the slaughterhouse." How much longer must it go on?

* * *

The halt of the German drive at Fort Souville on July 12th created a wave of optimism. A feeling of victory was in the air. The French Academy drew up a message of "admiration, gratitude and respect" to the Second Army; the Italian Chamber hailed France as the savior of Europe; King Alexander of Serbia came in person to thank the combatants of Verdun; the French ambassador at St. Petersburg was deluged with visits and congratulations. Meanwhile the Russian General Brussilov had broken through the Austro-Hungarian front, and Romania had decided to enter the war on the side of the Allies. Great Britain (where conscription had been adopted on May 25, 1916) sent enthusiastic praise to French General Headquarters at Chantilly, and promised to increase its war effort. The Somme offensive had got off to a good start, at least on the French section of the front. Both in the Ministry of War and the corridors of the Chamber of Deputies it was felt that the situation was propitious and that the defensive victory must be exploited to the full. There was a clamorous demand that the enemy be allowed no breathing space but be driven back without delay.

At Verdun this clamor from the rear reached the willing ears of Nivelle and Mangin. The intelligent and affable Nivelle, who got on so well with visiting deputies and had replaced the cautious Pétain in the command of the Second Army, must have thought that a real victory at Verdun, or at least the reconquest of all the lost ground, would give him a right to the honors to which he aspired. Mangin, the dashing fighter who suffered because on this muddy seesaw field of battle he had never been able to communicate his offensive spirit to the troops under his command, acquiesced enthusiastically. And so, losing no time, he launched his attack on July 15th, after a preliminary bombardment by 417 guns, medium and heavy.

"Four hundred and seventeen were not enough. We were nowhere nearly ready."

Whose words are these? Pétain's, of course. His voice, then clear and strong, seemed doomed to say the sort of thing that no one liked to hear. "We made a mistake. You don't remember, but we didn't have enough big guns or planes. We were not ready."

We have come to a new crisis, the final act in the Battle of Verdun. This narrative has attempted to follow the development of the battle itself rather than build up a case against any of those responsible for it. It is nonetheless important to note the attitudes of the principals at the most decisive moments in the battle.

Pétain has openly criticized the unfortunate July 15th offensive: "It was a mistake to entrust command of the sector to the commander of a recently arrived division not adequately prepared for so heavy a task." Later: "The local command entered too hurriedly into an engagement which turned out unsuccessfully. More thorough preparation was called for, because of the damage wrought in the Souville sector by the German attack of July 11." This is clear enough. But it is clear also that Pétain formulated his criticisms after the offensive and not before. How much power his position as commander of an army group gave him to delay or cancel the offensive is difficult if not impossible to ascertain. But, on the strength of the evidence, it was not until the offensive failed that Pétain pronounced: "It was inevitable."

There is no question, however, that on July 18th Pétain seems to have awakened to the fact that he was in fact commander of the Central Armies Group and to have abandoned his reticence. He informed the generals under him that henceforth he himself would decide and organize all important attacks on the Verdun front, "because of the means which, as commander of an army group, he had at his command." More expressly he recommended making better use of the artillery, by "the choice of targets, control of the range and communications with the attacking infantry." At the same time he asked General Headquarters at Chantilly for two 400 mortars with which to destroy the forts of Douaumont and Vaux, both of which had to be retaken in order to disengage Verdun.

"I was promised satisfaction for the early autumn, and I decided to wait until then to carry out our major counteroffensives. So it was that the months of August and September passed without any important action in the Verdun sector."

*   *   *

Twenty and even fifty times a day men said that it could end only in disaster. A short-circuit or simply a smoker's carelessness could cause an explosion. And yet, only a quarter of an hour before the mine went off, conversations were going on in the dark, just as usual.

"Furloughs? I don't give a damn about them. They can keep their furloughs. I don't intend to take any."

The voices should have echoed, since the speakers were in a tunnel. But the tunnel of Tavannes was stopped up at both ends, and both air and ground were so foul that every sound was stifled.

"Last time I took a furlough I said to myself that just to be aboveground would be heaven, even for someone as broke as I was, just to live without being afraid every minute of being killed. When I saw the Eiffel Tower I started to cry. I got to my street and my house, and in the hall the concierge said, 'It's good to see you.' But she gave me a funny look, all the same. 'I'm going to wash up,' I told her, 'to scrape off some of the glorious mud of the trenches.' But she said it wasn't worth my while to go upstairs because I didn't live there any longer. My wife had moved away, but the concierge couldn't tell me where. Of course, I hadn't heard from her for quite a while but that didn't surprise me. Neither of us was much for letters. My wife, did I say? Well, she'd flown the coop; I guess you knew that was coming. Of course, it's happened to plenty of other men before me. When I went to the municipal building of the Eleventh Arrondissement to get her allotment cut off and to ask about a divorce, they didn't bat an eyelash. Used to it, I guess. Well, I had a whole week, so I went to some friends near the Bastille and they put me up. Not that they were so very much better off than I was. They had only two rooms, and I slept on a mattress on the floor. I wasn't a very cheerful guest; I was in the way, and it cost them money to feed me. I spent most of my time walking around the streets, and after three days I didn't have enough money to sit down in a café; I had to perch on a park bench like an old man. Every time I sat down beside a woman, she got up and left, as if I still had lice on me. And so I came back twenty-four hours before my furlough was over. The next time was even worse. . . .

The railway tunnel ran right through and under the fort of Tavannes, which the Germans were bombarding. But since no projectile could penetrate the side of the hill, it was a place of complete safety, serving as brigade head-quarters, a storehouse for munitions, and living quarters for the reserves. Obviously it was crowded, and only the living quarters had any light. Electric current was produced by a gasoline motor, and the live wires had no insulation. Several men had been electrocuted, but the real danger was of an explosion. The northeast entrance to the tunnel was under German fire. As to sanitary conditions, one detail will suffice: any man who stayed more than a few days caught something called "cesspool jaundice." The only aperture that might have let in some fresh air had been sealed up in order to prevent the penetration of poison gas.

"Next time I had a furlough it was for two weeks, but at least I knew what it was going to be like. Broke again, of course, but I had an idea of what to do about that. I took a job on the assembly line at Panhard. I worked every day except the two Sundays. As for getting a place to stay, I went to the police station in my precinct and they gave me a so-called room ticket, with which I got a small single-bed room on a sixth floor. I paid an old woman living across the hall to cook my dinner and wake me up to go to work in the morning. In the evening I was too tired to go out except on Sunday. Every now and then I stopped somewhere for a glass of beer. As for women . . . well, I'd rather not talk about that. I didn't make enough money at the factory to buy myself any beauty queens. . . . So that's the story of my two furloughs. . . . Now here I am back with you, sitting in shit, or something very like it. . . ."

The tunnel had originally been equipped with a system of pipes for draining off the moisture left by the passage of the steam engines and what accumulated on the walls. But in turning it to military use the pipes had been blocked off, and now there were marshy spots on the ground, which attracted swarms of flies. "I'm going to clean this place up," said the divisional general in command of the sector at the end of July. But his sanitation officers had opposed the idea, saying that to stir up the mud and the polluted water would only increase the danger of an epidemic. So all that was done was to scatter a little lime here and there. Now it was the 4th of September. It is not because of a love for sordid details that the tunnel of Tavannes has been so unsparingly described. The tunnel and its condition have something symbolic about them.

It was true, as Pétain says, that "the months of August and September went by without the occurrence of anything important in the Verdun sector." From his bird's-eye point of view, the historian will agree. But the fighting men saw things at closer range. For each one of them these months were studded with important and almost unbearable events. It was at just this time that the feeling grew among them that the war would go on forever. "The hell of Verdun" lay not so much in the hardships endured as in the sensation of their infinity, an infinity close to the torments of hell. More than one veteran has recounted that by this time he had reached the conclusion that the war would never be over. Everything was organized to keep it going; too many people were making money out of it: the munitions makers, their wives and mistresses, the draft dodgers with well-paid jobs in factory offices, the petty profiteers, the army behind-the-lines of wine sellers and camp followers, the rapidly promoted generals, the Ministry of War officials who got a rakeoff on the munitions orders, the newspapermen . . . in short, everybody.

It seemed clear, by now, that neither opponent could really crush the other, and yet what government, after calling for a total victory, could settle for a negotiated peace? It would have meant admitting the absurdity of the slaughter, and provoking the soldiers on both sides to ask what was the reason for it all. It was better to let things drag on. The Allies were gaining new adherents to their cause, but the Germans were doing the same thing. Why shouldn't the rest of the world come in? The war might last for a hundred years.

The men who turned these melancholy thoughts over in their minds did not know that a major counteroffensive was under way, that Pétain had asked for two 400 mortars with which to smash the forts, that he was accumulating heavy artillery and planes, that he was organizing better liaison between them and rotating the infantry units more rapidly. They could not have known that Mangin was writing a report to Nivelle in which he admitted that it was better to give up the continual small counterattacks for the sake of a few trenches or a hundred yards of ground and to concentrate on thorough plans for a major attack. They could not have known that, between Bar-le-Duc and Saint-Dizier, special assault troops were being trained on ground laid out to resemble the one on which they would actually fight and that, for instance, every man in the battalion allotted to the attack on Fort Douaumont would know exactly what he would have to do when the time came, without hesitation. In other words, a miracle had happened, and the French command, for once united, was preparing the counteroffensive destined to disengage Verdun as painstakingly as the Germans had prepared their attack in February.

During August and September, then, the common soldiers were unaware of these things, partly because they were not informed and partly because during the months "without the occurrence of anything important" they were engaged in operations described as "mopping up of a German pocket" or "conquest of the point of departure for an attack," namely, the ridge between Thiaumont and Fleury, operations less spectacular, from the air, for instance, than the clash of two armies, but just as deadly when seen from the level of the ground.

At this point in the battle the description of the battlefield as "lunar" is no longer exact. The surface of the moon, so well known from enlarged telescopic photographs, does have craters that resemble shellholes, but these depressions have raised lips around them, and the general impression is that of a relief. The aerial photographs of the Verdun area taken in August and September 1916 present a very different picture. The most remarkable are those of the village of Fleury, which changed hands sixteen times in twenty-six days. If examined in the proper order they show, before the battle, a well-defined little village, at the juncture of several country roads; then a group of ruins; next, something like the X-ray plate of an ailing organ; then a vague blot, and finally nothing at all, that is, nothing but complete identification with the surrounding landscape, which has no resemblance to the surface of the moon but has been hammered perfectly flat. The desolation is so complete that it is mental as well as physical, like an abstract painting expressive of a total misery of mind.

The memory that has remained most intense among those who lived through the summer of 1916 at Verdun is expressed in a single crude word: putrefaction. "We all had on us the stench of dead bodies. The bread we ate, the stagnant water we drank, everything we touched had a rotten smell, owing to the fact that the earth around us was literally stuffed with corpses. Among the total of half a million French and German dead it has been calculated that at least 150,000 were never buried, but were simply absorbed into the ground. In these summer months the putrefaction of the Verdun battlefield reached a climax; it was as bad as the infamous hill of Vauquois in the earlier months of the war. No such state of things ever existed in any other war, before or since, nor is it likely to reproduce itself. The image of human beings reduced within a fraction of a second to nothingness, as they were at Hiroshima, the pictures of burned and maimed survivors and the knowledge of the damage done to their unborn children, the accounts of the minutes and hours immediately following the explosion, all these lead us to believe that the scene was one of tragic confusion like that of 1914–1918. But in all history there is no other example of a war waged for so long a time over such a small area, covered with the multitudes of the dead. Within the framework of this war, Verdun marks a climax.

Like all horrors, this one had a grotesque, surrealistic side. A veteran recounts that when he was sent to the Verdun region in 1917, a year after the great battle, he saw on the obliterated site of Fleury a wooden cross with the identification tag of a dead soldier called, let us say, Pierre Durand attached to it. A hundred feet away, amid a pile of heterogeneous debris—balls of rotted bread strung on a wire, bits of gnawed cheese, empty ration tins, strips of clothing, smashed rifles, and other pieces of equipment—he came upon a human arm in a coatsleeve with, on the blackened wrist, an identification tag bearing the same name and number that he had seen a few minutes before. Such things defy understanding.

But we may begin to understand how and why the living soldiers of these months of August and September 1916 were willing, indeed glad, to hole up in such miserable billets as those of the tunnel of Tavannes. There, at least, they had shelter; they could sleep. And they were so tired that even the buzzing flies failed to awaken them.

At a quarter-past nine in the evening of September 4th the tragedy began. The men crowded into the improvised wood-framed living quarters felt their hearts pound when they heard the sound of the first explosions from the vicinity of the southwest entrance.

"The grenade boxes! It was bound to happen!"

Immediately there was a wild melée, as the cans filled with gasoline for the motors producing electric current exploded, setting up first a violent current of air and then a rush of flame. The wooden barracks began to burn, with fanning yellow flames, while a dragon of black smoke wound its way through the tunnel. Some of the men did not even have time to cry out before they were asphyxiated. Meanwhile there were other explosions. The smoke billowed all the way to the east end of the tunnel, with blackened, burned, panic-stricken men fleeing before it. At the exit they burst into hysterical tears when they saw a hail of German shells pouring down just outside, their aim directed by the smoke. A colonel, revolver in hand, shouted threateningly:

"Get out of the way! Let the first-aid squad get through."

In spite of their masks and oxygen apparatus, men of the first-aid squad could not advance into the smoke, which carried with it an odor of burning flesh. That night, when they finally penetrated the tunnel, heaps of charred bodies blocked their way. The fire smoldered for several days. Between five and six hundred lives were lost.

*   *   *

Rain began to fall early in September. The summer heat had barely had time to crack the evil clay of the ground, and scattered, half-filled ponds dotted the landscape here and there. Now the days were rapidly growing shorter, and rain fell incessantly from the gray sky, soaking the earth and loosening the corpses and the debris buried in it. Sometimes the floor of a trench gave way, and bodies, both French and German, came to the surface and floated away. Reserve troops, on their way to the front line, walked through communication trenches where they were hip-deep in water, which had turned suddenly cold. The soldiers asserted that the combination of cold and wet was quite enough to kill them, without any need of enemy shells or bullets.

On October 4th a colonel sent to inspect the front lines saw a strange sight. The French and German trenches, which were some twenty yards apart, were both filled with three feet of water. Both sides had established a truce; they had come out and sat down on parapets, staring sadly across at one another under the downpour that fell, quite indifferently, upon the living and the dead of both sides.

In the rear, the rain blotted out the features of the mean landscape, peopled the camps with soldiers who trudged around wearing sacks or pieces of camouflage cloth over their heads, and stifled the smoke in the village chimneys.

In this widespread atmosphere of doubt and discouragement there appeared, not suddenly, but with striking spontaneity, signs of a positive will, of something new. Just as men were getting used to marching along the edge of roads no longer able to bear any wheeled traffic, squads of workers came with stones to repair them. Many such roads were repaired and opened: from Faubourg-Pavé to La Chapelle Sainte-Fine, from the ravine of Pas du Gravier to the vicinity of Thiaumont, through the Bois des Essarts and elsewhere.

Farther still to the rear masons, carpenters, and railway workers enlarged the freight yards of such stations as Baleycourt and Landrecourt. As soon as the new rails were laid, long trains of freight cars filled with building materials and flatcars carrying heavy guns began to pull in. There were logs, boards, and bags of cement, which had to be unloaded and hauled by horses and donkeys to the front, right to the combat area where, in rain and mud and often under enemy shells, engineers dug shelters and trenches, which often they had to reconstruct half-a-dozen times over when bad weather or bombardment destroyed them.

All this, of course, was the groundwork for the counteroffensive, the preparation of the forward positions from which it would take off. It was begun under the worst possible climatic conditions, and yet it continued, day after day, tirelessly and without respite, at an increasing tempo, as if guided by a will that would not be thwarted by any obstacle. This will was the will of Pétain, and also of Mangin. Pétain had vowed not to attack without adequate and proper preparation, and he had personally organized the growing movement of men and matériel. Nivelle had adapted himself to this methodical procedure, but the man who directly carried it out was Mangin. The old colonial remembered that he had been not only an intrepid leader of men but also an administrator and a builder. He set himself to providing the means necessary to attain the end, and applied the energy he had once put into a charge to the detailed staff work the counter-offensive demanded.

German shells fell on this amazing and progressively larger workshop on the right bank of the Meuse, but they fell less and less frequently as the days went by and the French heavy artillery began to find the range and cripple the German guns. The French artillery was now firing at a greater rate and with heavier metal than the German. Even in bad weather French fighter planes were able to protect the heavy biplanes that acted as range finders. The Nieuports flew with impunity over the German lines, and destroyed the famous German observation balloons long before they had risen to the full length of their cables, while the French balloons hovered, in relative safety, in the gray sky. In the air as well as on land the scales were being tipped on the French side.

On October 9th a small procession of automobiles drew up in front of the stone steps of the town hall of Souilly. Out of the second car emerged an easily recognizable figure, that of Joffre.

"Are you satisfied with what has been done?" he asked Nivelle. "Do you think we have a good chance of success?"

"Plans are complete, down to the last detail, General. Everything will be all right."

Mangin was there too, every wrinkle in his face eloquent of happiness. At last his counteroffensive was his to carry out. He told Joffre of his complete faith in the colonial troops under his command.

On October 12th Clemenceau, the Tiger, came, roundly cheered by the soldiers who were there to greet him. Of all the visitors to the front, Clemenceau was the most popular. The men liked his looks, his gruff but cordial manner, and even his dress: the worn overcoat, the wool scarf pulled up over his ears, the shapeless hat, the leggings, all of which gave him a relaxed and casual air. (Poincaré, in his military cap, never managed to look at home in it.) Moreover Clemenceau had a nose for the real danger spots, and demanded to be taken to them.

"Have you got everything you need?" he asked Nivelle. "Show me the plan of attack."

Nivelle, as we know, was a first-rate interpreter. He had a knack of making his listeners, even if they were completely ignorant of military science, feel that they understood the whole story. Now he pointed at the map and read from the operation orders.

"Eight divisions. Three will form the first line of attack. On the left the Thirty-eighth, under Guyot de Salins, which has Fort Douaumont as one of its objectives; in the center the One Hundred and Thirty-third, under Passaga; on the right the Seventy-fourth, under Lardemelle, which is to be the Seventh, Ninth, and Thirty-sixth. In the rear, as a reserve, the Thirty-seventh and Twenty-second."

"And what have the Germans got lined up against you?"

"Seven divisions, but echeloned one behind the other. We will be too quick for them."

On October 15th, Nivelle gave the word to Pétain, who passed it on to General Headquarters, that everything was ready. On the 17th Nivelle issued an order of the day to the Second Army, in which he said: "An exceptionally heavy bombardment will overpower the German artillery and open the way for the assault troops." This promise was maintained. On October 21st, the opening day of the bombardment, 650 French guns spoke simultaneously: 20 of them of a caliber between 270 and 400; 300 of a caliber between 120 and 220; 331 between 65 and 105 caliber. Against them, the Germans were credited with 800 guns. But this numerical superiority was compensated for by the fact that the French had by now established a more efficient liaison between their infantry and artillery and a greater accuracy in range finding. On October 22nd these matters were successfully put to the test. A feint was made, the apparent start of a full-scale attack. Immediately 158 German guns, hidden or camouflaged, replied. Having been located, they at once became targets, and sixty-eight of them were put out of action for the day of the real attack.

The men who had been trained for the last three weeks under simulated battle conditions, between Bar-le-Duc and Saint-Dizier, were moving up to the front lines. They trudged slowly through the communication trenches, with a certain down-at-the-mouth air. "For all of us Verdun was terrifying. We knew that every regiment that had ever fought there had suffered fantastic losses. We marched in silence, each one of us thinking to himself: 'Shall I come back or be left dead on the field of battle?' " Such reflections are understandable.

One very concrete condition made the marching slow, and that was the load each infantryman had to carry. Of course, on a battleground such as Verdun, where wheeled transport was impossible, men had to be equipped not only to fight but also to feed themselves and to dig holes for shelter. Nevertheless the amount of equipment seems to have been grossly overestimated. Many veterans even today remember with feeling that even the normal weight was almost more than a man could carry. They speak of something between sixty and eighty pounds. Here is what the soldiers of the 321st Infantry, assigned to the assault of Douaumont, were allotted *besides* their regular equipment, and their rifle cartridge belt:

Two gas masks
One pouch containing biscuits
One pouch containing dried meat and chocolate
One pouch containing hand grenades
One two-quart canteen of wine
One two-quart canteen of water

One blanket rolled in tent cloth
One shovel
Two sandbags

Only men of peasant stock, accustomed for centuries to bearing inhuman burdens, could have marched to battle under conditions like these.

On October 23rd Pétain, Nivelle, and Mangin came, all together, to a final decision. The opening day was to be October 24th, the hour, 11:40 in the morning.

*   *   *

Hundreds of thousands of shells had fallen on Fort Douaumont. Its roof was a gray, indescribably battered surface, and in aerial photographs its hexagonal outline was no more than a shadow, like the ghost of some buried Sumerian city. Yet the interior had nothing tomblike about it. The Germans had established order, cleanliness, and even electric lights with reflectors. The bunks were neatly lined up, the telephone worked, and the gas masks were regularly tested. Major Rosendahl of the 90th Reserve Infantry, the commander, was a stickler for discipline, rightly regarding it as the only safeguard, in such cramped quarters, against untidiness, discouragement, and defeatism. Sixty wounded men were under care in the infirmary.

After October 21st communications with the outside were rendered difficult by the continuous French bombardment, but the major did not seem to be worried. There were abundant reserves of food and ammunition, and the concrete walls showed no sign of giving way. October 23rd seemed to dawn reluctantly, with a sodden gray sky. Beginning at eight o'clock the bombardment grew in intensity, and there was no question of venturing outside. The Germans went about their usual routine, but as time went on they looked more and more frequently at the vaulted ceilings. They had only to touch the walls to be aware of the rocking of the ground. "It can't get any worse than this," they said to themselves, and yet five minutes later the noise and the shaking of the walls were more violent than before.

The first shock came at 12:30. For what seemed like an interminable length of time, but which was actually no more than a second and a half, the rumble of the artillery was smothered by a new sound, a sort of low hoarse roar that seemed to come from high up in the sky. This was followed by a surprisingly mild explosion, then a dull thud, and finally a deafening clap of thunder, accompanied by a rush of displaced air. As they stood motionless in the casemates or corridors, the defenders had a feeling that a meteor had exploded in the fort. Actually, it was the first shell from the French 400's.

The sixty wounded men instinctively tried to raise themselves into a sitting position as soon as they heard the first roar, but a second later they were all dead. The shell crashed through eight feet of concrete and landed in the middle of the infirmary. Several minutes went by before their comrades could locate the hit and reach the scene. They were greeted by flames and by the intensified noise, coming through a hole in the roof, of the regular bombardment.

Ten minutes later another of the 400's fell. The men in Casemate Eight looked at each other when they heard the hoarse roar just above their heads, but they too had no time to move.

The hoarse roar was unbearable. It recurred every quarter of an hour, with monstrous regularity. Major Rosendahl realized that those of his men who were not killed would go mad. After the fall of the fourth of the 400's he ordered the entire garrison to go down to the underground shelter. Strange to say, the electric light was still working.

The fifth shell shook the underground shelter from top to bottom, but it was impossible to guess where it had landed. When they heard the roar of the sixth shell, the garrison understood that their safety was illusory. Passing through the gaping roof, the shells would eventually penetrate the shelter. The sixth shell went through the same pattern as its predecessors—a hoarse roar, a mild explosion, a dull thud, a clap of thunder—but this time these were followed by a series of staccato bursts like that of a machine gun, and then a succession of explosions. The shell had landed in the munitions storeroom.

The soldiers put on their masks. Some of them moved as if to make for the outside. But shells loaded with poison gas were falling in front of the only two passable exits. At two o'clock the lights finally went out. The masked men, standing against the walls, crouching or lying in the darkness, had stopped counting the 400's and had lost all notion of time. Poison-gas fumes were fanning out through the fort.

At four o'clock noncommissioned officers, in voices stifled by their gas masks, passed on the commander's orders: "All men not strictly indispensable are to evacuate the fort. Those qualified as indispensable were a detachment of engineers, assigned to putting out the fire in the munitions storeroom. To the evacuees the idea of making their way through the hail of shells outside was terrifying. What chance did they have of running more than a few yards? But to stay in the underground shelter, into which more and more poison gas was seeping, meant certain death. In an impressively disciplined manner the soldiers filed out, with the noncommissioned officers standing by. By six o'clock the order had been executed.

The attempt to put out the fire was ill-fated from the start. In the light of the flames the engineers, unable to fight the conflagration in any other way, had recourse to bottles of soda water intended for the wounded. Toward eleven o'clock in the evening Captain Soltan, who had been left in command of the small fraction of the garrison still remaining, gave orders to set up a machine gun at the northwest entrance to the fort, which was still usable. Ten minutes later, in spite of their masks, the machine-gun crew had fainted. The 400's had stopped falling, but the shells loaded with poison gas were more numerous than ever. Several machine-gun crews in succession collapsed at the northwest door. By midnight everyone left in the fort was more or less intoxicated by the gas, and many were vomiting.

The final evacuation took place between four and five o'clock the next morning. The scene was worthy of Goya's *Disasters of War*. In the light of the raging fire and the oncoming light of dawn, a line of men, staggering and vomiting, carried their unconscious comrades on stretchers through the hail of French shells, with one chance out of twenty of survival. Not a single wounded or dying soldier was left behind.

And still the fort had not surrendered. Toward eight o'clock in the morning a group of twenty German volunteers, led by a certain Captain Prollius and two junior officers, moved in. Under the hail of falling shells Captain Prollius surveyed the situation and posted his men at the fort's various exits. Everywhere the battlefield was swathed in fog.

* * *

There exist some amazing photographs of the French counteroffensive of October 24th. In the dense fog overhanging the front the infantrymen formed a ghostlike procession, weighed down by their heavy equipment.

Where the fog was thickest the men emerged from their parallel starting trenches several minutes before the allotted time and lined up, in perfect safety, in front of the parapet. The Senegalese troops, in particular, gathered in little knots waiting for the attack orders. The French artillery could be heard to the north; the Germans were making practically no reply. The officers' eyes were glued to their watches, and at exactly 11:40 the first units started forward.

The plan was to cover a hundred yards every four minutes, with a pause at an intermediary interval to straighten out the line. A rolling barrage was to prevent the Germans from coming out of their shelters.

"The foggy weather made it quite extraordinary. The officers had to guide themselves with compasses. Everything seemed to be going so well that we felt as if we were out for a stroll. This lasted for several minutes."

Ulysse Lenain, a private of the 401st Infantry, belonged to an advance patrol sent out before eleven o'clock. After a few minutes of advancing through the fog he saw on his right, and slightly behind him, a group of Germans with three machine guns. They stared at him, but since he had no rifle, only hand grenades, they must have taken him for a deserter, for they let him go by. He took refuge in a shellhole and waited until he saw the first wave of French infantry coming through the fog. Then the Germans began shooting. Ulysse Lenain threw two grenades at them. They flattened themselves out on the ground, then got up and started shooting again. Lenain saw the advancing French line waver. He threw another grenade, then rose out of his hole and, grenade in hand, rushed over to within three yards of them.

"If you fire again, you're as good as dead," he shouted.

Some of the Germans were obviously suffering from combat fatigue, and raised their hands.

"Come ahead!" Lenain called through the fog to his comrades. "I've got them."

He had taken seventeen prisoners, including two officers, and three machine guns. For this feat he received the Legion of Honor at General Pétain's hands.

The attacking troops proceeded slowly because of the heavy load they carried and the slippery condition of the muddy, pitted soil. Though the fog masked their movements, it had its disadvantages also. The Eighth Battalion of the Colonial Infantry of Morocco was one of the units appointed to capture Douaumont. The Moroccans advanced in good order, led by their commander, Major Nikolai, who did not lift his eyes from his compass for a single second. A sudden German barrage blocked the way just ahead of them, but they went right through it without hesitation. Their reputation meant more to the Colonials than casualties. On they went, without seeing much of anything around them. The distance seemed long to cover, and Major Nikolai noticed that the differences in the terrain did not correspond at all with what was on his map.

"Battalion, halt!"

What was to be done with a battalion lost in the fog? Neither to the right nor to the left was there any sign of a fort. The Moroccans were ready to follow their leader blindly, but it was better that he should not be blind. Besides, shells were falling all around.

"Where the devil are the Germans, anyhow?"

Fortune has a way of smiling on the brave. At just this moment a lone German private appeared out of the fog, was surrounded, captured, and questioned. Fort Douaumont? He had just come from it. He motioned with his arm.

"Take us there, on the double. Battalion, forward!"

The steel of the major's helmet and revolver had thrown off the compass needle.

*   *   *

In spite of the noise of the rolling barrage, the Chasseurs of the 107th heard someone call out from close by, "Help! Help!"

It was a call that all of them had heard a thousand times before. But there are ways and ways of crying for help, and this one was heart-rending. A few seconds later they found out where it came from, from a man who had sunk up to his waist in a mudhole.

"Throw away your rifle! Get rid of your knapsack!"

It was easy enough to give advice from the firm ground on which they were standing. But the poor fellow was wrapped in equipment like a living mummy. The mud was rising, and anyone venturing closer risked being sucked down himself. The Chasseurs made a rope out of their rifle straps and threw it to the sinking man. But with the first pull it gave way. There could be no doubt about the fact that he was heavily encumbered.

"Braid the rifle straps together, and find some boards."

Where were any boards to be found? Several soldiers went off to look. It was a ridiculous situation, especially in the middle of an attack. The minutes seemed interminable. Finally they returned with some boards six inches wide and several yards long and laid them in the mud on either side of their helpless comrade.

"Lean on these. That way you won't sink deeper."

The man leaned his hands and forearms on the boards.

"Come on, fellow; you're getting out of it!"

The man pulled himself up, until his legs were almost out of the mud, paused for a brief rest, and then, with a dreadful sound, plunged back in, this time up to his shoulders. The situation was becoming desperate, and German shells were beginning to fall.

"Go ahead! Don't worry about me. You've done the best you could."

But this was impossible. A man could be shot to death beside you a thousand times, but the idea of letting a comrade die by slow degrees a few yards away from you was out of the question. Even a wild animal would not do it. The Chasseurs went almost mad. They dashed about, bringing back pieces of wood, scraps of iron, rolls of barbed wire, and threw this miscellany into the mudhole. Everything was implacably swallowed, until finally a roll of barbed wire held at the surface, signifying that the hole was full. Others among the Chasseurs had braided their gunstraps together, and now six of them hauled their comrade up. When finally the mud let him go, there were tears running down his cheeks.

They patted his heaving back. "We wouldn't have left you, old man. We'd rather have died than do that."

* * *

The Moroccan infantry regiment had the hardest mission of all. The Fourth Battalion was to capture and establish themselves in the German front lines. The First Battalion was to pass through it and encircle the fort; the Eighth (which we have already glimpsed in the fog) was to make the final assault on the fort itself.

There were, among the Germans, as we have seen, men whose morale was at a low ebb and who were ready to surrender, but there were others with an iron will, resolved to do or die. The machine gunners the Fourth Battalion ran up against even before reaching the enemy lines were of this second kind. A stupid rumor said that the German machine gunners had been chained to their weapons to prevent their running away. Chained they were, but by courage and endurance; this is the evidence given by Sergeants Gras and Ducom, who fought them that day. It was plain from the start that they had no idea of giving in.

The men of the Fourth Battalion were Senegalese. To the average Frenchman the Senegalese soldiers of those days inspired a mixture of curiosity, paternalism, and fear. When they laughed, displaying two rows of white teeth that contrasted with their black faces, people said:

"Overgrown children, that's all they are!"

"Overgrown children, if you like, but watch out! Have you seen their knives?"

"For mopping up a trench, there's nothing like them. They scare the Germans to death."

Some people spoke of their stringing the ears of their victims, like beads, into a necklace. In battle they had the reputation of formidable fighting men, who on occasion disappointed. They excelled in dashing assaults, but they could not be relied on to hold a difficult position. And they were, quite naturally, susceptible to dampness and cold.

The Senegalese soldiers of the Fourth Battalion of the Regiment of Colonial Infantry of Morocco had marched through Verdun tossing their knives up in the air and shouting, "Douaumont! Douaumont!" The name meant nothing to them; perhaps they thought of it as belonging to an evil spirit they must put to death, or else to some protective divinity. In any case, it had become, through repetition, a sort of verbal totem.

When they came to the German machine gunners who had held fast through the rolling barrage and had not flinched under the first hand grenades, the Senegalese hesitated. The fog and mud were unfamiliar; they had not expected to meet the Germans so soon, and they could not understand why shots were coming at them from both flanks as well as from the front. As they continued to stand their ground uncertainly, the major in command of the battalion intervened.

"Who is the idiot commanding this company?" he shouted.

Then he himself, in the full excitement of battle, led the company forward. Soon afterward the machine guns were silent, and the battalion occupied the German front-line positions, according to plan. According to plan also, the First Battalion passed through them, moving through the fog with a compass to guide it. Suddenly, the compass was no longer necessary. The fog was thinning out and lifting. The battlefield was not completely clear, but the visibility had increased. Three hundred yards ahead was the unmistakable outline of Fort Douaumont.

The First Battalion was alone. The Eighth Battalion, assigned to the capture of the fort, had lost its way in the fog. It was once again on the move, but meanwhile the First Battalion had to decide whether to wait for the Eighth's arrival or to attack. Waiting did not enter into the Colonial's vocabulary. Overall strategy may call for temporizing, but tactics almost never. Captain Dorey gave orders without hesitation. One company was to attack on the southwest side, the second to make a frontal attack, and the third to act as reserve. Audacity does not mean throwing all one's forces away.

"Forward on the double!"

Men loaded with a combat pack weighing sixty or seventy pounds, with straps that cut into their chests, broke into a run. They did not run like greyhounds, but it was a miracle in itself that they could run at all. Sometimes they slipped or stumbled on the muddy ground, but somehow or other they regained their balance and went on. These men who had set out from the rear in a somber frame of mind, each one asking himself, "Shall I be one of those that come back alive?" unhesitatingly charged the fort.

Toward half-past two in the afternoon officers watching the battle through their field glasses from the heights of Souville saw the silhouettes of French soldiers on top of the fort. The First Battalion of the Regiment of Colonial Infantry of Morocco had met up with a few men from the 321st Infantry, who had come up from the right to join them. Soon afterward, the remnant of the German garrison surrendered.

*   *   *

Here is where I shall end my story of the Battle of Verdun. This is the moment of its logical culmination, its final significance. The significance I shall try to define briefly, as I see it.

The war of 1939–1945 is still close enough so that the reader can remember how it was won. Strategic air attack destroyed centers and lines of communication and sources of supply behind the lines. Then tactical attack smashed all obstacles in the way of advancing tanks and infantry. Superiority in the air spelled success. I am not guilty of oversimplification if I venture to say that, at Verdun, artillery played the same role that aviation was to play in the later war. Heavy artillery played the strategic role, field artillery the tactical one. Where the firepower of the artillery was lacking, either an offensive or a counteroffensive could lead only to an infantry massacre. The French began to win only when their artillery was stronger than that of the Germans. Until this happened their commanders could do no more than plug the gaps with human lives.

Fort Vaux, abandoned by the enemy, was recaptured without a fight on November 2nd. Other events, entailing bitter loss of life, and much hardship and sorrow, took place in the Verdun theater during the months that followed: the attack of December 15, 1916; the offensive of August 1917; the attack of the First American Army on the famous salient of Saint-Mihiel, and many of what are called minor operations. In December 1916 the temperature went down to four degrees below zero; soldiers barely alive under a coating of icy mud gazed on the frozen corpses around them. Surgeons amputated countless hands and arms, feet and legs, which were not only frozen but afflicted with incurable gangrene as well. Then, once again, came the spring rains, turning the battleground into a mass of putrid mud; then summer, teeming with flies; and once more the biting chill of the autumn and winter of 1918. I do not mean to glide over the sufferings and deaths of the months after October 1916 as if they were historically unimportant. But after the October counteroffensive the Battle of Verdun was, strategically speaking, ended. It spilled over into the mainstream of the war, whose subsequent ramifications are outside the scope of this volume.

It is not easy for me to break off my story of the battle.

I have long been a victim of its fascination. Ridiculous as it may seem, since I took no part in the First World War, I feel as if I had lived through these unendurable months.

"Sir, what you say is no surprise. In the thirties, when I was twenty-five years old, my wife and I kept a café, at Lemmes on the 'Sacred Way.' There was even a milestone with an old helmet hung on it before the door. The café was not very big, but it gave us a living, because of the visiting veterans, the fellows who came to see the places where they had fought. There were group visits, organized by tourist agencies and veterans' organizations, but also many, many single individuals, from every class of society, who came by train, automobile, and bicycle. I remember one fellow—he must have been very well off—in a car driven by his chauffeur, a survivor of the same unit. They sat down here together, and he paid for a couple of omelets and a bottle of white wine. In the evening, after their visit, the two ate another meal together; then they got back into the car, one at the wheel, the other in the back seat, just as when they had arrived.

"Some fellows used to arrive dressed in their old uniforms, pretty nearly everything but the helmet and the insignia. What they were looking for, of course, was their old trench or shelter or the shellhole where their best friend had died beside them. Why, some of them brought along camping equipment and cooking utensils, and spent the night in their old dugout. Every now and then they got their heads blown off when their fire heated up an unexploded shell or hand grenade. But nobody seemed to bother. My wife and I used to listen to them talk. They exchanged tips as to the location of a trench or a battery emplacement: 'I was in Death Ravine. . . .' 'Which one do you mean?' There seem to have been at least a dozen by that name.

"And would you believe it? Germans came too. As time went by, nobody called them *Boches* any more. They ate something in a hurry, without very much conversation. They didn't talk to the Frenchmen, but every now and then they exchanged nods. Yes, there were pilgrims that came back every year. They covered on foot as many as fifteen or twenty miles a day. Some of the campers stayed as long as a week; it seemed as if they couldn't tear themselves away. They actually enjoyed it."

Who has not had a feeling of nostalgia for a place where he has endured great pain? The former café proprietor could have gone on talking forever; he was a victim of the same fascination as I, the fascination of a somber lodestar. In the infinite, such stars—which we often imagine as dead—are burning. And everything that they touch is consumed by fire.